An Exposition of the Late Controversy in the Methodist Episcopal Church
by Samuel Kennedy Jennings

Address:
HardPress
8345 NW 66TH ST #2561
MIAMI FL 33166-2626
USA
Email: info@hardpress.net

AN EXPOSITION

OF THE

LATE CONTROVERSY

IN THE

Methodist Episcopal Church;

OF THE

TRUE OBJECTS OF THE PARTIES CONCERNED THEREIN,

AND OF THE

PROCEEDINGS BY WHICH REFORMERS WERE EXPELLED, IN
BALTIMORE, CINCINNATI, AND OTHER PLACES;

OR,

A REVIEW

OF THE

Methodist Magazine and Quarterly Review,

ON PETITIONS AND MEMORIALS.

BY SAMUEL K. JENNINGS, M. D.

TO WHICH ARE APPENDED,

Remarks on an Article, entitled

ASBURY'S LIFE,

WHICH APPEARED IN THE

METHODIST MAGAZINE, &c. FOR JANUARY, 1831.

BY A LAYMAN.

BALTIMORE:
PUBLISHED BY JOHN J. HARROD.

PRINTED BY WILLIAM WOODDY,
No. 6 S. *Calvert street.*
::::::::::
1831.

Entered according to the Act of Congress, in the year 1831, by JOHN J. HARROD, in the Clerk's office of the District Court of Maryland.

PREFACE.

In presenting a republication of so much of our review as has appeared in the Mutual Rights and Christian Intelligencer, together with a compilation of the papers taken from the Mutual Rights, extracts from which have been printed in the Narrative and Defence in justification of the expulsion of Reformers; we have acted in obedience to the demands of our friends generally, as made known to us by our late General Convention; and of many individuals who have repeatedly called for a collection of the documents in explanation and justification of the measures which have served to institute and establish the Methodist Protestant Church. It would have been much more consistent with our personal ease, having continually pressing professional engagements to fulfil, to have retired from the controversy. But the reiterated declarations of the leading men in the M. E. Church, and the repeated publications which have issued from their presses in New York and Baltimore, &c. have had a tendency to impose upon the public very erroneous opinions respecting the motives and labours of the friends of Reform. It, therefore, became our duty, to forego considerations of personal ease or interest, and continue our labours for the cause of truth and Mutual Rights.

It was our original intention merely to suggest to our readers, the probable existence of a conspiracy for the expulsion of reform out of the M. E. Church, and to introduce so much testimony only, in support of the suggestion, as would serve the intended purpose, with the least possible reference to any thing personal. But since the publication of that part of the Review which was printed in the Mutual Rights and Christian Intelligencer, a number of essays have appeared, which we think have made it necessary to prefix the introductory chapter. The facts and considerations which this chapter supplies, will prepare the reader very satisfactorily to understand the remaining developements, which constitute the first part of the work.

The essays which, together with the accompanying notes and explanations, fill up the second part, at the same time that they present the papers to which the chief men engaged in the prosecution of reformers, made objections, will be found to be so full of the proper kind of information, that to the careful reader of the first part, they will present an epitomized history of the struggle through which reformers had to pass, in rousing the attention of the Methodist community to a subject so important.   It will be found, moreover, that the papers which were deemed so highly offensive by the friends of aristocratical power, are well written, and afford good evidence of the abilities of their respective writers.   To those who have not read the Mutual Rights, they cannot fail to be greatly interesting, and such is the effect of the arrangement which the occasion has produced, that the whole subject is presented with renewed interest, even to such as have been attending to the controversy.

The propriety of having appended the essay upon the subject of Mr. Asbury's intended Biography, will be obvious to every reader who will consider, that the personal injury which was aimed at us, was expected materially to affect the cause in which we are engaged.   We had long ago determined silently to "suffer wrong;"—and so long as it might have been permitted to remain an affair of mere private and individual interest, we were ready to endure, with "*all long suffering.*"   But having become conspicuously identified with the just claims and pretensions of the Methodist Protestant Church, when our reputation is assailed with design to injure the common cause, we are constrained to appear and answer.

CONTENTS.

CHAPTER XVII.

INTRODUCTION.

It is now extensively known, that more than thirty ministers and members, of the Methodist E. Church in Baltimore, were excommunicated for being members of the Union Society, and publishing and patronizing the periodical, which was known by the title "The Mutual Rights, of the ministers and members of the Methodist Episcopal Church." It ought also to be known, that this memorable transaction was intended to *expel reform* out of the church, and that the measures which were adopted, were contrived and conducted, with the hope, that the real object could be concealed, and the public be induced to believe, the church authorities had only exercised commendable discipline upon those thirty and more individuals, for publishing and aiding in the publication of certain essays and papers, said to be calumnious and inflammatory. The exposition and review will disclose some curious and important things, in respect to the management, by which the men in power accomplished their intention; and will satisfactorily unravel the policy, which was expected also to insure the approbation of the community.

The Editors of the Quarterly Review, &c. have laboured hard to set aside this imputation, and justify the proceedings of the prosecution.

The Baltimore Annual Conference considered those proceedings to have been so commendable as to merit the apellation, of "wholesome and sound discipline."

To develope the true design of the church authorities, to show how great the injustice done to reformers, and how necessary the struggle which brought upon them the displeasure of the government, are the objects and end of the review.

In conducting our investigations, facts, known to be incontrovertible, are stated as such. Inferences, taken from facts and circumstances, are so presented, that their value or intended pur-

2

port cannot easily be mistaken. In pursuing the obliquities of the prosecution, it has been found necessary, in some instances, to introduce probabilities into the argument; and considering the circumstances in which the reviewer has been placed, this will appear to have been both admissible and proper.

Certain preparatory movements induced us to believe, that an attempt would be made to sustain the contemplated expulsions, by means of a publication, to be modified as circumstances might indicate; and which, accordingly, turned out to be, the NARRATIVE and DEFENCE, &c. &c.

The incidents which excited attention to this point, and the fact, that the man who was believed to be the chief agent in the business, who made the extracts from the Mutual Rights, and wrote the Narrative and Defence for the prosecutors, were all in view, when the remarks which were made on this point, were written.

There was positive proof of a conspiracy, for the purpose of securing our excommunication, by an unanimous vote of all the official men in the station. The pains which were taken to gain this point, strengthened the conviction, that the occasion would require a competent agent, to give to the intended operations, their proper direction and effect. Moreover, there were signs of the existence of such an agency, which were not of doubtful interpretation. The review therefore, inevitably turns attention to this matter.

The printing committee, who superintended the periodical, intended no personal attack upon the preachers, from the Bishops down to the least important individual among them. They designed a benefit, and not an injury, to the Methodist Episcopal Church. It was their purpose to bring about an improvement in her government, and nothing more. It therefore, became our duty to review the extracts and comments, which were made by the agent of the prosecution, and show, that the alleged calumny and inflammatory imputations, which he has placed to the account of the Union Society, are in reality the productions of his own genius;—and, that it required his utmost skill to make the Narrative and Defence, to answer its intended purpose. It was necessary, that it should wear the appearance of a faithful history of the citations, the charges and specifications, the character and manner of the Defence of the accused, and of the final decisions; and in order to make the whole, the more to assume the appearance of honesty or plausibility; to take time, to plan and manage as circumstances might indicate; to introduce "an under-plot," and a collateral plot, &c. &c. We therefore considered it necessary to ferret out and disclose the more important parts of these secret machinations.

It was deemed highly important, that our views of the proceedings, should be submitted to the public. Because, if we erred in our opinions respecting the design of the prosecution, and of the measures which were taken for the accomplishment of that design; nevertheless, as we had very cogent reasons for adopting those opinions, sensible men will admit, that we ought to have been excused for refusing to appear before a tribunal, which we conscientiously considered, not only illegal, but also disqualified to do us justice; and the more especially so, when we did not believe that we had transgressed any known law. If our opinions were right, it will be still more clear, that submission to such a trial as necessarily awaited us, would have been an unpardonable dereliction of principle and duty. The review will prepare the reader to perceive the propriety of our course, and to appreciate the protest of the reformers.

So far as our exposition has been published in the Mutual Rights and Christian Intelligencer, although its ultimate intention was but imperfectly understood, it has given great offence to those who are implicated; and in order to prevent its effect, another effort has been made, of the same kind, and by the same genius, which brought forth the Narrative and Defence. Doctor Bond, in particular, has taken great umbrage at the mere insinuation, that he was the agent of the power party, as well as the writer of the "plain statement of the whole affair, &c." It is perhaps due to Dr. Bond, and the public, that the reasons should be assigned for having exhibited him in that relation to the prosecution;—for we have no inclination to misrepresent him, or misconstrue his writings.

The Doctor, in a late publication, says our inferences in respect to this point, were taken from two circumstances only. If those two were all that had weight, it might perhaps be inferred, that the reviewer had indulged in unfounded and reprehensible suspicion. There are, however, other circumstances, which came into the account. We had in fact, nine or more considerations, which taken collectively, approximate to a demonstration of the reasonableness and truth of our opinion. They are the following:

1st. When the lay members of the Baltimore station, met in the conference room, a short time previous to the General Conference of 1824, and appointed a committee, to prepare an address or memorial on the subject of a lay delegation to be submitted to the conference, Dr. Bond, at that time a preacher, insisted on being admitted among them, as a layman, that he might be placed on the committee. As he had not then been ordained, his request was granted, and he officiated as secretary.

The result of their labours was the production of that memorable paper, which surrendered all claim to a lay representation, as a matter of right, and proposed to rest the whole subject upon the ground of expediency. In the instant, when that part of their report was read, which contained this fatal proposition, we considered it a known surrender of the cause of reform; and we have continued to view it in the same light, until now. Prior to that time, the Doctor was an active patron to the Wesleyan Repository, probably, one of the writers for that work. Since that time, we have not known any act of his, which favoured our cause. This circumstance indicated *"disaffection"* to the work of reform, and had some influence, we admit, in modifying our feelings in view of the second consideration.

2d. When the chairman of our printing committee, and Mr. McCaine, were called on to meet Bishop Hedding, in the conference room, and answer to his demand of the proper name of Timothy, they found him attended by Bishop George, Rev. John Davis, and doctor Bond.

This incident occurred some time within the first week in April, 1827. The expulsions in Tennessee had then taken place. Likewise those in North Carolina; and the latter had received the confirmation of the Virginia Conference. Moreover, we had received intimations, that the Baltimore Conference, which was then at hand, was expected to deal with Rev. D. B. Dorsey. Under all these stormy appearances, we think the Doctor ought to have excused us, if we then began to think, that something more was agitated in the cabinet, than the single inquiry, who was Timothy.

3d. Soon after the suspension of the Rev'd D. B. Dorsey, doctor Bond, as the champion of the power party, wrote and caused to be published, "An Appeal to the Methodists, &c." in opposition to the principles and objects of the Reformers. In the introduction to a "brief review" of this appeal, Mr. Shinn has the following remarks. "How can a man sit down calmly to examine, and impartially to answer a book of sixty-nine pages, when he expects the arm of authority to be upon him, before he shall have arrived at the middle of his investigation? Our opponents have systematically commenced the work of suspension and expulsion; they are using all imaginable efforts to enlist against us the passions of the people; and the doctor's performance, coming out at this time, appears but too well calculated to fan the flame. We may reasonably expect, it will be used for the accomplishment of this object, as extensively as possible." If so well calculated for such a use, with the two preceding reasons in view, were we not pardonable in thinking, the "Appeal, &c." was written for the very purpose mentioned by Mr. Shinn? However much we might have endeavoured to "hope all things," the doctor soon gave us conclusive proof, that our apprehension concerning his agency, was but too well founded.

4th. Doctor Bond convened the meeting at the corner of Pitt and Front streets. His own account of it is, that his object was to make a publication under the sanction of this called meeting, in defence of the Baltimore Annual Conference, in the case of Rev'd. D. B. Dorsey. The meeting was held on the 7th August, 1827, thirty-two days only before we were summoned by Mr. Hanson, to appear and answer to charges, which were preferred by the seven prosecutors. The doctor's publication was made, and it received the sanction of the meeting, with the following preface, viz: "At a very large meeting of the male members of the Methodist Episcopal Church, in Baltimore City and the East Baltimore stations, exclusive of the members of the Union Society, convened by public notice given in ALL our churches, and held in the city of Baltimore on the 7th day of August, 1827; brother William Wilkins being called to the chair, &c. the following preamble, resolutions, and address to the ministers and members of the church in the *United States*, were freely discussed and adopted, with only three or four dissenting votes."

A part of the address is as follows, viz: "The opinion of the Conference, that the Mutual Rights was an improper work, was not founded on its being a work on church government, &c. &c. * * * * but it was founded on the FACT, that the Mutual Rights was a work, in which anonymous writers were permitted to *abuse* and *defame* the travelling preachers—to deprive them, if possible, of the confidence and support of the people of their charge, by holding them up to public odium, and by *misrepresenting* both their actions and motives."

On the 8th September, 1827, we received information, that charges had been preferred; and a part of the second specification reads thus:—"The Mutual Rights of the ministers and members, &c. contains much that inveighs against the Discipline, &c. * * * ; and that is *abusive* or *speaks evil* of a part, if not most of the ministers of that church," &c. &c. Is it not clear to the most ordinary apprehension, that when this large meeting, almost unanimously, voted for the part of the address above quoted, doctor Bond, who had called the meeting, written the address, and caused it to be freely discussed, had by this measure, secured their approbation of the intended charge as stated in the specification? The large meeting voted, that it was a FACT, that writers were permitted in the Mutual Rights, to *abuse* and *defame* the travelling preachers, &c. by *misrepresenting* both their *actions* and *motives*. The prosecutors charged us with publishing, in the Mutual Rights, * * * much that is *abusive* or *speaks evil* of a part, if not of most of the ministers, &c.

In another part of the address, and which in like manner, had the vote of doctor Bond's called meeting, we find the following, viz: "The present agitations may be consequent upon some general declension, in reference to the *strict administration of that* WHOLESOME DISCIPLINE, which governed our fathers, and distinguished them as '*a peculiar people.*' The present storm may be necessary to *defecate* and purify the church from *Laodicean, lukewarm* professors." Hear what the doctor's address proposed, and for which he obtained the approbation of almost the whole of this large meeting!" "*Strict administration of discipline to defecate;*" that is, to purge off the dregs, and by so doing, to purify the church from lukewarm professors. Can any reader fail to see, the proof of an agency, making preparation for our expulsion?

The doctor called a large meeting, which was attended by almost the whole of the male members of the church, including in course, the official men, and so secured their vote, upon points which involved all that was necessary, to ensure success, in the contemplated "defecation" of the church. Surely it was an act of the utmost preparatory importance; and, if there were no other testimony, this one measure proves, that he was, not only an agent, but a very provident and efficient agent, by whose management in this single instance, we were obliged to know, that we were condemned, before we were cited to trial.

5th. About one week after the prosecutions were commenced, doctor Bond, "ventured alone and without the knowledge of the prosecutors, upon the business of negotiation." He "had not yet relinquished the hope, that some *conciliatory course* might be *devised*, by which the *necessity* of further proceedings before the CONSTITUTED AUTHORITIES of the church, might be removed." In *narrating* and *defending* about this affair, thus far, the doctor wrote according to the truth of the case. He wrote what he felt on the subject. "He ventured upon the business of negotiation:" that is, to take the management of the business into his own hands. He hoped, that he would be able *to devise* a conciliatory course, which would put an end to the necessity of further proceedings. With this intention, he proceeded like an autocrat, to prescribe the terms which he saw fit to *"devise."* But in order to conceal the true extent of the power, which he felt himself at liberty to exercise, he appended to the terms which he dictatorially offered, a clause, a kind of *rider*, under the authority of which, in case of his detection, he intended to claim the privilege of being considered a mere mediator, who had not consulted either of the parties. See Narrative and Defence, pages 24 and 25. The reader will find this part of doctor Bond's agency, resumed in another place and treated to all necessary extent.

6th. When doctor Green arrived in Baltimore, *he having been sent for* to perform a part in the great drama of "defecation," doctor Bond had immediate notice of his arrival, with a request to meet him at Mr. Warfield's. In the course of the evening, doctor Bond found it convenient to attend; and the two doctors were together till a very late hour. On the following morning, we received doctor Green's first communication, dated 15th January, 1828. In this letter he says, "I have not mentioned this subject to any of your *stationed* preachers;" leaving us to infer, as a thing of course, that he had mentioned it to doctor Bond only.

This inference seems to be still more reasonable, because we had an opportunity to see his communication, addressed to the president and members of the Quarterly Conference, then in session, which was dated 16th January, 1828, and reads as follows, viz: "Whereas certain charges have been preferred, &c. * * * and whereas I, as a *disinterested* member of said church, have *volunteered* as a mediator, &c. * * * * as there is a negotiation now pending, between doctor Jennings and myself, in relation to terms of reconciliation between said parties, &c. * * * * and as such a reconciliation is desirable, and has been *sought on your part, with anxious vigilance*, and would now be hailed by each one of you, &c. * *.'' Doctor Green had no proper authority for this assertion. In fact it was not true. If the unqualified mandate of the prosecutors, to dissolve our Union Societies and discontinue our periodical, was *seeking* reconciliation, we must admit they sought it, in that manner; and if one application in this unlawful and repulsive way, was a proper expression of *"anxious vigilance,"* this evidence of vigilance was afforded. Nothing bearing, even the name of reconciliation, had been intimated, excepting the terms dictated by doctor Bond to doctor J. S. Reese. These terms were all that any one of them had ever proposed; we were obliged, therefore, to come to the conclusion, that doctor Bond had made doctor Green acquainted with this circumstance, whilst they were together, the first night, at Mr. Warfield's. Hence it appears, that although doctor Bond had ACTED ALONE in his attempt at DEVISING *means of reconciliation*, he had prepared doctor Green to say in his letter, which afterwards was to be published in the Narrative and Defence, that a reconciliation had been sought on the part of the church authorities *"with anxious vigilance."* This circumstance was calculated to tell to great advantage. The church had sought for a reconciliation with the reformers, "with *anxious vigilance*," whilst the reformers, on their part, had continued to treat the church authorities with *"proud contempt."*

On the 16th January, 1828, when replying to doctor Green, we indulged a hope, that all was fair. But his second communication of same date, which was the day following his interview with doctor Bond, presented terms, which let us know, that he was nothing better than a sub-agent, who had come to act as an auxiliary to doctor Bond. The terms which he submitted, perhaps we ought to have said which he dictated, were in substance identical with those proposed by doctor Bond to doctor Reese. See Narrative and Defence, pages 124, 125. In a summary, they were as follows, viz:

1st. To suspend the publication of the Mutual Rights, until the result of our memorial to the General Conference shall be known. Or if it be continued, "it shall be conducted by a committee, in whose appointment the friends of the present administration and the friends of Reform, shall have an equal part, &c. &c.

2d. That the Union Society shall be dissolved, until the result of your memorial, &c. &c. shall be known.

Doctor Bond's terms, in substance, were as follows, viz: See Narrative and Defence, page 25.

1st. "When the convention shall have terminated its session, the Union Society shall be dissolved and not re-organized, in the present or any other form, until after the next General Conference."

2d. The Mutual Rights, if continued at all, shall be strictly confined, &c. &c. * * * each number in the proof-sheets, or the materials before they are printed, shall be submitted to three persons, *chosen mutually* by the reformers and the committee, who have preferred charges, &c. * * * who shall be authorized to expunge all exceptionable passages therefrom."

The reader is requested to consider, that doctor Bond's terms were prescribed to us, before the meeting of our convention. Those of doctor Green after the convention. He will make allowance for this difference, and he cannot fail to perceive the near affinity of the terms dictated to us, by these two doctors. We are now told, that doctors Bond and Green, were closeted upon another subject, and even that doctor Green so carefully regarded the principles of neutrality, in view of his delicate mediation, that he declined any conversation on that subject. If we rightly understand the signatures of the *"anonymous writers,"* who of late, are engaged on the part of the Methodist Episcopal Church, "to speak evil of ministers," but who have nothing to fear from the seven prosecutors, seeing they are on the side of power, doctor Bond passed this compliment, upon his coadjutor, doctor Green. We must be excused, in claiming the privilege of placing this to the same account, on which we have entered a similar item, which occurred about the time when our mediator, who left his home "with intention to volunteer, &c." "without being solicited to do so by any one,"—was announced to the Quarterly Meeting Conference. He and doctor Bond had been together the greater part of the preceding night; and yet, when notice was given of his arrival, &c. doctor Bond arose in Quarterly meeting and inquired, *"Who is this doctor Green?" Is he the man who preached, &c. &c.?*

All such matters could be conducted "without any itinerant suggestion or influence whatever." And these "gentlemen" may succeed in persuading the people of their fellowship, that they practised no obliquities;—in the mean time, all disinterested persons will admit, that we had too much cause to doubt their

3

candor, and consider them the secret agents of the government; the more certainly so. when we now state openly, as we might have done at the commencement of the review, that doctor Green, himself, told Rev'd. Mr. F. Stier, that *he was sent for.* Moreover, one of the doctor's pupils, gave similar information to Mr. J. J. Harrod's family.

7th. After the expulsions had been accomplished, agreeably to the intention "to defecate the church," so clearly "indicated," by the address and vote of the Pitt street meeting, Doctor Bond wrote the Narrative and Defence, in justification of "that wholesome discipline which governed our fathers, and distinguished them as a peculiar people." This fact, is itself, an irresistible proof of the doctor's agency. Indeed, few agents have manifested a warmer interest, or greater zeal. And judging from the high commendations which have been bestowed on it, by the editors of the Christian Advocate, &c., at New York, those who were most deeply interested, considered the agency to have been executed most admirably.

8th. Another consideration, which had weight in inducing the opinion and belief, that doctor Bond took an active part in *planing* and *managing* matters, was the marked caution which he evinced, in order to escape the imputation. We will explain, by referring to two or three of the occurrences of those times.

1. In his attempted negociation with the Union Society, through doctor Reese, he *"wished it to be distinctly* understood that *he acted alone* and as a *mediator,* and that he had not *consulted* with any of the old side brethren on the subject, &c. &c." By the by, as he felt himself at liberty to *"devise"* and dictate terms, which might accomplish all the purposes of the prosecution, and so "remove the *necessity* of further proceedings, &c." there was no need of consultation.

2. When our protest was advertised, as in the instance of doctor Reese, above stated, so in this, he was looking on with "anxious vigilance;" and perceiving that the publication of the protest called for his help, he gave to Mr. Samuel Harden "the first suggestion of the necessity" of submitting to the public, a "plain statement of the whole affair," so soon as the trials should be ended. Perhaps if we knew all, we might say, he dictated, that such a publication should be announced, in order to counteract "our novel procedure."

Our friends know, that immediately after our interview with Mr. Harden, we told them, that a publication would be made by the power party, with intention to justify their proceedings. It is an affair of very small moment, that Mr. Harden has ventured to contradict our assertion that we learned their intention as to their contemplated plain statement, &c. from him. In their attempt to avoid Scylla, they have run into Charybdis. The doctor thought it important to get away from Harden's unintentional disclosure; but in managing the affair, it escaped his notice, that he was furnishing proof positive of his agency in the case. He says, *he* gave to Mr. Harden, the first suggestion of the necessity of such a measure. Surely his own testimony may be safely admitted.

8. Dr. Bond was the writer of the Narrative and Defence, and notwithstanding he has said, the part he took in aiding the prosecutors, was generally known, and to no one better than to the writer of this Review, it is a fact, that we knew nothing more about it than will be found in this publication. We think it probable, however, that the review provoked the public acknowledgment, that he was the writer. Would it not have comported more strictly with candor and truth, if he had affixed his own proper signature to the work? It would then have been concluded as follows, viz.

THOMAS E. BOND,
for the seven prosecutors.

And every reader would have been prepared to judge how far, *laymen*, *unassisted*, had been the agents in the "defecating" work. Instead of this plain and honest procedure, the names of the seven prosecutors are all subscribed, as if they were the authors of the book.

9th. Dr. Bond's agency is fairly deducible from the disingenuousness of the Narrative and Defence. Although an avowed "plain statement of the whole affair," perhaps a more unfair *exparte* account of things, has not been published in the United States. This imputation will be supported by the review of the extracts and comments which will be seen in the sequel. It is not intended, however, to confine the charge of disingenuousness to the extracts and comments. It is stamped upon the face of the book, more or less, upon almost every page. We will select one example, which for the present may serve as an illustration of our complaint touching this point. Our protest was based upon his "appeal to the Methodists, &c." and the address which he caused to be issued from the Pitt street meeting. No subject, therefore, could have been more familiar to him. That protest presented a very important difficulty to the prosecution, which he ought to have met and answered fairly. The subtile evasion, to which he had recourse in this particular, is the example of subterfuge to which we now invite attention. See Narrative and Defence, pages 30, 31, 32, and 33.

The second part of our protest, which was formally entered before the extraordinary tribunal, CONSTITUTED by the Baltimore station for the purpose of securing our expulsion, and the publication of which, induced doctor Bond to give "the first suggestion of the necessity of publishing the Narrative and Defence," was drawn up in the following words, viz: "I now enter my protest, because of the impossibility of a fair and disinterested trial,—for that, my sentence is already pronounced, by the men who are to sit in judgment. For confirmation of this, I refer to doctor Bond's book, (Appeal to the Methodists, &c.) pages 44, 45. 'The history of this controversy,' says he, 'bears irresistible testimony to the position, that a profession of religion will not save us from the consequences incident to opposition and contest among the professors. Let any man look over the pages of the Wesleyan Repository, and the Mutual Rights, and doubt this position, if he can. He will see the *merciless gladiators, cutting* and *thrusting without pity or remorse.* He will see a periodical work, * * * which the heat of debate, and the *mortification of disappointed ambition,* has converted into a *vehicle* of *anonymous slander* and *misrepresentation, &c. &c.*' * * * * * * * * * And I am warranted in saying, that the sentence here pronounced in doctor Bond's book, is likewise the sentence of every active old-side man in the station. Of these official men, who are to judge of my case, it *certainly* is. For proof, I refer to the pamphlet, whose manuscript, written by doctor Bond and the rest of the committee, had the sanction and vote of the meeting, at the corner of Pitt and Front streets; a meeting of the old side brethren, when and where, these three brethren of the committee, acted and voted with them, as *they themselves* now *admit*. Read (the address,) on pages 2 and 3. 'The opinion of the conference, (Baltimore Annual Conference is meant) that the Mutual Rights was an improper work, &c. &c. * * * was founded on the FACT, that the Mutual Rights was a *work* in which *anonymous* writers were permitted to *abuse* and *defame* the *travelling preachers, &c. &c.* * * * * * * by misrepresenting both their actions and their motives.' Here is proof positive, that the Mutual Rights, is already under sentence of condemnation. And I am constrained to say, this semblance of a trial, is intended to condemn me, in like manner." The difficulty which this protest presented has never yet been met; and it is impossible to reconcile it with the principles of common justice, much less with those of christian benevolence. In order to escape it, the Doctor says, "the protests chiefly rested on the want of conformity in the appointment and in the proceedings generally, to the practice which obtains in courts of criminal jurisprudence." Every reader must perceive that this statement is not true. Our protest rested on the notorious fact, that all the men concerned, had prejudged our case. Having made the above misrepresentation, he makes a fine flourish in view of it, affecting to shew how reformers, "after their fashion," would bring the church into all the uncertainties of the law. "Instead of the little book of discipline, give them as a substitute, massy folios of common law, and statute law, with commentaries of learned length and reports of ponderous magnitude,"—"ecclesiastical lawyers,"—"courts," judges, clerks, &c. &c. "to keep them to all the rules of special pleading, and legal technicalities." This learned display may have entertained the friends of the prosecution. In view of our protest, it is without meaning, except only, that it "indicates" a probability, that doctor Bond was the author of the charges and specifications. He proceeds to inform us that the prosecuting party "considered the church judicatories, as merely moral tribunals, in which a few plain pious men were deemed capable of deciding, whether an accused brother had violated his religious or social obligations." * * They think "that men of plain common sense, with the *necessary piety* and *integrity,* were fully competent to judge in such matters, both of the *law* and the fact." And what does all this signify? We suppose this is the Doctor's argument to prove, that the three local preachers selected to condemn us, possessed enough *piety* and *integrity;* or perhaps, that they possessed all that was "necessary," to fit them to join in the preparatory meeting, vote for "defecating" the church of the publishers of the Mutual Rights, and then sit in judgment to confirm their own previous decision. This procedure, according to the Doctor, is such, as "men of plain common sense" with the "necessary piety and integrity" will pursue. We are constrained to pray, "from such expressions of common sense, piety or integrity, good Lord deliver us!" After all these and other fancies equally evasive, at length he affects to

march right up to the difficulty. "In the cases under consideration, the objections were, first, that the members of the committees, &c. at a meeting held at doctor Roszel's academy, partici-
pated in the appointment of a committee to prosecute. Secondly,
that they had voted for certain resolutions and an address, at
the Pitt street meeting." He denies, however, that such committee was appointed; and says they were *requested to inquire* into
the causes which had produced the existing agitations, &c. &c.
It matters not. The seven men were sufficiently "indicated" by
the *request*, to feel themselves called to the service of the prosecution. In doctor Bond's view of things, however, there seems
to have been a difference.

"The second objection," respecting the vote at Pitt street, he
admits, "is more specious, and requires particular consideration."
In view of this, it appears that the Doctor and we are of the
same opinion. "It requires particular consideration." At said
meeting, all the official men had voted it to be a FACT, that the
Mutual Rights had published much, that abused or spoke evil of
ministers. On our trial, the same men are appointed to inquire,
whether it is indeed a *fact*. Now let us see how the Doctor
meets it, after admitting that it needs "particular consideration."
"In the address complained of," says he, *"no individual is named,* as being responsible for the publication in the Mutual Rights,
nor *is any opinion given, that the writers or publishers of that
work, ought to be expelled from the church."*
Can it be, that doctor Bond expected his readers to accept
this as an explanation? The prosecution charged us with "speaking evil of ministers"——because we aided, &c. in "the publication of the Mutual Rights, which contains much, &c. * * that
is *abusive*, or *speaks evil* of a part if not most of the ministers,"
&c. The address asserts it to be a FACT, that the periodical,
the Mutual Rights, was rightly considered to be an improper
work, because in it, writers were permitted "to *abuse* and *defame*
the travelling preachers;"——the pretended offence for which the
Doctor and his aids intended to expel us, and for which they did
expel more than thirty of us as soon as they could, and save appearances. But as they did not read out the names of the contemplated victims, nor say they *intended to expel* us; as they only
voted the necessity of *"defecating"* the church of luke-warm
members, they would have us to admit, that all was in accordance
with the law of Christ, "as ye would that men should do unto
you, do ye likewise unto them." As the Doctor says, the com-

mittee, although they voted for the address, had not prejudged the cases of the accused on the charges preferred against them, we must succumb and say, "so let it be." In order to expose clearly, the sophistry which he intended to serve his turn, in this case, let us inquire what ought to have been the proper subject of investigation before the court of inquiry. Had they prosecuted the writers of the objectionable papers, individually, the Editorial committee were bound to surrender the proper name of each, or answer in his stead. Or if they had intended to prosecute the committee, either individually or jointly as Editors, their names were known, having been publicly announced every year. The inquiry, therefore was not who were the writers, nor who were the publishers. It was only necessary to ascertain, whether the Mutual Rights *did* or did not "contain much that is *abusive* or *speaks* evil of a part, if not most of the ministers, &c. &c." The prosecutors asserted the affirmative, and it was their business to support that affirmation, by the necessary testimony. Those who stood charged would have asserted the negative, and in the event of a trial, it would have been incumbent on them to justify their papers or publications.

Although the Doctor endeavoured to escape by shuffling up this substitute for an explanation, he seems to have been impelled by a sense of justice to return to the only correct view of the subject, and concluded by saying, "whether the decisions which these committees have given in the cases submitted to them, have been *just*, will be left to the reader after he shall calmly and dispassionately have read the *extracts* from the Mutual Rights, upon which those who preferred the accusations relied to sustain them." And if the reader will be contented with doctor Bond's "extracts," and his comments upon them, it is very probable that he will also be satisfied, that the decisions of the committees were just. How many have already been satisfied with the accounts given of these matters in the Narrative and Defence, we know not. But all such are liable to a very mortifying censure; inasmuch as it will appear to have been an affair of no importance with them, how great the departure from principle and correct procedure, which marked the conduct of the men who sat in judgment, and prevented the accused from making a proper defence; all that was necessary to secure their approbation, was, that the prosecutors or their agent for them, was ready to tell a plausible ex-parte story. For it will be demonstrated by the review, that we were insulted by a mere mock-trial, and that the extracts upon which the Doctor relies for the justification of their proceedings, are garbled fragments only, of the essays from which they are taken, caricatured by his comments, and fitted up for the special purpose, of sustaining the Methodist Episcopal Church in the outrage practised upon us, with intention to exterminate reform.

We might have said, that we had ten reasons and more for considering doctor Bond an agent in the prosecution of the friends of reform. We will notice one fact only in addition. He was at the pains to attend the General Conference, at Pittsburg, the distance of 280 miles. What other business might have concurred, to make his attention there necessary at that time, we know not. But we had information from our friends, that his exertions were continued, until the General Conference had decreed the terms and conditions for the re-admission into their fellowship of such of us, as might be disposed to submit to them;—the same terms in effect, which he had attempted to impose upon us through doctors Reese and Green, as will be clearly seen in the conclusion of the review.

Taking all these circumstances and considerations into the account, can it be thought, that the strictest law of charity was transgressed, in admitting the opinion that Dr. Bond was a concealed agent of the power party, and the fast friend of the government of the Methodist Episcopal Church; or in signifying our apprehension, that by means of the two first meetings, one at Mr. William Brown's, the other at doctor Roszel's school room, a conspiracy was organized, and by the management of doctor Bond, in calling the third meeting at Pitt street, and obtaining an almost unanimous vote, that conspiracy was extended and strengthened, insomuch, that the leading men of the two stations of the city, were all pledged to help him to "defecate the church," of the friends of Mutual Rights?

The Doctor says, this account of the part he acted in the drama of "defecation" is intended to be "a personal insult without provocation." That "gentleman" has thought it necessary to commence a personal attack on us, expecting to divert the attention of the public from our review, the effect of which he foresees and fears. We have no time for personal contests, and it has been a source of regret, that the introduction of doctors Bond and Green, by name, was necessary. But we found them amongst the most prominent dramatis personæ in the performance of the grand display, of the manner how the "fathers" exercised *a strict administration of wholesome discipline*, and distinguished themselves as a peculiar people." They were very desirous to make the public believe, that the whole performance was conducted without "any *itinerant suggestion* or *influence whatever;*" and we paid to each of them, so much attention only, as the intended exposition required, and no more. We were particularly compelled to acknowledge the importance of the part which doctor Bond had to perform, and in the execution of which he acquitted himself so well, that we thought he richly deserved a benefit. He says of it, himself, that to have equalled our account of it, would have required the talents of a Talleyrand, or a Metternich. Surely then, we offered no insult to his understanding. We considered him the fast friend of the government of the Methodist E. Church. And this, it is presumed, is now one of his chief boastings. And as he was pleased to devote himself, after his own manner, to the support of the prosecutions, we assure our readers, that no part of his conduct, pending the whole of that transaction, was as reprehensible in our estimation, as is his recent attempt to conceal his agency. After having acknowledged, that he called the meeting at Pitt street, for the purpose of publishing under the sanction of the male members of the two stations, a defence of the Baltimore Annual Conference, in the case of Rev'd D. B. Dorsey. After having acknowledged the part he took in preparing, reading and discussing the address which denounced the Mutual Rights, and signified the necessity of discipline, "to *defecate*" the church, &c. After admitting that he made the extracts from the Mutual Rights, and wrote the Narrative and Defence, in justification of the "defecation," so soon as it had been accomplished by the unanimous vote, which the call of the meeting was intended to secure, we are obliged to think his further attempt at concealment, has the appearance of being at variance with christian candor.

He has endeavoured to elude the imputation of his agency, in regard to his having written the Narrative and Defence, by alledging, that the papers, from which the extracts were made, had been previously "indicated," in the charges and specifications, which had been prepared for the prosecutions. Those papers may have been previously indicated, and yet we are excusable, even now, in suggesting the possibility, that he aided in making out that "indication," with intention to comment on those parts of them, which he thought he could use to advantage; first, for

4

accomplishing the intended "defecation" of the church, by an unanimous vote of the Quarterly Meeting Conference, "a majority of which body had not read the Mutual Rights at all;" and in the second place, to satisfy the Methodist people, who in like manner were expected to see the extracts only, and without "reading the Mutual Rights, to adopt the conclusion furnished to their hands by the Narrative and Defence: and so by one effort, make all believe, that the church was greatly benefitted by his "defecation." It is unimportant who indicated the papers, and the merit of the Review is not in the least diminished, if we erred in supposing that the attention of the Bishops had been called to them by the Doctor, some months before hand, because it is known by the circumstances of Rev'd D. B. Dorsey's case, that the Baltimore Annual Conference and the Bishops who attended that conference, did turn attention to the subject, and clearly made known their disposition towards the Mutual Rights. Or if the proceedings of the conference were not sufficiently notorious by other means, doctor Bond's address, which was read and discussed at the Pitt street meeting and afterwards printed, fairly disclosed the fact, that the condemnation of the Mutual Rights by the church in Baltimore, would be in accordance with the views and previous decision of the Annual Conference.

One of their writers, doctor Bond, it is presumed, says "Having *slyly* assigned to doctor Bond, the contrivance and arrangement of the fearful conspiracy against reformers, Doctor Jennings now introduces him, as condescending to manage an *under-plot*, by proposing terms of compromise to the Union Society, which was afterwards to make a figure in the Narrative and Defence." As doctor Bond has attempted to shew "great delinquency, in our manner of touching this point, let us examine it again with more care. The statement, as it was printed in our review, is as follows, viz: "But before the trials commenced, doctor Bond took occasion, on his responsibility, to offer terms to the Union Society, which if accepted, he ventured to engage for the prosecutions, that they should be dismissed." And to make his charge of delinquency the more conspicuous, he exhibited his imaginary contrast, in two opposite columns. It was his intention, to leave an impression on the minds of his readers, that unguardedly and in violation of truth, we had asserted that he gave a pledge, when he was careful to be understood as acting the part of a mediator. And as he did, in preparing the

Narrative and Defence, so in this case, he makes his charge of delinquency look very specious. We reply, that neither the nature of the engagement, nor the value of the "pledge," was the burden of our story. It was our leading intention, in view of that part of the transactions of the day, to show how *important* doctor Bond felt himself to be, in respect to the prosecutions:—that he acted as the *chief man*. And to make known our reasons for taking such a view of his importance, we referred our readers to the Narrative and Defence, pages 24 and 25. There doctor Bond, speaking of himself, says, "he had not relinquished the hope, that some conciliatory course might be *devised*, by which, the *necessity of further proceedings before the constituted authorities of the church, might be removed.*" * * * "and that he VENTURED ALONE and WITHOUT OUR KNOWLEDGE (the prosecutors are meant) UPON THE BUSINESS OF NEGOTIATION." In accordance with this statement, made by the doctor himself, and in perfect agreement with the impression which it made on our minds, it is said in the review, that "he took occasion, on his own responsibility, to offer terms to the Union Society." So far from being untrue, is this comment upon the doctor's statement, that it is not as strong as it ought to have been. Instead of having said "he took occasion to *offer* terms," it ought to have been said, he took occasion to *dictate* terms. As to any thing that the brethren, generally, knew antecedent to that circumstance, doctor Bond had not made his appearance. It is obvious, however, from his own statement that he was on the alert waiting for the time proper for his entrance, when by *some device*, he ALONE, *without the knowledge* of the seven prosecutors, might render further proceedings before the constituted authorities of the church, *unnecessary*. And here it may be proper to remark, that the terms which he "DEVISED" and intended, and hoped to be able to impose upon us, first through doctor J. S. Reese, in the way of this "*under-plot*," and next in the way of a *collateral plot*, by the intervention of doctor Green, were the same which were again held out by Mr. Hanson, to the "defecated" victims; and finally, by the General Conference, as the only conditions of our return. And every intelligent reader, on examining these terms, the "DEVICE" of doctor Bond, will find, that they are so "*devised*" that had we acceded to them, when proposed by him, "*further proceedings before the constituted authorities of the church*," would indeed have been unnecessary. But why did the review present an "*unequivocal assertion*," that these terms contained a "pledge," that the prosecutions should be dismissed? Let it be remembered, that in our apprehension, doctor Bond was a chief agent, though concealed. We therefore, in reading the account which this agent gives of himself, find him saying, that *"without the knowledge or consent* of the prosecutors, he *ventured* ALONE *upon the business of negotiation."* Again in presenting his dictatorial terms, he says *"I am disposed to use* MY PERSONAL *influence* to procure a suspension of proceedings before the church, upon the *following conditions;"* and he told doctor J. S. Reese, it was his opinion, if the Union Society would come to the terms which he proposed, the prosecutions would be dismissed. Moreover, doctor Bond told a very respectable citizen, not a Methodist, that he was *authorized* to make the overture of terms to the Union Society, which he presented to doctor John S. Reese. As he did this, as he "ventured upon the business of negotiation *alone and without the knowledge of the prosecutors,"* and was nevertheless *authorized* to do it, we ask, who but those high in power, and yet out of sight in the transaction, could have given him the authority? We know that Bishop George was acquainted with the intended "defecation," whilst as yet the preparations were making, and we cannot forget, that doctor Bond and Bishop George attended Bishop Hedding, when the proper name of Timothy was demanded.

Contemplating the subject according to this view, we would ask, wherein consists our delinquency? Let us examine the subject in still another light. The object of the prosecution, according to our candid apprehension, was, to depose and annihilate reform. The terms *"devised"* by doctor Bond, if they had been received, could not have failed to have accomplished this purpose. But if they were obliged to rely upon the intended *"defecation,"* although it had received the vote of the Pitt street Meeting, yet it was possible, and the doctor could foresee the possibility, that our prediction to Mr. S. Harden might be fulfilled; and after all their care and pains and *"unanimity,"* in effecting a "defecation," Reform might continue to be very troublesome to them; as it has been, in fact, and will continue to be. But if the doctor's *device* could have taken effect, all would have been hushed into silence. And who but such a Talleyrand of an agent, would have conceived a device so cunning? And if the Union Society, had been silly enough to have been captivated by it, can the reader be persuaded to believe, that he was not ready *"to engage for the prosecution, that it should be dismissed for an advantage so great?* The agent, believe us, understood the object of his *negotiation* too well not to have secured it, if it had been in his power. And besides, all these considerations to disprove the accusation of delinquency, we did not pretend to quote the words of doctor Bond, in the terms and conditions which he devised and prescribed; we stated only our view of their meaning, and referred the reader to the Narrative and Defence, pages 24 and 25, that he might judge for himself, whether our view was correct;—whether a *negotiation*, thus undertaken, by such an agent, did not imply *engagement* on his part, for the fulfilment of the terms dictated by himself.

The doctor has accused us, with having commenced a personal attack upon him, without provocation. The reader will find, we have in no instance departed from the subject of our controversy;—in no particular, indulged in personal remarks, except only when he is personally identified with the question at issue. And as we hold him implicated, as one of the chiefs in the prosecution, as he was, in fact, the writer of the Narrative and Defence, it is useless for him to say we commenced the attack upon him. In a paragraph of that work, on page 66, he says, "doctor Jennings * * * * ought to have reflected, that as one of the editorial committee of the Mutual Rights, he had assailed the spotless reputation of men, who labored in the ministry * * * perhaps before he was born. * * * If there were any just grounds for the accusations, we should be grieved. * * * But when these accusations are totally destitute of truth, and only got up to subserve a party purpose—we cannot and dare not be silent. * * * That the allegations were not believed even by those who made them, is sufficiently obvious."

If this paragraph, which is one only out of many similar instances of attack, contained in the Narrative and Defence, was not a personal attack on us, because we were a part of the editorial committee; then, nothing said of doctor Bond in the Exposition or Review, is personal in respect to him, since he bore so important a part in the prosecution. With this concern we found him associated, and therefore have paid our respects to him,—and that because it was not possible otherwise, to do justice to the subject. Apart from the transactions by which we were expelled from the Methodist Episcopal Church, we have no intention of troubling him or any of his party.

AN EXPOSITION

OF THE

LATE CONTROVERSY, &c.

PART FIRST.

AN EXPOSITION OF THE LATE CONTROVERSY, &c. PROCEEDINGS BY
WHICH REFORMERS WERE EXPELLED, &c.

CHAPTER I.

Presents a brief account of the true cause of the expulsion of Reformers, by the rulers of the Methodist Episcopal Church in Baltimore.

THE readers of the Methodist Magazine and Quarterly Review, new series, No. I. having no other information than can be collected from that review, the "Christian Advocate and Journal," &c. of course, nine-tenths of the Methodist people will be induced to believe, that the Reformers of this city, of Cincinnati, of Pittsburg, Lynchburgh, &c. &c. in their late efforts to obtain the right of representation in the legislative department of the church, contended for a very different purpose.——That their main object was, to secure to themselves, what Mr. Emory is pleased to call, "the sweet liberty of inveighing and endeavouring to sow dissentions, without restraint;" of comparing Methodist preachers with the ancient Druids, the despots of Babylon, Egypt, and Tartary, &c.——That for their unchristian conduct in asserting this kind of liberty, they were expelled. That when they were called on by the church, to account for such unwarrantable conduct, they held the church authorities in "*stubborn,*" and "*proud contempt;*"—refusing to obey citations to appear before inferior tribunals, or despising the right of appeal to the higher. That, therefore, their cases were not entitled to the consideration of the Annual or General Conferences, although the latter condescended to propose terms of reconcilation and peace. That on the whole, they have no right to complain.——And that the Presbyterians, &c. by permitting reform preachers to occupy their pulpits, have refused to acknowledge the regularity of the proceedings, by which they were suspended and expelled; when at the same time, no proof of the contrary had appeared, but the complaints of such disciplined and deposed members.

Every impartial reader of the Mutual Rights knows this, to be a gross misrepresentation of the whole affair. And considering the extensive circulation and influence of the Magazine and Quarterly Review, it seems to be necessary to meet the unmerited aspersion, with an exposition of the whole transaction. This is the more necessary, because there are thousands of our friends who have not seen the fourth volume of Mutual Rights, which contains the principal documents. There are other reasons, which will be obvious in the sequel. As it respects us, the call for such a development as we are able to give, seems imperious, because

————————————————quæque ipse miserrima vidi,
Et quorum pars magna fui.————————————————

It has been the steady purpose of Reformers, from the commencement of their labours, to inculcate such views of church polity as are consistent with Christian liberty. They have insisted on the rightful claims of the people to self-government. And they have been particularly desirous to remove out of the way of the ministers of the gospel, all temptation to assume unwarranted authority, or a proud elevation over their brethren. So long as they could have entertained a hope of effecting any meliorating change in the government of the Methodist Episcopal Church, they would have been willing, that it should have been brought about in a gradual manner, and would have been satisfied with the most moderate concessions, that reasonably could have been accepted. They were particularly solicitous, that the General Conference might take the lead, in a work so important, and secure to themselves the high claims to just respect, which such a dignified course of conduct was calculated to procure. With such views and feelings they sent up memorials to the General Conference of 1824. The point which they urged more particularly, was the right of the people to a representation in the legislative department of the church. The bishops and Conference replied by a circular, saying, that if any departure from the institution as they had received it from their fathers, were intended, they must be pardoned, "if they knew no such right, if they comprehended no such privilege." This was a declaration of their unqualified determination to retain their power, undiminished. The only hope of Reformers for accomplishing any thing from that time, rested upon their success in gaining the attention of the people.

A periodical, entitled the Wesleyan Repository, had been issued in monthly numbers, for three years preceding the Conference, the principal writers for which had taken much pains, to prove to the travelling preachers, that the true interest of the church required the concession of a lay delegation. The work, however, was greatly opposed by those, whose best interests it was intended to subserve. It was, therefore, thought advisable, that it should give place to the Mutual Rights; and with intention to counteract a similar opposition to this periodical, and secure the greater unanimity amongst the Reformers generally, Union Societies were instituted, in various places, and recommended to the friends of reform generally. Aided by these necessary arrangements, the cause soon assumed a more systematic form, and produced a more extensive and obvious effect. After a perseverance of about three years, all who understood the subject, were well convinced, that the same measures continued, would extend the work throughout the United States. All were satisfied by the evidence daily afforded, that a sufficient circulation of the Mutual Rights, sustained by a corresponding organization of Union Societies, would soon produce an impulse in favour of correct principles, which would be irresistible. For the same reason, the travelling preachers and the friends of power, considered it necessary to bring about the destruction of measures, which they were obliged to see, were becoming every day more formidable. But as the publication had been permitted to go on without interruption for so many years, and as it was confidently believed that the people of these free states, would not sustain an open attack upon the liberty of speech and the press, Reformers generally supposed that the intimations given of an intention to charge them with a breach of discipline, with "inveighing" and "speaking evil of ministers," were without foundation. In this, however, they were greatly mistaken. The wise ones were maturing their plan of operations, and at length, they satisfied themselves, that extracts might be made from the Mutual Rights, which, with their intended comments, would be considered so offensive, as to ensure the condemnation of the periodical, with the Methodist community, and justify the expulsion of its editors and patrons. They concluded too, judging from other facts, when individuals had been subjected to church censure, that the characters and influence of their intended victims, would be so entirely destroyed, that their expulsion would rid the church of further trouble on the score of reform.

In order to bring about the official death of the local preachers, with the least observation, and prepare the people to give them up, most quietly, the preachers in charge of the Baltimore city stations, excluded them from their pulpits as unworthy of public confidence; and justified themselves to inquiring friends, by representing them as bitter enemies of Methodism, and dwelling with great emphasis on their late interference in the case of the Rev. D. B. Dorsey, who had been censured by the Baltimore Annual Conference, and left without an appointment for one year. For the dread offence of having recommended the Mutual Rights, and for having dared to assert his rights in the presence of the Conference, he was subjected to these penalties. The editorial committee, with intention to prevent such tyrannical proceedings, on any subsequent occasion, had published an account of them. This was particularly offensive to the travelling preachers, and perhaps served to hasten the contemplated expulsion of reform out of their borders.

5

CHAPTER II.

Statement of preparatory measures, and remarks upon them. The Pitt Street Meeting, &c.

When the leaders in this drama, were in readiness, they collected together in Dr. Roszel's school-room,* a number of those supposed to be favourable to their views, and selected seven of their most distinguished members, to act as prosecutors, who were to attend to the preparation of the intended charges and specifications, and proceed to our expulsion. And that our exclusion, and not our trial with intention to do us justice, was intended, will fully appear in the sequel. Before they began to cite us, it was determined to call a general meeting of the party, together with as many of the prosecutors as were then in the city, at the old Baptist church, at the corner of Front and Pitt streets, where they united in a common vote "that the *opinion of the Conference*, that the Mutual Rights was an *improper work*, was not founded on its being a work on church government, &c. but it was founded on the fact, that the Mutual Rights was a work, in which anonymous writers were *permitted* to *abuse* and *defame* the *travelling preachers;* to deprive them, if possible, of the confidence and support of the people of their charge, by holding them up to public odium, and by misrepresenting both their *actions* and their *motives.*"

By this public vote, all the active members came to a common understanding, that the Mutual Rights had properly come under the condemnation of the Annual Conference, and that this sentence had the approbation and sanction of the whole party. In this unanimous sentence, the seven prosecutors, the three local preachers who afterwards sat in judgment on the cases of the ten local preachers, as also, the committee, who in the like manner sat in judgment on the twenty-two members who have been expelled, were all present and voted, and of course virtually pledged themselves to stand by the prosecution. I may add here, that the paper which contained the above 'opinion of the Annual Conference, gave notice of the contemplated purpose to "defecate" the church.

After having made such ample preparation, every body must perceive, that nothing more remained to be done, but to get up such charges as should accord with the preparations; then take us one by one, identify us with the Mutual Rights, and the whole business of our condemnation was settled. The formality of charges and specifications, appears to have been necessary, merely to save appearances, make the act officially an act of the church, and lead the community into a belief, that the Reformers had been accused righteously, tried in due form, fairly condemned and justly punished.

*They had held a previous private council, at the house of Mr. William Brown, deceased.

Knowing as we did, that these arrangements were previously made, when summoned to appear and answer, it was as clear to our minds as a sunbeam, that we were called upon, not to be *tried*, but to be *excommunicated*. And as the excommunication of a few individuals, could not answer the purpose which the party had in view, we were obliged to see with equal clearness, if they were permitted to succeed, in this way, in Baltimore, that similar measures would be taken against Reformers, upon a scale sufficiently extended, to effect their excommunication throughout the whole extent of the Methodist Episcopal Church.

We could not consent to be tried before a tribunal, *constituted* for this purpose. To have done so, and by our own act to have given sanction to their proceedings, would have been to sacrifice principles, which every American and every Christian is bound to hold more dear than life. We therefore entered our protest, under conviction, that such a court could not have admissible jurisdiction in the case. The very circumstance, that it had become necessary to make the intended prosecution an affair of the party, in order to carry it on, to all candid and well informed minds, must be conclusive proof that a church court had nothing to do with the subject. The dispute in question, involved interests of great public importance, which the decision of such a court could not finally dispose of or settle, and upon which its sentence could have no adequate effect. And we did hope that the higher authorities of the church would sustain our protests, and wipe off the stain which this unprincipled transaction was tending to fix upon it. This we had good reason to expect, in as much as by the circular which issued from the General Conference of 1824, the bishops and Conference assured us, they "rejoice, that the institutions of our happy country are admirably calculated to secure the best ends of civil government," adding, "with your rights as citizens of the United States, the church DISCLAIMS ALL INTERFERENCE." The "liberty of speech and of the press;" the liberty to assert our ecclesiastical rights and privileges; the right to investigate and communicate the results of our investigations into the administration, and especially into the mal-administration of men in office and power;—these are some of the most important privileges, which are guarranteed to us by the Constitution and Bill of Rights of the United States and of the state of Maryland, and of course are rights, with which "the church disclaims all interference." And yet this prosecution was an attack, which by men with right views of the Constitution of the United States, will be considered an act of treason against our civil and religious liberties, at the same time that it trampled under foot and dishonored this sacred pledge, given us by the bishops and General Conference.

It is said there was no intention to infringe upon our rights in any of these respects, but to call us to account for a licentious abuse of those rights. This is the aspect which our prosecutors are desirous their proceedings should wear. This, Mr. Emory would present as the "gist" of the offence.

32

CHAPTER III.

A statement of the case, as it ought to have been viewed by the committee.

We were accused as editors, &c. of a periodical. The principal design of the periodical was to shew, that in the organization and administration, of the government of the Methodist Episcopal Church, there are infractions made upon the natural and Christian rights of whole classes of her members. Under the protection of the Bill of Rights, and Constitution of the United States, and the State of Maryland, we asserted our right to take on us this office, and under the grand charter, which comprises and confirms the Christian rights of every member of the church of Christ, the Holy Word of God, we claimed the right, as members and as ministers of the church, to examine and "try all things;"—the government, its administrations, its practices; and to communicate through a PERIODICAL, the result of our investigations. It was our right and privilege as editors, to judge respecting the merits of any paper offered for insertion, and particularly to judge, whether it was intended "to speak evil of ministers." It is true we were liable to err, and if we erred, in the judgment of any brother, he had a right as well founded as our own, to make a becoming representation of our mistake; which done, there existed an obligation on our part, to make such correction as might have been reasonably and properly required; and this we always were ready to do.

Had the brethren waited on us, with a view to any such correction, they would have been received in love, and as far as their demands were reasonable and proper, they would have been granted. But they never took any step of this kind.

The meetings preparatory to the accomplishment of our excommunication, preceded any call upon us, in relation to the Mutual Rights. And when the prosecuting committee were ready to make a specious attempt to justify themselves in their intended course, they waited on us, to let us know, *that we must desist from the publication of the Mutual Rights, and abandon the Union Society, or they would proceed against us.*

From this conduct, it is obvious, that a correction of the manner of our publications, had no place in their thoughts.

The attack was made upon reform, and the design was to secure a continuance of the absolute power of the travelling preachers, by expelling out of the church, the friends of reform. The question at issue was an affair of opinion, and could not be settled righteously in this way. The court of inquiry in the first instance, was tainted with partiality and injustice. The judge, the Rev. Mr. Hanson, had written his opinion in a letter to Mr. Jacobs, of Alexandria—"I am disposed," said he, "to view the greater part of them, [the Reformers,] as holding a relation to the church, to which in justice and propriety, nay even in charity itself, they are no longer entitled."

CHAPTER IV.

Presents the absurd and truly ridiculous character of the prosecution.

The judge, the prosecutors, and the committee, were all of one party, and had all prejudged our case. If a majority of Reformers had been permitted to sit in judgment, they would certainly have decided in our favour. The whole court were anti-reformers, and they decided against us. And now we ask, what information has been gained by the inquiry and the decision of this court? That anti-reformers are opposed to our views, and had rather turn Reformers out of the church, than permit investigation to go on in it. And does this settle the question? Reformers have been labouring to prove that they have a just claim to a representation in the legislative department of the church. Anti-reformers sat in judgment on their claim, and expelled the claimants from their communion for asking it and daring to produce evidences in proof of the importance of its being granted. And all the while, that these formalities and severities of a church court were going on, it was still a question of opinion. And what is worse, it was making the opinion of the three local preachers, who sat as our committee, to be the measure of the judgment of the whole Methodist Church on the great question at issue.* It was even worse than this. It was declaring to the world, that great polemical questions are settled in the Methodist Episcopal Church, by expelling those who dare to think differently from the travelling preachers, and that the travelling preachers can enlist their members to sustain them in it, even to the withholding from their people, the liberty of speech and of the press.

How obvious is it, that a party difference cannot be settled righteously in this way! When any question which is agitated concerns none, but those who are permitted to act in the case, it might be put to the vote of a majority. For example, if no one out of the station of Baltimore, had been interested, a meeting of all concerned, might have effected a temporary arrangement, by putting the question to vote in a friendly manner. But all communities are forever changing, both in their constituent materials, and in the opinions of their members. Of course the very nature of human society, implies the necessity of freedom of inquiry and of opinion;—and no arrangement, short of a frequently elected delegation, for the purpose of regulating conventional principles and rules of conduct, can maintain a form of church or state government, which shall do equal justice to the opinions of an extensive fellowship. How very far therefore, would even the vote of a ma-

*These three preachers, were John W. Harris, Samuel Williams and Thomas Basford. We thought them well meaning men; but as to their qualifications for sitting in judgment on a case of so much moment, we must say, we pitied their temerity. All who know them, will testify, that they can barely sustain themselves as local preachers in the Methodist Episcopal Church, of the most ordinary attainments.

jority of the Baltimore station, have fallen short of doing justice to the opinions of our vastly extended community! And ought not the sense of justice of the people or preachers to have led them to admit, that the friends of reform had the right to inquire and think, as well as they?

CHAPTER V.

The prosecution violated all the fundamental rules by which judicial proceedings should be regulated.

It is settled in this country and in Great Britain, that in all judicial proceedings, the tribunal which determines both the law and the fact, should be impartial. According to judge Blackstone, "should be like Cæsar's wife, not only pure, but unsuspected." Hence the establishment of certain rules of the courts, to guard against the want of integrity;—against the prejudices and partialities to which all human tribunals are liable.

Upon any trial for the *least* offence, which can be charged by the most enlightened and impartial grand jury, not an individual of those who served on such grand jury, can be legally permitted to act and determine as one of a traverse jury, upon the guilt of the persons so charged. Not one would be permitted in this country, even if the whole grand jury had been composed of bishops, presiding elders, itinerant or local preachers, trustees or stewards. Yet in this case, after taking the vote as it was done, at the meetings at Roszel's school-room, and at the corner of Pitt street, where *all* served as grand jury-men, they were under the necessity of dropping the intended prosecutions, or of exhibiting the novel proceeding, of making up all their committees, out of the men who had previously decided and published their decision on the case in question; which every reflecting man in the nation, will consider out of character. For nothing can be more rational, than to believe and expect, that those who *voluntarily preferred charges*, would declare the charges true, which they themselves had with great assiduity prepared.

Again, it is an important rule in criminal proceedings, that the law in all penal cases, shall be construed strictly and rigidly, against the government and in favour of the accused. Considering the circumstances and the materials, in view of the men who constituted the court of inquiry, what prospect had the accused, of availing themselves of the benefit of this rule? In fact, every question was decided against them.

Another indispensable rule, is, that the character of the offence, as charged, shall be made out so specifically, as to enable the accused, not only fully to comprehend its nature, but clearly to perceive, what evidence may be necessary for him, on trial; that he may not be liable, either to mistake, or to be entrapped in preparing for and making his defence. In this case, we had the absurdity of a vague reference to all that is published in three large octavo volumes, and part of a fourth, in extenso, and more particularly to fifteen long essays, containing more than one hundred and fifty pages, with not one sentence definitely specified. Nay more, when some of the accused requested that the offensive papers might be read, in order that the supposed defamatory words might be designated, it was peremptorily refused by the court.*

This is a faithful description of the view which we we recompelled to take, of the official members of the city station. It was a time of excitement; and the colouring may be sufficiently strong, but it is honest, and as free from prejudice, as possible in existing circumstances. Here, we leave them for a little, until we shall have taken a brief notice of the District Conference, the tribunal before which, we were willing and prepared to appear upon the merits of the case.

CHAPTER VI.

The District Conference dissolved, in order to place the local preachers under the authority of the Quarterly Meeting Conference, the members of which had been pledged by the vote at Pitt street, to stand by the prosecutions.

It was known to us, at least two months before hand, that it was a part of the plan of the dominant party, to dissolve the District Conference, and compel the suspended local preachers, to appear, for trial, before the Quarterly Conference;—before the same men, who had with one consent, prejudged our case and published their judgment, in the famous pamphlet which issued from their Pitt and Front street meeting. We also knew, that if a majority of votes in favour of a dissolution of the conference, could not otherwise be obtained, the coloured preachers would be called on to vote. The editor of the Review says, it has been affirmed that they voted, and it has been denied. Had he turned to the Narrative and Defence, page 112, he would have read the following statement, made by the prosecuting agents of the church. "He [the President, Rev. Joseph Frye,] then requested that all who were in favour of the motion would rise up, and stand till they were counted; nineteen white members and ten coloured, arose in favour of the motion." It gave us but little concern, that the coloured men also had been enlisted against us. But, the transaction went far to satisfy us that we had taken a true view of the object of men in power, and that we were correct in our former declaration, that the prosecution was put in

----

* These rules or principles, by which the jurisprudence of our country is regulated, are in perfect accordance with the dictates of common sense. They are introduced in this place, to show how the Methodist Episcopal Church authorities regard principle, when it is at variance with the designs of men in power.

motion by "persons at a distance, high in authority."*   Some objection was made, to the propriety of calling on the coloured
preachers to vote in the case; when one of them arose and declared in justification of his rights, that he and others had waited on
the Bishop, when he was last in the city, and the "Bishop told us,
said he, to go to Conference and insist on our rights; for we had as
good a right to vote, as any man in the Conference; and if he were
in the chair, he would call to order and put down any one who
would oppose our right to vote."   The transaction afforded additional proof, of a concerted design, in which the bishops, presiding
elder, the preacher in charge of West Baltimore station, and the
whole body of official men, were confidently expected to sustain
their proceedings.

We have good cause to believe that the prosecutors, or at least,
the agent, knew they would be sustained by the General Conference;   and, as shall be shewn more distinctly by and by; that
they relied upon the Narrative and Defence, which they intended
to publish.

We considered it to be inconsistent with our responsibilities to the
friends of reform, in view of the great question at issue, to acknowledge the legality of the prosecution before the committee, or
court of inquiry, and therefore we had entered our protests. Nor could
we see any good cause for changing our course.   We therefore
determined not to appear before the Quarterly Conference.   The
brethren in like circumstances were of the same opinion.   All
concluded it would be a waste of time, and an improper avidity of
humiliation, to wait upon the Conferene to hear a formal condem-

* This was our view of the affair at the time when it occurred and when
we commenced our Review.   We have since learned, that Francis Watkins,
the coloured man who so boldly asserted his right to vote on the occasion, by
his manner, made an impression that he had recently received such instruction from Bishop George.   In this there was a mistake.   Some friends of the
prosecutions, had waited on the coloured preachers, and urged them to be in
place and vote.   We are now of the opinion, that the Bishop's view of their
privileges, had been presented for their encouragement, until Watkins and
others, had associated it with the pending transaction.   In confirmation of
this conjecture, on an application made to him about the first of the present
year, for his own account of the matter, he replied, perhaps hastily, that he
had reference to an interview, he and others had with the Bishop, not a very
long time before the District Conference.   But when requested to make a
statement of it in writing, he asked for time, to see Mr. Hanson, &c. and returned with a written reply, referring the interview with the Bishop, to some
time between 1824 and 1826.   On application to John Fortie, he produced a
journal, kept by himself, by which it appears, that it took place in March,
1826.   In course, it was not intended for the occasion to which it was applied;
and F. Watkins had probably by the influence above noticed given to it an
erroneous association.   It is, however, a matter of no importance, although
the agent would wish now to have it so.   If this incident had not occurred
at all, the issue would have been the same.   Independent of this, we knew,
that Bishop George approved the prosecutions, and took pains to predispose
some of our friends to approve our expulsion, when it should be accomplished.   Besides, the final decision of the General Conference, has put the subject altogether at rest.   By that act, the prosecution with all its absurdities
and severities, received the approbation of the Bishops and Conference.

nation of the Mutual Rights, when it was already known that its condemnation was certain. All concluded, that the General Conference, when they should be made acquainted with these circumstances, even if every member of the Conference should be hostile to reform, for the credit of Methodism and their own reputation, ought to interpose, reverse the decision of the Quarterly Conference, and devise some plan for our restoration;—one in which we could safely and honorably concur.

At the time appointed, the Quarterly conference met, and after having exhibited an extra scene, which occupied several days, in which a certain Dr. Green was the ostensible actor, who affected to have come an unsolicited and disinterested mediator, and whose terms for our return to submission, we shall have occasion to notice; the Quarterly Conference proceeded to the reading of the selections made from the Mutual Rights, adding we presume, their sapient comments, as published in the Narrative and Defence; and so effectually did they answer the intended purpose, "that on motion for our expulsion, there was not a dissenting voice."

CHAPTER VII.

Memorial sent up to the Baltimore Annual Conference.

Agreeably to our contemplated course, when the time for the meeting of the Annual Conference was approaching—in April, 1828, we prepared and sent up the following.

MEMORIAL TO THE ANNUAL CONFERENCE.

"This memorial of the undersigned, late ministers and members of the Methodist Episcopal Church, in the city of Baltimore, and who have recently been expelled from the fellowship of said church, respectfully sheweth, that we believe we have been unjustly deprived of our membership, for the following considerations:

First. We consider it to have been a grievous encroachment on our rights, to require us to withdraw from the Union Society, and to demand the suppression of the Mutual Rights, as the only condition on which we could avoid a church prosecution.

Second. We consider it to have been a violation of the discipline, and an unjustifiable neglect of a well known duty of the preacher having the pastoral charge of the station, to have received accusations against us and summoned us to trial, without having previously used all his personal influence to restore and preserve peace.

Third. We consider it altogether inconsistent with any proper sense of justice, that we should have been subjected to trial for publishing papers, the authors of which, being members and ministers of our church, were left unmolested; although the names of

6

some of the writers were made public, and no demand had been made for the names of those who were not known. This consideration is greatly strengthened by the fact, that some of the papers to which exceptions were raised, had been published two or three years previously, and during all that time the characters of such of us as were official members, had been regularly passed, without exception, by the quarterly meeting conferences, of which our prosecutors were members.

Fourth. We consider it altogether unreasonable that the preacher in charge, did not allow time to the chairman of the editorial committee, to correspond with the writers of the papers complained of, before he was compelled to appear and answer;—thereby subjecting him and all of us, to the necessity of entering our protests against the illegality and injustice of the procedure.

Fifth. We consider it very objectionable, that after the question upon church government had produced so much excitement, as to lead to the acknowledged formation of two parties; one party should have been permitted to enlist the church authorities, to aid them in the expulsion of the other party;—which of course produced the reproachful consequence, that the whole of the proceedings were inevitably conducted in an exparte manner.

Sixth. When cited to trial, the committee ought to have been devoid of partiality or prejudice; this we presume will not be denied;—but the fact was far otherwise. The preacher in charge selected the two committees from brethren who had previously voted at a select meeting, that we were "enemies of Methodism." Moreover, when asked by the Rev. Mr. Hanson, if we had any objection to the committee, and after their own acknowledgment that they had voted as aforesaid, yet Mr. Hanson declared them fully competent, and they were retained, notwithstanding our solemn protestations against such a procedure.

Seventh. We consider it highly objectionable, that although the preacher in charge was respectfully requested, in accordance with the general if not universal practice, of all the courts of enlightened jurisprudence, to direct the reading of the particular words, sentences, paragraphs, or sections, which were to be relied on, as proof of objectionable matter; yet Mr. Hanson, in reply to the request to order the reading of such parts of the Mutual Rights, as were expected to sustain the charges, declared it could not be admitted, and the committees were permitted to retire with all their prejudices, taking with them the Mutual Rights, in extenso, on which to form their decision, without having given an opportunity to the accused, to explain, or even to remove wrong impressions; and this consideration acquires additional strength, from the fact, that the explanations of the writers themselves, which ought to have been had in the case, were also precluded, the undeniable importance of which, will still more fully appear, by reference to a late paper, written by the Rev. Mr. Shinn, in reply to the Narrative and Defence, &c. and to facts which transpired in the course of the trials, &c.

Eighth. Had we been required to correct any thing that was erroneous, in previous numbers of the Mutual Rights, or to apologize for any severity of expression, or to explain, or to rectify any thing that might have led a reader into error, we hereby declare, (as was declared in some of the protests,) that we should most gladly have done so, both as a matter of duty, and for the sake of our brethren, but these were not the conditions proposed to us, either by our brethren, who accused us, or by the preacher, who expelled us. They required us to abandon the Union Society, and to suppress the Mutual Rights, the most proper medium through which the evils complained of, if they really existed, could be corrected.

Ninth. It may be asked, why did not the lay members appeal to the Quarterly Conference? To this we answer, that having protested against the legality of the whole proceeding, we deemed it improper. The impropriety of an appeal to that tribunal, must have appeared with irresistible force to any, knowing as we did, that nearly all of its members had been actively engaged in getting up the prosecution, and had united in *condemning* us in their Pitt street publication.

Your memorialists forbear to state numerous other facts developed in the course of the prosecutions and trials, calculated in their tendencies and issues, not only to degrade us, but to widen the differences among brethren; and to bring lasting, and just reproach on the co-ordinate executive branches of the Methodist Episcopal Church.

We, therefore, request the conference, in the name of Him whom we all profess to serve;—by their attachment to the principles of righteousness and the interests of their lacerated Zion, to interpose and restore us to the enjoyment of our former standing in the church of our choice and affections, from which, we have been unnaturally severed. Thereby they will render us an act of justice, and insure to themselves, an ever during acclaim from the virtuous and the good.

Your memorialists would finally state, that no malevolent affection has place in their souls, against either of the prosecutors, preachers, or committees.

At the same time, justice and propriety demand your immediate investigation of the official conduct of the Rev. J. M. Hanson, and that of the Rev. Joseph Frye, in reference to our particular cases.

That the great Head of the church may direct your deliberations in this, and all other matters which are interwoven with the best interests of Zion, is the sincere prayer of your memorialists.

Baltimore, April, 1828.

CHAPTER VIII.

Resolutions of the Baltimore Annual Conference, in reply to our memorial, with strictures, and a copy of a protest.

To this memorial, the Conference in their wisdom and fraternal wishes to recover us, returned the following resolutions, in reply.

RESOLUTIONS

Passed by the Baltimore Annual Conference, in reply to the memorial of the expelled brethren.

1. *Resolved by the Baltimore Annual Conference, in Conference assembled,* That ministers or members of the Methodist Episcopal Church, who do not obey the citations of the church to appear before inferior judicatories, in cases of accusation or complaint; or who neglect to avail themselves of the intermediate appellate judicatories, for redress of alleged grievances, are not entitled to come before higher judicatories, either as appellants or complainants.

2. That to sanction or countenance a contrary course of proceeding, would in the judgment of this conference, be subversive of WHOLESOME and SOUND DISCIPLINE.

3. That if the suspended local preachers in Baltimore, on the dissolution of the district conference, had appeared before the quarterly meeting conference, as cited, and objected to the jurisdiction of that body, if they thought proper to do so; in such case, on an appeal, this conference would have fully considered and decided on the whole subject, embracing the question of the legality of the dissolution of the Baltimore district conference and the jurisdiction of the quarterly meeting conference. But as those local preachers preferred to pursue a different course, and one, in the judgment of this conference, both irregular and disorderly, making inflammatory appeals to the public, declaring that they had no other alternative, and that a church court, even if righteously constituted, could not be considered to have admissible jurisdiction in such a case, this conference judge it both useless, and inconsistent with correct and necessary principles of discipline and order, in these circumstances to take further cognizance of the subject.

4. That the secretary be, and he hereby is directed to furnish a copy of the preceding resolutions to Dr. Samuel K. Jennings, and others, signers of the communication from Baltimore, addressed to the Conference.

Carlisle, Penn., April 18, 1828.

Is not this a queer thing? If the local preachers had "*appeared before the quarterly meeting conference and objected,*" they would have been permitted to *complain and appeal.* We had sent in a formal protest, addressed to the presiding elder, as will be seen presently, but as we failed in this act of homage, as we disregarded this important formality of the courts of the Methodist Episcopal Church, as we failed to APPEAR before their honours, it was fatal to our cause!!

PROTEST.

TO THE REV. JOSEPH FRYE, PRESIDING ELDER.

"We the subscrbers, having been informed by your note of the 12th instant, of your intention, to bring before your quarterly meeting conference of the Baltimore city station, the charges and specifications heretofore alleged against us, and on which the church authorities of this station, have already once acted and ordered our suspension; and that you say, this will be done because the "district conference refused to hold its regular session." We hereby inform you that as the district conference met, was legally organized, and for one whole day and more continued in session, according to Discipline, it was, therefore, your duty to have continued the session until the business was finished. Instead of this, you arbitrarily received a vote of the minority of the attending white members, for a dissolution of the conference, and pronounced it dissolved, accordingly.

We, therefore, PROTEST against your right to bring the charges and specifications alleged against us, before the quarterly meeting conference.

1st. Because we consider you have acted without law or precedent; and that the provision to which you refer, as made by the Discipline, has in view those districts *only*, in which the local preachers "shall refuse or neglect to hold the regular sessions" of their district conferences. In this case, the preachers had actually met and commenced their regular session: moreover, a majority of the white members in attendance, were in favour of continuing the conference.

2d. In thus arbitrarily compelling us to appear before the quarterly conference of the Baltimore city station, you would subject us to the great injustice, of being tried by men, who were our prosecutors and judges in the first instance, together with those, who had virtually pledged themselves to sustain the prosecutions: first, by appointing said prosecutors at the meeting, held in Roszel's school room; and secondly, by their vote for the publication of the Pitt street Address, in which they publicly declare us to be the "enemies of Methodism."

3d. Besides, in consequence of the course that you have pursued, the tribunal, designated by the Discipline, as the place of trial for local preachers, and before which we were ready to appear, ceases to exist; and you have no authority to bring us to trial before any other; our condition is altogether novel, and not within the limits of the jurisdiction of a quarterly meeting conference. Our case necessarily makes its appeal to the general conference, since there is no other tribunal which can have a right to say what shall be done, when a presiding elder shall have pronounced a district conference dissolved, notwithstanding a majority of those interested, shall have actually met, for the purpose of holding their regular session, declaring themselves meanwhile opposed to a dissolution.

4th. The illegality and impropriety of having counted the votes of coloured men, in deciding a question of this sort, within the limits of the state of Maryland, we presume will not be questioned

Samuel K. Jennings,	Thomas M'Cormick
Daniel E. Reese,	Luther J. Cox,
James R. Williams,	John S. Reese,
John C. French,	John Valiant,
William Kesley,	Reuben T. Boyd.

Baltimore, 16th January, 1828."

This paper was of no worth with the Annual Conference, because the local preachers had not *"appeared"* before the quarterly meeting conference.

After all these things, can any candid reader believe that the Annual Conference acted the part of an impartial tribunal, or that they pronounced a just judgment? We gave to that body, a faithful account of the conduct of the prosecution, as we honestly viewed it. And is it to be believed that a body of *disinterested* ministers of the gospel, perhaps seventy, if not one hundred in number, could have come to the *unfeeling* conclusion, that we were not entitled to one word of complaint, because we had not been sufficiently respectful towards prosecutors and judges, of whom we had complained, under circumstances so glaring? We did believe conscientiously, that these men had forfeited our confidence; that they could not have been impartial; and of course were disqualified to sit in judgment upon our cases. We therefore, solicited the interference of the Conference. But our supplications were of no avail. Those ministers of the sanctuary, notwithstanding the great love which they professed for us, thought it necessary to treat us, with these hard resolutions, in order to prevent the *"subversion* of *wholesome and sound* discipline."

It is the judgment of the Baltimore Annual Conference, that the proceedings of the Baltimore station, in our prosecution and expulsion, are fair expressions of *wholesome* and *sound* Episcopal Methodist discipline!* I am compelled to believe that these men expected their resolutions to be sustained by the "Narrative and Defence;" by the *official book* which contains the testimony as extracted from the Mutual Rights, so pressed and moulded by the explanations and pleadings of the prosecution, as to fit them to the intended purpose. And this was readily done. There was no offset. They had it all in their own hands. They managed the matter as they wished, and then, in this book, published a "plain statement of the whole affair;"—a history of this conspicuous instance of *wholesome* and *sound* Episcopal Methodist Discipline!

* With intention to "defecate," &c. ! !

CHAPTER IX.

The secret, unintentionally let out, that one leading object was, the destruction of our Union Societies.

THIS standard volume informs us, that "the formation of the Union Society was in fact, the organization of a schism, and that, had no Union Society been established, the discussion of the various projects of reform might have gone on, without producing any general excitement in the church; whereas, organizing these societies, incorporated the spirit of party." See Narrative and Defence, page 12. This is an acknowledgment of the truth of our statement. We are here informed what was in reality the "gist" of our offences. And it will be made very evident that the destruction of these societies and the discontinuance of the Mutual Rights, were the real objects to be accomplished, and that, because they considered these the only effectual means for securing the attention of the people;—the means, but for which, *"no general excitement in the church could have been produced."*

To accomplish the intended devastation of these offensive (because they were efficient) works of reformers, it was important, to find some one, a fast friend to the government of the church, having sufficient zeal, and a competent degree of ingenuity, so to manage matters, that in the event of a refusal on the part of the reformers, to receive the dictates of the intended prosecutors, and a consequent recourse to expulsion, the Methodist Episcopal community and the world, might be made to believe, that the church took no authoritative step to *prevent reform;*—that the prosecutions were entered upon and carried into effect, by *lay brethren,* "without any itinerant suggestion or influence whatever;" they (the lay brethren) being offended, not with our labours to bring about reform, but with the manner in which we were endeavouring to accomplish our object.

CHAPTER X.

Some uncertainty how far the agent had previously progressed in making preparation for the Narrative and Defence.

WE are not informed with positive certainty, that the entire plan of the intended book, was laid, antecedent to the appointment of the seven prosecutors; but we are fully satisfied, that some one or more, had been employed in making the selections from the Mutual Rights, which constitute the pith of the Narrative and Defence. It is very probable, that they were made and submitted to the five Bishops, and some other distinguished travelling preachers, who were in the city, a short time before the first caucus was held at Mr. William Brown's. And we cannot avoid the supposition, that it was previously understood, that this selection when it should appear, would serve to justify a course of prosecutions and expulsions, if that should become "necessary" for the accomplishment of their object. The knowing ones had their eyes on this, when they met at Dr. Roszel's school-room. And when we called on Mr. Harden, and took occasion to intimate the possibility of scandal to the Methodist Episcopal Church, if they should go on with their contemplated prosecutions; he said in reply, "we are prepared to meet all consequences, and when we shall have wound up our proceedings, and laid before the public, *such extracts from the Mutual Rights, &c.* as we shall be able to make, together *with our comment upon them*, we have no doubt about being sustained by the public." *

With this view of things, we are prepared to understand why there was such a disinclination to hear the reading of the exceptionable papers, when called for, by brethren on their trial, and why Mr. Hanson declared it unnecessary.

With a strong conviction of the correctness of this view, a few days after having read our protests, &c. before the seven prosecutors, the preacher in charge, and the committee, we considered it our duty to publish them. This publication was immediately followed by a notification of the intention of the prosecutors to "publish a plain statement of the whole affair."

"Doctor Samuel K. Jennings having endeavoured to forestall the opinions of the Methodist public, by publishing the proceedings in his case, before the decision of the Committee could be known—all who feel any concern in the matter, are respectfully requested to suspend their judgment, until the proceedings shall have termi-

* Mr. Harden has given a certificate, contradicting this statement; and alleges, that he could not have had any allusion to the Narrative and Defence, because they had not at that time determined to publish such a Narrative and Defence, nor until the publication of our protest had made it necessary: And to sustain himself, he appeals to his coadjutors in the prosecution. This conversation had with Mr. Harden, was published in October, 1828, whilst it was fresh in our recollection; and many of our friends know, that we reported it to them, immediately after it took place. We still assert it to be true, as then published. There was no witness present. We affirm and appeal to our publication made more than two years ago. He denies, and sustains himself by a declaration, that they had not then determined to publish the Narrative and Defence. Here we are at issue. Immediately after our publication appeared, Mr. Harden came out with his contradictions, and claimed a *"faithful* detail, and correct statement of *all* the leading points * * * the *whole truth."* And then in view of the WHOLE TRUTH, took his imaginary exceptions. We reviewed his paper and proved by himself, that we did not differ. What we wish the reader to observe particularly, is, that Mr. Harden in view of the *whole truth,* did not then pretend to deny this very prominent item. We will not say that he did not then foresee, that a denial of this "leading point" would be necessary, to save the reputation of the agent. But we will say, he acted unadvisedly, and cannot have been well informed, respecting the hazard and difficulty of attempting to prove a negative: moreover, that he must have great reliance upon his weight of character. We will only add, that he himself has seen fit to suspend the scale and compel us to be contented, to let the public judge.

nated, **when** a plain statement of the whole affair will be published.

GEORGE EARNEST,   ALEXANDER YEARLEY,
JACOB ROGERS,   JOHN BERRY,
ISAAC N. TOY,   FIELDER ISRAEL.
SAMUEL HARDEN.

October 3, 1827.

CHAPTER XI.

The Quarterly Conference unanimously condemn the Mutual Rights, and it is admitted by the Agent, that a majority of them had not read the work at all.

THE "plain statement" turned out to be the Narrative and Defence. The selections introduced into it, were read before the Quarterly Conference, "and such was the effect produced by the reading of the passages from the Mutual Rights, on which the charges rested," together with the agent's comments on them, "that although much difference of opinion was known to have previously existed among the members, in reference to the cases before them, there was no dissenting vote on the motion to expel." This appearance of unanimity was thought important, in order to make the Narrative and Defence, look by so much, the more respectable. To secure this unanimity, Mr. Hanson removed six class leaders, and by so doing, "cleared the way for an unresisted exercise of the intention of the government party."

The intention was, to make the impression that the prosecutions were not only instituted and conducted by *"lay brethren,"* but that these lay brethren were *unanimous;* of course that they were altogether in the right, and Reformers altogether in the wrong. For how could the entire body of official members of the Methodist Episcopal Church in the city of Baltimore, the great seat of Methodism, be unanimous on a subject so momentous, if there were any possible room for doubt? There was deep policy in securing this unanimous vote. But unhappily for the scheme, the means which were used to bring it about, serve to lay it open to public view.

On the 29th page of the Narrative and Defence, the same which records this wonderful unanimity, we read, "It is now ascertained, that a great proportion of the Conference, so far from having made up their opinion before the trials, ****** had not even read the Mutual Rights at all, and therefore could not have made up a premature verdict." This is an important disclosure. It is an acknowledgment, that the Narrative and Defence contains ALL that *"a great proportion of the Conference"* knew about the Mutual Rights, consequently all that they knew about the designs, operations, or offences of Union Societies or Reformers. That they had heard just so much, as our prosecutors saw fit to read, and no more. That they had heard their own side only, without correc-

7

tion or contradiction. The prosecutors who had been appointed
by them, had made out charges and specifications to correspond
with the selections previously made. And having now officially
given to them their intended personal application, they submitted
the whole to the Conference; and of course, they all with one accord approved their own handy work, and affixed to it the seal, of a
unanimous vote for our expulsion. What a triumph! What a
memorable unanimity!!

To give to this unanimity the more importance, the Narrative
and Defence says, a great proportion of them, had not read the
Mutual Rights at all; and therefore, could not have made up their
opinion before the trials. Here, without intending it, they acknowledge that they ought to have read the work, before they
made up their opinion. But they must have forgotten, that a great
proportion of these same men, had united in the vote at the Pitt
and Front street meeting, where they reiterated and adopted the
opinion of the Annual Conference, "that the Mutual Rights was
an improper work ****, a work in which anonymous writers were
permitted to abuse and defame the travelling preachers," &c. &c.
bearing witness against themselves that they had made up an
opinion before the trials, and that, when they did it they had not
read the work at all! And here they acknowledge, moreover, that
they commenced their prosecuting operations under the influence
of the opinions of the Conference, although they have told the
world in this same Narrative and Defence, that the prosecutions
were instituted and carried into effect by *lay brethren,* "without any
itinerant *suggestion or influence* whatever."

After all these acknowledgements it is very obvious, that "a
great proportion of these men" moved under the direction or influence of the master spirit. They confided the cause to those
who would manage it, expecting to be sustained by the intended
Narrative and Defence. For, surely, they could not have known
the ruinous fact, that this "plain statement of the whole affair" is
nothing more than an exparte account of matters, and that in view
of the Mutual Rights, as a whole, the extracts and comments, present a very incorrect account of the spirit and works of the friends
of reform. That this is the fact, will be seen by the careful and
candid reader, before we shall have concluded this review.

CHAPTER XII.

*They did not intend to effect any correction of our manner of publish-
ing, &c. but to expel us. Their patience was worn out.*

It is not probable that our prosecutors foresaw, that a dissolution of the District Conference, would lead to a resolution on our
part, not to appear before the Quarterly Conference, and by so
doing, afford them the opportunity of reading their extracts, without opposition or contradiction. But they were prepared, and had

no doubt of an "unanimous vote for our expulsion." This *unanimity*, in aid of the Narrative and Defence, was to enable them, the more certainly to persuade the Methodist community, that the expulsion of the reformers was not at all intended to interdict the freedom of speech and of the press, but was a godly execution of "*wholesome* and *sound* discipline." That they were moved, by the very pious and laudable design, of correcting the licentious abuses of liberty, practised by the Union Societies. The merits of this pretension, shall be more fully examined.

Two things can be demonstrated. 1st. They had no intention to correct the manner of our publications. 2d. They did not intend to permit us to remain in their fellowship, unless we would consent to give up reform. See their Narrative and Defence, page 17.

After a dissertation on our resolutions respecting the proceedings of Baltimore Annual Conference, in Rev. D. B. Dorsey's case, they say, "it was evident now, to the most incredulous, that these measures could not be the work of reformers, but of revolutionists. Their object could not be to amend, but to destroy."—— All hope of returning peace was now cut off, and those, who all along discouraged the enforcement of discipline on the *offenders*, ****** began reluctantly to yield to the *absolute necessity* of the measure. In fact, human patience, even the meekness of christianity" [as far as it had influence over the official members of the Methodist Episcopal Church in the city of Baltimore,] "could endure no more." That is to say, it was considered necessary on all hands, to put down the reformers; "to enforce the disciple on these *offenders*." What else could they do? Their *patience* was worn out. Their *meekness*, that peculiar grace of the christian, had been put to a test, so severe, that it, too, had failed. No preacher, itinerant or local, nor lay member, had ever in person, or by letter, expressed to us any dissatisfaction, respecting the spirit or manner of the papers that had been published in the Mutual Rights, although their *patience* and *meekness* had been so sorely tried, for almost four years: except only, that bishop Hedding called on us a short time before the prosecutions were instituted, for the proper name of Timothy. The name of Timothy was given to the bishop; and that unimportant transaction, includes the whole of the correspondence, which the rulers of the church ever sought, or condescended to hold with us, all the time that their patience and meekness were wearing out!

On page 18, Narrative and Defence, we read, "And they," the committee appointed to prosecute, "determined forthwith to visit the members of the Union Society to *admonish* them of their error, and expostulate." They could not have been in very good frame of mind, to undertake *fraternal* visits and *persuade* brethren to give up reform, when, by their own confession, the labours of reformers had put their patience to the rout, and their "meekness could endure no more."!! Here we pause to consider, that the patience of these administators of *wholesome and sound discipline* was worn out, but not by having "taken us individually alone," and

expostulated with us without effect, till our "obstinacy" had worn
out their patience;—not by having taken with them one or two more
and with pains in brotherly love, laboured again and again, to excite
in us the desired repentance.   There was no disposition for such
procedure.   There was "*an absolute necessity to enforce the discipline on the offenders.*" They had no thought of making peace;
"*all hope of returning peace was now cut off.*"   Their peace making
graces "could endure no more," and like other angry masters, they
now determined to *command* the peace, and enforce it too;—to compel us to be submissive or expel us out of the church.
It was soon rumored abroad through the city, that such a resolution had been adopted; in consequence of which, one of our
brethren, a local preacher, had an interview with a distinguished
member of the prosecuting committee, and requested information
on the subject.   "You and your friends," said he, "are members of
the Union Society, and say you will not leave it.—You publish the
Mutual Rights, and say you will not discontinue that publication.—
You also say you will not *withdraw* from the Methodist Episcopal
Church.   Now we are reduced to one of two alternatives; either to
let you remain members of the church, and go on peaceably publishing the Mutual Rights, by which you agitate the church, or
expel you.   We have come to the *determination*, to take the latter
alternative, and *expel* you."   As might have been expected, every
member of the Union Society was roused at the threat of being
subjected to such magisterial Coercion: and whilst they were de-
liberating how they were to meet an attack of this sort, if it should
be made, which they could hardly believe would be attempted, all
their doubts were ended by the following note, which had the signatures of the seven prosecutors in due form, and was addressed
to Mr. John Chappell, President of the Union Society.
"The undersigned, believing that the members of the Baltimore
Union Society, have violated the discipline of the Methodist Episcopal Church, and being desirous to have a friendly interview with
them individually, previous to instituting charges against them, *if
necessary.*   We respectfully request to be furnished with the names
of the members of said Union Society."

CHAPTER XIII.

*The "friendly interview" sought for by the prosecutors, was an oppor-
tunity to make their most arrogant demands.*

We were now officially informed, that the church officers had
already organized their prosecuting committee, with intention to
institute charges "*if necessary.*"   It only remained for us to be informed, on what ground the *necessity* would be made to rest, in
order to judge of their entire design.   And this information was
soon furnished by the prosecutors, who proceeded to make their
visits.   Two of the seven waited on the writer of this review.

See Narrative and Defence, page 20. It was not their object, as may be seen by reading their book, to ask in a friendly way, nor even authoritatively to require, any correction of some one or more of the essays which had been published; nor to require the names of any of the writers of them; nor to ask or require any change in the manner of conducting the periodical. They came to let him know, that it was *"necessary"* that he should use his influence to effect a dissolution of the Union Society, or withdraw from it, and cease to publish the Mutual Rights. "In as much" said they "as the Union Society and Mutual Rights, have become so completely identified with the evils of which we complain, we deem it *indispensable*, that you should dissolve your connexion with them." The points upon which the *necessity* turned, were now presented. The Union Societies had "incorporated the spirit of party." Through their aid, the Mutual Rights had produced much excitement, and bid fair to extend it far and wide. The reformers were not children, whose works were likely to be abortive. They had employed ways and means, which were not to be resisted. It was *"necessary"* therefore, that they should be met by the arm of power and compelled to obey the dictates of their masters. In the most unqualified manner imaginable, the two prosecutors let him know, that their opinion must regulate his conduct, and that obedience on his part was *"indispensable."* And yet they said "they did not wish nor require him, to make a sacrifice of conscience or of principle." He might *call* himself a *reformer*, and speak, write and petition, "in a temperate and christian like manner, in favour of reform!!" That is to say, he must do what they had commanded; and although he had laboured much, for four years, to establish Union Societies, and give effect to the periodical, he must instantly, at their bidding, turn round and destroy the one, and disgrace the other, and then, save his reputation, and conscience, and self respect, if he could, by calling himself a reformer still. And if he would let them be judges of what he might say, and write, and petition, after this explanation of what they deemed necessary, he might still speak, and write, and petition!! He felt commiseration for the men, who in their great zeal to maintain the power of the travelling preachers, gave such proof, how little they understood themselves, when they talked about making a sacrifice of conscience or principle. These men, under circumstances so highly offensive, waited on him; not to ask in a becoming manner, what they had a right to ask, the correction of any misstatement, which they were ready to specify and prove to be incorrect, but to dictate a destruction of all our labours, and to let us know, that we must obey their commands, or expect expulsion! They probably considered it a godly visit. We viewed it at the time, as an insolent interference with our rights, as christians and American citizens. And we now say, the *"wholesome and sound discipline"* which they were preparing to execute, was a conspiracy against the rights of reformers, for which intelligent Methodists throughout the United States, ought to be ashamed, since it has had the sanction of the General Conference.

We ask the intelligent reader, now carefully to consider the demand, to which, in their opinion obedience was so *"necessary,"* so absolutely indispensable? Had it been any affair of individual interest or of individual misunderstanding, it would have been an easy task for us to have suffered wrong. Even, if it had been a misunderstanding, which extended no farther than that portion of the Union Societies, which resided in the city of Baltimore, important as the effect would have been, we should have considered it a duty to signify to them our readiness, to endeavour to be accommodating. But the case was altogether different. The editorial committee had been engaged in the publication of the Mutual Rights, nearly four years. During the whole of that time, we had been of the committee. Our list of subscribers had been greatly extended, and was receiving daily accessions. Thousands read our paper with interest. The Wesleyan Repository had been so resisted by the friends of power, that that it had become necessary to exchange it, for the Mutual Rights. Experience had demonstrated the necessity of sustaining the periodical, by the organization of Union Societies. Such, indeed, had been their effect, that we were entirely satisfied with our prospect of success, and the proceedings of the power party prove, that they were no less apprehensive of the ultimate result. Were we not bound by every consideration of justice and propriety, to say to them in reply, that we considered their attempt at coercion, in this matter, altogether out of the way? In fact, if obedience had been the price of personal safety, the price would have been considered too dear. It is believed, we would not have yielded the rights for which we contended, under existing circumstances, to have saved our lives.

CHAPTER XIV.

The transaction which doctor Bond has named "an underplot."

VERY soon after this visit, the intended charges were laid before the preacher. But before the trials commenced, doctor Bond took occasion, on his own responsibility, to offer terms to the Union Society, which if accepted, he ventured to engage for the prosecutions, that they should be dismissed. See Narrative and Defence, pages 24, 25.

The first intention of this overture, was, if the Union Society would agree to meet it with their approbation, to accomplish the same objects, the dissolution of the Society, and the destruction or neutralization of the Mutual Rights. "The Union Society shall be dissolved" said he in his proposals, "and not re-organized in the present or any other form." And all papers intended for publication in the Mutual Rights, "shall be submitted to three persons, chosen mutually, by the reformers and *the committee who have preferred charges against some of them*, who shall be authorized to expunge all objectionable passages therefrom." Of course no paper could have been published unless it had the approbation of men, in the confidence of the worst enemies of reform. And every candid reader must see, that such an arrangement was more offensive, than the demand made by the prosecutors themselves. What man, not under the influence of blind passion, could have proposed to his fellow citizens, terms so degrading? But these propositions were not terms of a brotherly compromise, offered in the true spirit of conciliation. Charges were already preferred against us, and the dread consequences of excommunication were held up, in terrorem, over our heads. So that these appearances of accommodation, were in reality inquisitorial dictations, of the most offensive kind, made the more repulsive, by the obliquity which marked the manner of their introduction.

There was also a second intention in making these overtures. If the Union Society should reject these terms, then this *kindly* interference of the doctor, was to make a fine figure in the Narrative and Defence, and be additional proof of the *"obstinacy"* of reformers.

CHAPTER XV.

The appendage to the "underplot," which is noticed in the introductory chapter, as the collateral plot.

For the same purposes, and to give still greater formality and notoriety to their pretensions to make peace, *doctor Green was sent for.* They would then be prepared to say, that these two doctors, both disinterested, had used their influence to prevail on the reformers to accept terms of reconciliation, but they had *"obstinately"* rejected them both.

Had doctor Green come to use his influence in *reviving the patience* and *meekness* of our prosecutors:—had he exerted himself to dissuade them from their tyrannical and repulsive proceedings, that they might seek an understanding with us, upon principles of equality and brotherly love, then indeed he would have merited the reputable appellation of a mediator. But, as he came to reiterate the same offensive propropositions, which were obviously intended to effect the utter destruction of reform, we were compelled to consider him an insidious enemy. And that his mediatorial propositions, were drawn up under the influence and advice, if not the dictation of doctor Bond, we can have no doubt. A note was picked up among the papers swept from the conference room, addressed to doctor Bond, bearing date the same day that doctor Green wrote his first letter. It was to inform doctor Bond that doctor Green had arrived, and to request him to come up to dinner or soon afterwards. And, although doctor Green says in his second letter, "I set out from my family and my home, with intention to volunteer as a mediator in this case, without being solicited to do so, by any one. Yet he was sent for.

After the receipt of the last letter addressed to us by doctor Green, we wrote the following general reply, which perhaps he did not receive. At any event, it is not recollected with certainty, whether it was forwarded. It is now published, because it presents the subject of his correspondence and mediation, in the light in which we then viewed it.

"January, 1828.

Dear Sir,
"As you addressed to me, your letters of introduction, to what you saw proper to offer as your volunteer work of mediation between the contending parties, in the Methodist Episcopal Church, you will permit me to trouble you with one in the conclusion.

"Your first was written in a style and manner, which very much prepossessed me in your favour, and led me to expect, that, as you had come a hundred miles to volunteer as a mediator, you would inquire into the amount of our grievances; take measures to hear our explanation of the principal occasions which had produced those publications, which, it is alleged, provoked the old-side brethren to institute their prosecutions; inquire into the propriety or impropriety of their proceedings;—by an equal consideration of the claims or complaints of each, and a dignified, impartial and christian like attention to both, ascertain which side had greatest cause of complaint, and in full view of the whole, act the part of a real and trust-worthy mediator. But I am sorry to say, that your second communication compelled me to change my opinion:— That it destroyed all my hopes. For instead of any thing like a mediation on just and equal principles, you made it obvious, that you had *volunteered*, to unite your talent and influence, with the power and authority of the city station, with an intention to induce reformers to receive the same dictates, which we had unanimously considered tyrannical, had firmly rejected, and in view of which, had determined to become martyrs for the cause of emancipation in the Methodist Episcopal Church. Indeed, I am not at all surprised to learn from a brother, who obtained the information from yourself, that you had spent much of your time with doctor Bond; because the terms which you offered, were in substance and in their intended effect, the same that he had assumed the liberty to offer to us, on *his* own *individual* account.

"I must frankly say to you, that the pains you have taken must be considered by all well informed men, to have been produced, not by any wish in the character of a disinterested mediator, to do an act of equal justice to us and the prosecutors; but by an intense zeal to save the church from merited scandal; either by bringing us to submission, and by so doing, justify the "constituted authorities of the church;" or in case of failure in that purpose, afford them an occasion to say, we were *obstinate* and perverse, in refusing an overture of peace. I hope, sir, you will not flatter yourself or your party, (for you must excuse me in identifying you with our adversaries,) that because you have seen fit to call your *dictates, honourable terms of reconciliation*, that disinterested men will consider them in that light. The world will know by the first exposition of the transaction, that you have evinced no concern for the honour of reformers, but the *utmost* solicitude for that of the men in power. But what is most strange and most strongly confirms the truth of the above imputation, is the fact, that when your own judgment had led you to anticipate our intention to propose a committee on our part, to meet a similar committee on the part of the Quarterly Meeting Conference, and which was rejected on the part of the prosecution, you persevered in offering your own offensive proposals to the oppressed brethren, in your letter to the chairman of our committee.

I repeat it sir, if you left home with intention to be a mediator; by mingling with our persecutors, either imperceptibly or by design, you forgot the object of your visit, and undertook the office of a minister for the tyrannical party, in order to aid them in their endeavours to establish their authority over us, in a measure to which we had refused to submit. It is very clear, that the object was to secure an acknowledgment of guilt on our part, in order to justify "the constituted authorities of the church," and at the same time, effect the destruction of all our means of future success;—and thus save the Methodist Episcopal Church from her deserved reproach, and retain to her the same dominion with unabated authority. But, sir, your party has taught us to be wary, and by the blessing of God, we have escaped your snare. With sincere good wishes for your *personal happiness,* and the most ardent prayers, that the men in power may see their mistake, I subscribe myself, S. K. J.

CHAPTER XVI.

The Destruction of the Mutual Rights and Union Societies,—the Alpha and Omega of the prosecutions.

THE two prosecutors officially appointed to wait on us before citing us to trial, said, inasmuch as the Union Society and Mutual Rights, had become so completely identified with the evils of which they complained, they deemed it indispensable that we should dissolve our connexion with them.

On the evening of our trial, Mr. Israel, on the part of the prosecution, came out in the same open and candid manner in which he gave the desired information when called on by brother James R. Williams, and said, "we regret that this course was unavoidable; we had no other alternative; we were driven to this course. We have been told by the members of the Union Society, that they must have lay delegation. They also say, they never will withdraw from the church. Lay delegation we believe, is not practicable or expedient. With these views, we never can agree; we are as distant as the poles. The Mutual Rights has produced wranglings, disputations and divisions; it has produced two parties. Every

8

religious community has a right to form its own discipline; and its members are not at liberty to disturb it. While they remain members of the church, they have no right to form, or be members of the Union Society." These laconic sentences;—his communication to J. R. Williams, with respect to their determination to expel us; together with the requisition of the prosecutors officially made to us, by which it was declared *indispensable* that we should dissolve our connexion with the Union Society and Mutual Rights, prepared us to know with certainty, that our views were correct, and that we had only to choose between the most disgraceful submission to their dictates, and expulsion from their fellowship.

After hearing our protests, the prosecutors were ready, without any proper investigation, to turn over the whole affair, *en masse*, charges, specifications, and Mutual Rights *in extenso*, three entire volumes and part of the fourth, to the committee, to carry home with them, to read at their leisure, to cogitate and to confer, until they should be ready to decide, whether we had or had not a right to form and be members of the Union Society, or to publish the Mutual Rights: or more properly to be ready when called on, to perform their part in executing the "wholesome and sound discipline" which was intended to secure our expulsion, by an "unanimous vote," even if the most of them should not have found it convenient to read the Mutual Rights at all.

We know not when the committee made their report. In the mean while, their other preparations were going forward. Dr. Bond had an opportunity to submit his propositions, as before specified. And then came doctor Green, the object of whose visit has been stated. The interference of these two Doctors proves, that they greatly desired the destruction of the offensive institutions, to be brought about entirely at our expense. If they could have prevailed on us to accept their terms, which would have been a "surrender at discretion;" then the prosecution would have been justified, the rectitude of all their measures admitted, and in course, "their *responsibilities* would have set very lightly upon *them*." And considering how prolific their ingenuity in preparing their indictment; their charges so precise and so fully embracing the objects they were intended to accomplish, we are not surprised, that doctor Green was employed to second doctor Bond, in his endeavours to persuade us to submit, and in the attempt at persuasion, so to manage and conduct his correspondence that in the event of a failure with us, it might constitute a part of the Narrative and Defence, and co-operate with all the other things which constitute that book, to make an impression on the public mind unfavorable to our cause. They were very desirous, that their proceedings should be thought in accordance with "*wholesome and sound discipline*." Reformers, however, were not to be wheedled by their ingenious devices, and the quarterly meeting conference proceeded to read the garbled extracts; and, as was intended, condemned us "without a dissenting voice."

The following extract from a copy of their decree, as officially furnished, confirms the foregoing views.

"Resolved, thirdly, that the Rev. Samuel K. Jennings be expelled from the Methodist E. Church, unless he *withdraw, forthwith*, from the Union Society, and promise not to be engaged hereafter, in *any publications* that inveigh against our discipline or government, or speak evil of ministers," &c. A copy of these resolutions was sent to each of the expelled preachers and members: See Narrative and Defence, page 29. It is true the Mutual Rights is not named in the resolution. This was carefully avoided, not only in this, but in all their subsequent papers. The work had then been officially condemned, so that the resolutions not only included the Mutual Rights, but every other possible publication, intended to find fault with the discipline or the government of the Methodist Episcopal Church.

The above decree was soon followed by a letter from the Rev'd James M. Hanson, which, after giving his views of the trial, &c. concluded as follows:—"You must therefore, plainly perceive, that the only ground on which expulsion from the church can be avoided, is an *abandonment* of the *Union Society*, with assurances that you will *give no aid in future to any publication* or *measure calculated to cast reproach upon our ministers*, or occasion breach of union among our members.

Be good enough then, my brother, to answer, in writing, the following plain and simple questions: 1st. Will you *withdraw forthwith* from the *Union Society?* 2d. Will you *in future withdraw your aid from such publications* and *measures*, as are calculated to cast reproach upon our ministers and produce breach of union among our members?" [Mutual Rights or any other paper or book, or any thing else of whatever kind, which can promote reform.*]

JAMES M. HANSON.

From the whole evidence it is indubitable, that in the beginning of the prosecution, and in its conclusion, they had one fixed and determinate purpose to accomplish, which was, the destruction of the Union Society and the Mutual Rights. There was no desire on their part to rectify our opinions. If we would have agreed to the demolition of those two things, we might afterwards have called ourselves reformers; so said our prosecutors; so says the Narrative and Defence. But at any event, those were to be destroyed. And it is now as clear to our minds as any other proposition, that the selections were made, not to review and demand a correction of any paper; but to heap together in their own way, the things which they could use to the best purpose, in the construction of the Narrative and Defence, and by it, make the people believe we had so far outraged all order, that they were warranted in expelling us, after their own manner. And yet we believe these men had a zeal for God, in all this absurd procedure.

The seven prosecutors, the preacher in charge, towards whom we have never felt any personal hostility, although he seems to think otherwise; the local preachers who sat as the committee of

* In annexing the explanation contained within the brackets, we only wish that the reader may mark the comprehension of the resolution.

inquiry in our cases, and the members of the Quarterly Meeting Conference, all seem to be satisfied in the opinion, that there was sufficient evidence in the Mutual Rights to prove us guilty of hav· ing enveighed against the discipline and spoken evil of ministers of the Methodist Episcopal Church. Such is the nature of their hierarchy, that Methodist ministers are unavoidably identified with their discipline and government. Hence when fault is found with any part of their system or its administration, a Methodist, commonly considers, not only one, or a few, but the whole ·body of the itinerant ministry to be assailed. The zeal of these men for the honor of their establishment, regulated by the influence which the principal leaders had over them in the transaction, seemed to have turned their chief attention to the necessity of getting the church rid of the influence of reform. Hence their ingenious pains to identify the evils of which they complained with the Union Society, and Mutual Rights. They intended to dissolve the one and suppress the other, and so put an end to the investigation: but still, they felt it necessary, if possible, to make the pubic believe that their only object was to restrain or punish the licentiousness of the press; and that they had no objection to a temperate investigation into the principles and practices of ecclesiastical government. But we shall show that in their zeal for the government, they forgot the proper design of "wholesome and sound discipline." That they were so eagerly intent upon the chase of reform out of their borders, that they overlooked the course prescribed by the word of God, for effecting the reformation of the offenders, and that it was their glaring departure from the rules of conduct by which they ought to have been regulated;—their executive usurpation of legislative authority, and that too intended to have an *ex post facto* operation, that subjected us in self defence, to the unavoidable necessity of protesting against their procedure.

CHAPTER XVII.

The Commencement of the Prosecutions.

THE prosecution commenced with the following citation, viz:

BALTIMORE, Sept. 8th, 1827.
"*Dear Sir,*—You are hereby informed, that charges have been preferred against you, by the following persons: J. Rodgers, S. Harden, J. Berry, I. N Toy, A Yearley, G. Earnest, and F. Israel. As it is desirable for the satisfaction of all who feel an interest in the matter, that a hearing should be had as soon as practicable, it is hoped that Tuesday evening next, at 7 o'clock, will suit your convenience. Yours, respectfully,

JAMES M. HANSON."

What a fearful aspect does this citation wear! A posse commitatus of seven leaders, stewards, and trustees, all united to give their charges weight!! Never did the government of the Methodist Episcopal Church in Baltimore, assume such a formidable appearance!!! We wrote to Mr. Hanson, requesting a copy of the charges, which was sent on Monday evening, the 10th of the month. The charges were as follows:

"The Rev. Samuel K. Jennings is charged with endeavouring to sow dissentions in the society or church, in this station or city, known by the Methodist Episcopal Church, and with the violation of that general rule of the Discipline of the said church or society, which prohibits its members from doing harm; and requires them to avoid evil of every kind; and especially, with violating that clause of said general rule, which prohibits speaking evil of ministers."

These charges exhibit a formal statement of "the evils of which they complained," and if he was chargeable with the alleged offences, he was so chargeable as an individual, without any implication of the Union Society. The offences, so far as they had existence, were committed by the publication of certain papers in the Mutual Rights, the specification of which, was all that was necessary or proper.

CHAPTER XVIII.

The proceedings illegal in their commencement;—in violation of a positive precept of our blessed Lord Jesus Christ.

If these general charges, "the evils of which they complained," had been accompanied with definite references to the words, sentences, paragraphs, or sentiments which they deemed exceptionable, as the specifications, without the attempt, sophistically to identify them with the Union Society and Mutual Rights, and especially if the two prosecutors had not made their previous demand, the accusation would have had the appearance of a personal prosecution, and we should have been bound to appear and answer, in the customary way. But even under such circumstances we should have had great cause of complaint, because they had not proceeded according to the word of God, which directs that an attempt should first have been made to obtain a satisfactory explanation, in a private and friendly manner. If any brother had aught against any one of us, it was his duty to have come to such individual himself alone. And why himself alone? Because brethren are equal, and such an interview, to do any good, must take place on terms of equality, christian love, forbearance, and all long suffering. And any man who is not furnished with these pre-requisite graces, is unfit to minister reproof. Instead of regarding this rule, with becoming reference to its divine authority, they came two together and made a demand, for doing which, they had no authority from the word of God, or from the book of Discipline; a demand, which shall be shewn in the sequel, they themselves have admitted they had no right to make.

CHAPTER XIX.

The proceedings violate the Discipline of the Methodist Episcopal Church—form of first Protest.

WE had good cause of complaint, also, because they had not proceeded, as the Discipline directs. According to the general rules, upon which they pretended to base their charges and specifications. "If there be any, who habitually break any of them, (the General Rules,) let it be known unto them, who watch over that soul, as they who must give an account. We will admonish him of the error of his ways. We will bear with him for a season." Who are they who say this? The travelling preachers. They make these promises. They have given the pledge, that the preacher in charge, whoever he may chance to be, in whatever circuit or station, shall perform this duty. And it is clear, that the duty properly devolves on the preacher in charge, who is appointed by the bishop and conference, to watch over the souls which pertain to his pastoral oversight. Mr. Hanson was bound by the general rules, if he had been informed that we had transgressed any of those rules, to have first admonished us, and then to have borne with us for a season, before they could have proceeded according to the Discipline, to subject us to church censure. But this was not done; and we shall shew in the sequel, that he had already disqualified himself to do his duty. After all these glaring instances of default, in their proceedings, when we appeared in obedience to the citation, above stated, we were informed by the prosecutors, that they "had nothing personal against Dr. Jennings; that they entertained for him the highest respect. But the *Mutual Rights*, had produced wranglings, disputations, and divisions." And the members of the church "while they remained members, had no right to form Union Societies, or be members of them." After these declarations made by the prosecutors, with the charges and specifications before us, we were obliged to see, that the prosecution was not intended to be personal, but to effect the destruction of Union Societies and the Mutual Rights, and that in order to accomplish this purpose, they had resorted to the device of identifying them "with the evils of which they complained." For such a course of procedure we knew there was no existing rule of Discipline. And as the intended decision, was to have a general effect, according to their design and expectation nothing short of an entire destruction of reform, we entered our protest in the following words:

"A church court cannot have admissible jurisdiction, in any case, the merits of which, necessarily involve questions and interests of great public importance, which it has not the power to dispose of or settle, and upon which, its sentence can have no adequate effect. Its jurisdiction is, and forever ought to be, confined to cases of immorality, heresy, and the settlement of differences which may chance to occur between two or more individuals, on account of some personal altercation which such individuals are not prepared to adjust by agreement, between themselves. In affairs of this sort, the church has a Scriptural and common-sense right to interfere, because the whole effect of her decisions in such cases is completely within the control of her authority and influence. But the charges and specifications to which we are called to answer, so deeply involve the interests, rights, and privileges of thousands, in many different places throughout the United States;—interests, rights and privileges of vast and national importance, that in despite of sophistry, they will be considered by disinterested judges, to constitute a case entirely new, and for which, no adequate provision is made in our code of discipline. The general conference has never yet fairly deliberated on the fundamental principles involved in it, and therefore, there is no law to regulate your proceedings, or justify your decision.

"The manner in which this prosecution has been gotten up, is altogether new, and unknown to the oldest Methodist now living. A catalogue of the names of seven, the most important official men in the station, stewarts and trustees, men of wealth and influence, in one phalanx of prosecutors, might have served to intimidate the fearful, or perplex the ignorant, and it may have some affect upon the minds of the men appointed to act as the committee, but it does not change the true character of this prosecution. It carries with it, prima facie evidence, that they themselves consider the case new, and one which requires new measures. It proves that they were at their wits' end to bring forward their cause, dressed in a garb, which might give it the appearance of familiarity;—of an old acquaintance of the judiciary of this station. But a discerning community, whose eyes are anxiously turned upon these proceedings, will understand the subject, and will sustain us in our *protests* against such unheard of acts and doings—against the *competency*—against the *right* of this tribunal, to try the questions which are involved in this case; and if this court, shall proceed, notwithstanding this protest, we will consider it an executive usurpation of *ex post facto* legislative authority. But we sincerely hope, that whilst we are as yet at the threshold of this undertaking, brethren will reconsider their purpose, dismiss the prosecution, and not set up a precedent, which of all others, is the most dangerous to the pulic welfare and safety."

CHAPTER XX.

Their specifications proved to be sophistical and unsupported by Discipline.

THE correctness of the foregoing views will appear still more clearly, on a careful examination of the two specifications, which were intended to sustain their attempt, to make out the identification so necessary, to give to their proceedings the appearance of legality. Specification 1st. "Because the said Samuel K. Jen-

nings, while a *member* and a *local preacher* of the Methodist Episcopal Church aforesaid, did heretofore attach himself to, and become a member of the Society, called the Union Society of the city
of Baltimore; which Union Society, is in *opposit'on to the discipline*,
in whole or in part, of the Methodist Episcopal Church aforesaid."
    This specification is a piece of scandalous sophistry. It pre-
supposes the existence of two rules of discipline, which had no
being. The first supposition is, that the discipline prohibits the
formation of Union Societies. The second supposition is, that
the discipline forbids the members, and more particularly the local
preachers, to "attach themselves to, or become members of such
Union Societies." As this is a point of great importance, we will
be indulged in proceeding in a further examination of it, with tech-
nical exactness. The specification, may be considered, to contain
two syllogisms. The first would read thus. The discipline of the
Methodist Episcopal Church, prohibits the formation or existence,
of Union Societies. This is the major proposition. The minor
in course, would read thus: But a Union Society has been formed
in Baltimore. Then comes the conclusion. Therefore the Union
Society in Baltimore, is in opposition to the discipline of the
Methodist Episcopal Church. We deny the truth of the major
preposition, and demand the proof; the chapter and paragraph, of
the discipline, which contains the prohibition. It is not to be
found.
    The second syllogism would read thus. The discipline of the
Methodist Episcopal Church forbids the members, and particularly the local preachers of that church, to attach themselves to, or
become members of the Union Society. This again is the major
proposition. Then comes the minor in course: But "Samuel K.
Jennings, while a member and local preacher of the Methodist
Episcopal Church aforesaid, did heretofore, attach *himself* to, and
become a member of the society, called the Union Society of the
city of Baltimore, which Union Society is in opposition to the discipline," &c. The conclusion is, therefore, the said Samuel K.
Jennings, has violated this rule of discipline. We deny the truth
of the major proposition and demand the proof. It cannot be produced, and these prosecutors have themselves admitted it. See
Narrative and Defence, page 28. "The committee with whom the
conference committee were intended to negotiate, were appointed
by the *Union Society*, a *body* not *recognized* by our *discipline;* and
of whom the church could *demand nothing.*" With this acknow-
edgement staring them in the face, we say again, this first specification is a piece of scandalous sophistry, *devised* for the special
purpose, of making out their unlawful and forced identification.
    The prosecutors must bear with us a little, while we exhibit
them, at cross questions with themselves. In the specification, they
say, "The Union Society is in opposition to the discipline, in *whole*
or *part*, of the Methodist Episcopal Church." In the Narrative and
Defence, they say "The Union Society is a body not recognized by
the discipline." It follows in course, then not prohibited. And yet
they seem persuaded, that Union Societies, must be in opposition

to the Methodist Episcopal Church, if not *in whole* at any event *in part*. They were like Peter in Dean Swift's tale of the tub. If the necessary opposition, could not be established by any known and promulged rule, they could make it out by some rule of construction. It was all in their own hands, and they did *make it out*.

Let us now try the merits of the second specification, which reads thus. "Because the said Samuel K. Jennings, as a member of the said Union Society, directly or indirectly, either by pecuniary contributions or his personal influence, aiding, abetting, co-operating or assisting in the publication and circulation of a work, called the Mutual Rights of the ministers and members of the Methodist Episcopal Church, printed under the direction of an editorial committee (of which the said Samuel K. Jennings is, or lately was one) appointed by, or who are members of the Union Society aforesaid, which work or publication, called the Mutual Rights, &c. contains (among other things) much that inveighs against the discipline of the Methodist Episcopal Church aforesaid, in whole or in part, and is in direct opposition thereto; and that is abusive or speaks evil of a part if not of the most of the ministers of that church. The general tendency of which work or publication, has been, to produce disagreement, strife, contention and breach of union among the members of said church, in this city or station.

So much of this second verbose specification, as relates to personal accusations, we postpone for subsequent consideration, and confine ourselves at present, to the part which is intended to "identify the Mutual Rights with the evils of which they complain." Here we have another instance of the same kind of sophistry. The specification proceeds, as if the first had been established, intending to make the Union Society and Mutual Rights, offenders in common with "the said Samuel K. Jennings," who was "a member of said Union Society." The sophistry of this crafty *device*, consists in the supposed establishment of two points which were without foundation. It supposes the first specification to have been established, and takes for granted the existence of a rule of discipline, which forbids the publication of any book or periodical, in which any essay or paper, shall ever, on any account, be admitted, that shall be considered to "inveigh or speak evil of ministers." The major of the proportion would read thus: The Discipline of the Methodist Episcopal Church forbids the publication of any book or periodical, &c. as above. Then the minor would be, the Mutual Rights is a periodical which contains such papers. The conclusion; therefore, the Mutual Rights is forbidden by the discipline of the Methodist Episcopal Church. We deny the truth of the major and demand the proof. But they were so confident, that they had fully succeeded in their policy, that on their first approach, they came to demand a surrender of the Union Society and Mutual Rights. "It was indispensable that we should dissolve our connexion with them." That is,

9

we must submit to the heaviest penalty of which the case could admit;—the very same penalty, which they required as the satisfaction for the church, for the offences of which they pronounced us guilty, and for which they condemned us "by an unanimous vote." And yet it is "strange, passing strange," that these same men, when more cool and dispassionate, acknowledge they had no right or authority, to make any such demand. See Narrative and Defence, page 28. "How were the committee to know, what satisfaction to require for the church, of *those, whom the church had not yet officially decided to be guilty of any offence at all.*" And yet *before trial, without any official decision, they demanded what would have been in effect, a discontinuance of all further efforts to bring about reform, a violation of our engagements as editors of the periodical with more than fifteen hundred subscribers, and an acknowledgement of our having transgressed laws that had no existence and that the prosecutors had acted correctly as Christians and as Methodists, in all these unreasonable and unjust things.*

After collating those demands with the verbose and cunningly devised charges and specifications, and connecting the whole with the known previous arrangements to secure an unanimous vote for our expulsion, the propriety of appearing before our accusers, except for the purpose of entering our protest, will be clear and unquestionable.

CHAPTER XXI.

Correspondence with Mr. Hanson. His letters prove that a fair trial was not intended. It was an act of usurpation. A protest the only proper defence.

WHILST we were meditating as to the proper course to be pursued, a second note was sent to Mr. Hanson, of which the following is an extract.

——"I have to say to you, that the nature of my defence, will make it imperiously necessary for me to correspond with the several writers, for the publication of whose papers, as one of the editors of a periodical work, I am called to give an account. This circumstance, together with other very important parts of my intended defence, will necessarily require a good deal of time. A proper sense of justice on the part of the executive, therefore, will certainly protect me against the violence of being urged to too hasty a hearing.

I am, &c.   S. K. J."

Rev. James Hanson.

The following is an extract from Mr. Hanson's reply.

——"I am no less astonished, that you should think it all important to your intended defence, to have a correspondence with the writers of those pieces, which the brethren, above alluded to, have designated. The *sentiments* and *expressions* which are deemed *exceptionable*, have been *published to the world*, and *speak* for themselves. With the writers for the "Mutual Rights," scattered as they are over the continent, the charges in question have no immediate concern: nor is it easy to see, how these writers are to render you any assistance. They can furnish no testimony,—they can undo nothing, that you as a member of the editorial committee may have done; and without designing to flatter, I may be permitted to say, they can place the subject in question, in no light, in which it has not appeared to your mind, seeing that it has been with you a subject of close and deep deliberation for several years. Under these impressions, and desirous, for the good of all concerned, to bring the matter to as speedy an issue as is consistent with a proper sense of justice, it is deemed altogether unadvisable to fix upon any period for investigation, beyond Monday 17th, at 7 o'clock, P. M.

I am, &c.   JAMES M. HANSON.

This second appointment allowed us five days of grace to prepare for trial. But it is evident from the face of the letter, that his mind was already made up upon the subject, and that he had no expectation of a trial upon the merits of the papers;—that he intended to make no inquiry after the writers of them, nor to afford any opportunity of obtaining from them any explanation. Besides, at the time we had in possession a copy of a letter from Mr· Hanson to Mr. Jacobs, of Alexandria, a short extract from which was read with our protest, to prove that he could not act the part of an impartial judge. We now give a more extensive extract:

——"I was sorry my dear brother, extremely sorry, to find you, in your communication to the Union Society, sometime since, identifying yourself with a set of men, who are, I have no doubt, the most decided and violent enemies, that our church has on earth;—men who have spared no pains, and paid no regard to any of those maxims, which ought to govern the conduct of christians towards one another, in striving to render the church odious in the eyes of mankind. And who are those mighty reformers, after all the mighty dust, that has been raised? Why, a few men who have retired from the hardships of an itinerant life; 2d, a set of men, who have never contributed in any considerable degree, either to the organization or prosperity of the church, and whom their quarterly conferences would never have recommended as proper persons to be licensed to preach, in the Methodist Episcopal Church, had it been known, they would take the course they have taken.. 3d, A few travelling preachers, some of whom perhaps have been disappointed, in not getting into the General Conference.————4th, A few of the laity, who by great names and pretty sounds, '*lay delegation* and *Mutual Rights*' for instance, have suffered themselves to be led away,"&c.————"*More than two years ago*, I was led to fear there was corruption at the very root of radicalism, and although I had rather favoured some of their views, I felt and avowed the most decided opposition, to others. Since my appointment to this station, I have had an opportunity of observing their movements more closely, and making myself better acquainted with their spirit, and I hope I shall not offend my brother Jacobs (whom I yet sincerely love) when I tell him, that I am disposed to view the greater part of them, as holding a relation to the church, to which in justice and propriety,—nay even *in charity* itself, they are no longer entitled."* Compare Mr. Hanson's commenting reply to the note asking an opportunity to correspond with the writers of the exceptionable papers, with this, his letter to Mr. Jacobs, and who will say his judgment was not made up, or that he was not disqualified to sit in judgment upon our cases? Compare the previous arrangements to secure "an unanimous vote" with the demand of the two prosecutors for the destruction of the Union Society and Mutual Rights, and then look at the sophistry of the charges and specifications, and who will doubt the predetermination of all concerned on the side of the government, to expel us, if we would not consent to give up the Mutual Rights and Union Societies. In view of the whole of these matters, we considered the prosecution in all its circumstances, unlawful, and calculated to scandalize the church; we therefore met the prosecution with a solemn protest.

The sophistry of the device for identifying the charges, &c. with the Union Society and Mutual Rights, has been made evident to common sense. Hence it appears that this surreptitious mode of procedure was expected to supply the want of a rule of discipline to justify their proceedings; and in course, that it was "*an executive usurpation of legislative authority*," intended to have an *ex post facto* operation. It brings to our recollection, an occurrence which took place in one of the upper counties of Virginia, about thirty-eight years ago. A county-court lawyer, who had long had great influence over the court, was urging a point in favour of his client with very great earnestness, when the opposite council arose and objected to the whole argument, on the ground, that it was not sustained by common or statute law, or any act of the State Legislature. The zealous advocate replied, "Gentlemen of the jury, that can make no difference as to the merits of this cause;

---

* The reader will bear in mind the fact, that this preacher, after '*thinking evil*' of us for more than two years, and justifying his evil thoughts by a closer observation for several months, having become our *pastor*, and we think, having been placed over us that he might "maintain *wholesome* discipline" amongst us, but who never in all that time, had called on any one of us in person or addressed us by letter; this man sat in judgment with his court, to expel *us* for "speaking evil of ministers." He had said of us, that we "*paid no regard to any of those maxims which ought to govern the conduct of christians towards one another, &c.* Was it not evil speaking of us, to say we paid no regard to any law of Christ? Could he have said any thing more comprehensive? As to christian maxims, we were perfect out-laws. According to this mode of "divine expounding." A travelling preacher may say what he pleases, of those under his pastoral care;—being an "*expounder*" he is not bound to be a keeper of the maxims which ought to govern the conduct of christians towards another!!"

for if what I have advanced is not the law, it ought to be the law, and what then is the difference?'' So with the prosecutors in our case: they appear to have thought, if there is no rule in the Discipline of the Methodist Episcopal Church which forbids the existence of Union Societies, or the publication of periodicals favourable to the work of reform, there ought to be such a rule, and what was the difference?

CHAPTER XXII.

A fair trial under existing circumstance, was impossible.

It is probable, that the government party were of opinion that we entered our protests, because we wished to evade a trial. This mistake, it is hoped, will now be corrected; as a fair trial, under the existing circumstances of the case, was absolutely impossible. For the present we dismiss the consideration of the identifying specifications, and return to the general charge so far as it admits of personal application. We were accused of speaking evil of ministers, in the character of Editors of the Mutual Rights. And for the proof, reference was made to numbers 1, 7, 25, 27, 29, 30, 32, 33, 34, 36, and 37, of that periodical.

Now suppose we had consented to be tried as the prosecutors proposed, what plea could we have entered in the case? Even admitting that we had been misguided in our judgment in respect to the character and abilities of the writers, and had erred materially as to the true spirit and meaning of their papers: admit all this—and would it have been a proper course, for us, the editors, to have plead guilty to the papers of those writers, without first having written to them for their views? Suppose, again, the writers to have been such men as Mr. Snethen, Mr. Shinn and others, notorious for integrity and truth, on whose judgment we could rely, and who in course were always ready to answer for themselves,—would it have been right, in view of all these considerations, for us to have plead guilty to charges predicated upon their papers? Would it have been proper for us to have entered the plea of justification, and offered the truth in evidence, when we were not permitted to correspond with them on the subject of their papers respectively? Every reasonable man will perceive what ought to have been done, had the church court been disposed to dispense justice. The prosecutors were not ignorant of it. See Narrative and Defence, page 76. "The doctor's defence, then, ought to have been a very different thing from what we find it. Instead of declaiming on reform, and the iniquity of endeavouring to prevent it, he should have set himself to prove the truth of the allegations, made by him and his *associates*, against our Bishops and other ministers. If he had shewn them to be true, the charge of EVIL SPEAKING could not have been sustained," &c. Then it follows, from their shewing, that "we ought to have set ourselved to prove the truth of the allegations made by our *associates*." And how were we, how were the editorial committee to do this, without the help of the writers? We wrote to Mr. Hanson, stating, "that the nature of our defence will make it *imperiously* necessary for us to correspond with the several writers, for the publication of whose papers, as editors of a periodical work, me are called to give an account"—adding that this would require time. Mr. Hanson, the judge and ruler of the court, replied, "With the writers for the 'Mutual Rights,' *scattered* as they are *over the Continent*, the charges in question have no *immediate concern;* nor is it easy to see how these writers are to render you *any assistance*. They can *furnish no testimony*. They can undo nothing that you, as a member of the Editorial committee, may have done," &c.

We were cited to trial on the 7th of September, to appear on the 10th. The time was extended to the 17th, beyond which, said Mr. Hanson, "it was deemed altogether unadvisable to fix upon the period for investigation.

Two points were thus previously settled by the judge. First, that in view of the intended course of proceedings, the court had pre-determined that the writers of the papers had no immediate concern with the charges in question, And secondly, that "they could furnish no testimony." They say we ought to have set ourselves to prove the *truth* of what our *associates*," the writers, had alleged. By whom were we to prove it? Not by the writers, said Mr. Hanson, nor by any testimony that they could have furnished. The "writers of the papers have no immediate concern with the charges"—"they can furnish no testimony." And in order to foreclose the possibility of obtaining or offering any such testimony;—the only testimony of which the case could have admitted—he limited the period allowed us to prepare for our defence, to the 17th—one week only—when he knew the writers were "*scattered over the continent.*"

With such unquestionable information, with respect to the spirit and intention of the prosecution, three things "rested upon us with the force of moral obligation."

1. We owed to ourselves sufficient respect to avoid a sophistical snare, intended to fix on us the scandal of "*evil speaking*," without affording us any possible means of defence or escape.

2. We owed to Reformers throughout the United States, they being absent, a refusal on our part to acknowledge them guilty of evil speaking, especially when we were officially informed by Mr. Hanson, that no opportunity would be allowed us to give them notice of the sweeping charges, which were to settle the principles by which every man of them would be liable to excommunication, at the nod of the travelling preachers.

3. We owed it to the Methodist Episcopal Church, to give them an opportunity or an occasion, by the interposition of the General Conference, to disavow and correct such unwarrantable and unjust proceedings. And from what has been submitted, our readers cannot fail to perceive that the only alternative left us, was to enter our protest against their surreptitious attempt to make a sub-

stitute for law;—against their unjustifiable arrangements to secure our condemnation by an unanimous vote;—and against the avowed prejudice of the preacher in charge. It must be particularly clear that we would have done ourselves and our cause, irreparable injustice to have submitted to such a *mock trial*, when we had certain information that it would terminate in our condemnation, upon a charge for publishing papers, as editors of a periodical, when at the same time we were not only not permitted to correspond with the writers of those papers, but were also informed by the judge of the court, that they could be of no service to us;—that they could afford us no testimony.

If our laymen had not been placed under the protection of the protest, we now know by the subsequent developement of facts, that condemnation awaited them, by "an unanimous vote;" and that nothing but the publication of the protest, could have prevented an impression, almost universal, that they had been righteously expelled. If the Local Preachers had gone to trial, upon the premises, it is equally clear, that we would have shared the same fate. It is true, we might have appealed to the Annual Conference: But what would that have availed us? The fate of Rev. D. B. Dorsey, who had only recommended the Mutual Rights, too well foretold what would have been the decision of that body, upon our appeal. The fate of our memorial let us know how they would have disposed of our case. Notwithstanding all the glaring improprieties which so amply justified our protest, the Annual Conference decreed, that in as much as we had dared to protest, and had not submitted to be caught in their snare in the inferior judicatories, we were not entitled to the poor privilege of uttering a complaint, much less of presenting an appeal. To have countenanced our protest, in the judgment of the Conference, would been "subversive of wholesome and sound discipline." And after the Annual Conference had condemned the Rev. D. B. Dorsey, and the Quarterly Meeting Conference, in the City of Baltimore, had condemned the Local Preachers by "an unanimous vote," would not a reversion of the sentence have been doubly "subversive of the *wholesome and sound discipline?*" It is obvious that an appeal to the Annual Conference would have been worse than useless, because it would have given the General Conference a better apology for refusing us a hearing, if a majority of that body were disposed to enter into the views of the Annual Conference.

The ultimate and chief design of the protest was to ascertain whether the Methodist Episcopal Church, as a body, were prepared to sustain the proceedings of the prosecution, which was gotten up in Baltimore station, and which, in the Narrative and Defence, the prosecutors say, was instituted "without any itinerant suggestion or influence whatever."

The great impropriety of proceeding against the Editors of the Mutual Rights, and not against the writers of the offensive papers, must be obvious; especially, as we could neither plead guilty, nor justify, in reply to the charges. It it equally obvious, that an honest intention to do justice and try the charges upon the merits of the publications, would have led to the prosecution of the writers, and not the Editors unless they had refused to give up the writers' names. But the prosecutors in this case, included many members of the Union Society, who were neither Editors nor writers, and they found us all equally guilty, and all were condemned for the same things! They knew who were some of the principal writers, and by a proper application to the committee might have known them all. They referred to papers written by Mr. Snethen; in course they knew he was one: why did they not bring him to trial? Or if they were determined to hold us implicated with him, why did they not give us time to call on him? He informed the public, that if at any time before these trials, notice had been given him, either verbally or by letter, or in the Mutual Rights, no man need to have been prosecuted or expelled on his account. "I would," said he, "have taken all my burden on my own shoulders."—"As the case now stands, I am not convinced, that I have misstated any fact—or that I have drawn false inferences from my premises." Mutual Rights, Vol. IV. page 351.

They knew Mr. Shinn was also one. Why did not they prosecute him? Why expel more than thirty members of the Union Society, because his papers were published in the Mutual Rights, and permit him, unmolested, to take his seat in the General Conference?—They knew if he were called on to answer for himself, or if they gave us time to write and receive his answer, in explanation of his papers, that they would be obliged to meet something like the defence which was published in the Mutual Rights, Vol. IV. page 257—287. Why did they not demand the name of Vindex and prosecute him? They knew that of these men, each for himself, could defend his papers, and heap disgrace upon any that would dare to bring him to trial. It suited their purpose better to identify the evils of which they complained with the Union Society and Mutual Rights."—With the writers for that work, "*scattered as they are over the Continent,* the charges in question," said Mr. Hanson, "have no immediate concern." The immediate concern of the prosecution was by means of "the charges in question,"· supported by their own comment on the papers, without explanation, to ensure "an unanimous vote for turning us all out of their fellowship, as the publishers and patrons of the periodical. Whether the writers could justify or not, was no part of the question, and gave them "no immediate concern." The leading purpose of the prosecution, was to expel us all, unless we would *"withdraw forthwith* from the Union Society, and promise not to be engaged, *hereafter, in any publications* that inveigh against *our discipline or government,"* &c.

CHAPTER XXIII.

Declaration that we were expelled without a trial. A memorial makes this known to the General Conference.

HAVING given our views of the transaction by which so many local preachers and members of the Methodist Episcopal Church were excommunicated, with the real, though covert intention, to put a stop to the work of reform, but with the avowed and ostensible intention, to bring to trial and punish the editors and patrons of the periodical, for "inveighing," &c. and "speaking evil of ministers." We now make our appeal to all well informed christian people, and to disinterested citizens of the United States generally, in a *solemn declaration*, that *our cause has never yet been tried.* All who have read, know, that we have clearly demonstrated, that a fair trial before the church court of Baltimore in our case, was impossible. In course no man can judge between our accusers and us, unless he will take the necessary pains, to read the four volumes of the Mutual Rights, and make himself acquainted with the nature and circumstances of the controversy. We have already stated the considerations, which made it "a duty which rested upon us, with the force of a moral obligation," to meet the prosecution with a *solemn protest.* These considerations were submitted in substance to the General Conference, as the subjoined memorial will shew; and we now say, the General Conference ought to have interfered, in some way, which might have served to wipe off the scandal from the Methodist Episcopal Church;—the scandal of having *expelled so many local preachers,* and *people without a trial, and without just cause.*

Our protests were intended to open the way for our contemplated memorials to the Annual and General Conferences. And although we had no good reason to expect any relief from the Annual Conference, a memorial to that body was considered necessary to precede our application to the General Conference. The resolution of the Annual Conference not to "subvert" *Baltimorean,* "wholesome and sound discipline," was such as we might have expected, when we knew their proceeding in the cases of the Rev. D. B. Dorsey and W. C. Pool. But we had a right to expect something better from the General Conference. And in view of such an expectation, on the 17th April, 1828, we wrote the following letter to brother Shinn.

BALTIMORE, *April 17th,* 1828.

Dear Brother,—In answer to your highly esteemed favour, I will say, that a restitution of our membership, together with such an acknowledgment of our rights and privileges, as our friends may consider a satisfactory guarantee for our safety, and which of course will make our return honourable, at the same time that our cause will be saved and protected, would assuredly be very desirable to us

10

all. Not so much, however, permit me to add, for any personal consideration, as for the reputation of Methodism. Individuals who understand the importance of the question at issue, will be found generally, perhaps in every instance, to have within their reach, resources sufficient for their own personal comfort.

The late transactions of Baltimore, must be considered by men of sense, every where, to be sufficient cause of scandal, to awake every intelligent Methodist in the United States. And I am still willing to believe, there will be found in the General Conference, men not so infatuated, that they cannot perceive, how loudly, a due regard for their own reputation calls upon them, to take such measures, as may be effectual to extenuate the offence which has been committed against our rights and liberties, and relieve the Methodist Episcopal Church from the reproaches, which, otherwise must inevitably fall upon her.

With intention to bring the subject before the General Conference, a memorial will be prepared and forwarded, and a letter will be sent to some one of our friends, which will communicate our views, respecting any concessions which ought to be admitted on our part, &c.

I am respectfully, your *brother*, &c.

SAMUEL K. JENNINGS.

Copy of a Memorial from the expelled members, addressed to the General Conference, assembled in Pittsburg.

"To the bishops and members of the General Conference of the Methodist Episcopal Church, in Conference assembled.

Esteemed Fathers and Brethren.

The memorial of the undersigned, late ministers and members of the Methodist Episcopal Church, in the city of Baltimore, respectfully sheweth.   That for upwards of three years last past, a periodical called "The Mutual Rights," has been published in said city, under the direction of a committee of ministers and members of said church, which periodical had for its object, the discussion of the propriety and utility of introducing an equitable representation from the ministry and membership, into the legislative department of said church.

Your memorialists beg leave to state, that most of the prominent writers for said periodical, are itinerant ministers of the said church, all of whom we verily believe, are ardently attached to the interests thereof, and whose only object, in furnishing contributions for said periodical, was to obtain a well balanced form of government, that said church may become the glory of the present age, and the just admiration of posterity.

Your memorialists further state, that no formal charge was preferred against either the authors, or editors, by any legal authorities of the church, during the aforesaid period of three years; but in the month of July last, a select meeting of some of the ministers and members of this station, was held for a particular purpose, and after that purpose had been subserved, a motion was made, and carried, to appoint several persons, to examine the Mutual Rights, to ascertain if the Discipline had not therein been violated.

Your memorialists would represent, that about the month of September last, the committee just referred to, called on some five or six members of the Union Society, individually, and demanded of each, an abandonment of the Union Society, and that they should withhold their aid from the Mutual Rights, as the exclusive terms on which a prosecution was to be avoided. Those brethren on whom the demand was made, did then, and do now believe, that the requisitions were such as neither the word of God, nor the discipline of the church recognizes as terms, on which brethren in Christ Jesus, are to be continued in church fellowship; and were therefore conscientiously impelled to decline giving the pledges demanded.

A few days thereafter, charges and specifications, based on certain essays in the Mutual Rights, were handed by the prosecuting committee to the Rev. Mr. Hanson, against upwards of thirty members of the Union Society, which were sent by him to the accused, with citations to trial, without a prior visit from him to either of the accused, to reconcile the parties and to prevent the unhappy collisions and *exacerbations* of party feeling, consequent on a church trial involving so many individuals; and to prevent the justly to be deprecated issues, which followed.

The first person cited for trial, was the Rev. Dr. Jennings, the chairman of the editorial committee of the periodical. He respectfully requested of Mr. Hanson, time to correspond with the authors of the pieces, adduced as proof of the charges, but this was refused. He nevertheless appeared, and made the protest, accompanying this memorial, marked A, to which we solicit the attention of the General Conference. The most of the accused appeared, and entered their protests against the glaring absurdity of the procedure, as well as the prejudiced character of the committee of trial, more particularly the latter, who had aided in promoting the prosecutions, and moreover, had in a publication, for which they had voted previously, prejudged our cases.

A considerable time after the trial (so called) Mr. Hanson sent us a communication informing us, that the committee had found us *"guilty;"* the committee had reported that the charges and specifications were *"sustained,"* and in the said communication, reiterated the demand made by the prosecutors, as before recited, and which were afterwards renewed, by doctor Green. We cannot but consider it remarkable, that such a striking sameness of demand should be made, at three different periods, and by three persons. Suffice it to say, that Mr. Hanson's demand was declined on the part of the accused. A short time after the members were expelled, and the local preachers were suspended. The local preachers determined to take their trials at the district conference, as provided by the discipline. The district conference met, and after being organized, and ready for business, was violently and illegally dissolved. Now as we cannot suppose, that the general conference ever designed to transfer the business of a district conference, to a quarterly meeting conference, by such means as were employed on this occasion, and especially by the votes of coloured preachers, in a slave holding state, and without allowing the subject to be discussed, we sincerely believe that the dissolution was illegal and void, and that the quarterly conference had no jurisdiction in the case.

The lay members obeyed their citations, but they did not appeal for the same reason which served to make the local preachers more sensible of the injustice done them by the unlawful dissolution of the district conference; which was, that we all knew the members of the quarterly meeting conference, (with but very few exceptions) at a meeting called for the purpose, had by a vote, adopted a paper which was published by themselves, in which it was stated, that the Mutual Rights had been rightly considered by the Baltimore Conference, to be an improper work; because in it anonymous writers were permitted to defame the travelling preachers, &c. Inasmuch, therefore, as the principal charge was for speaking evil of ministers, and the specifications referred to the Mutual Rights, as the only evidence by which they expected to sustain the charge and specifications; it was a necessary conclusion, that they had already decided on the facts (so called) in our case. They considered all the members of the Union Society identified with the exceptionable papers, and of course we as members of the Union Society, were made the subjects of their denouncement. An appeal, to have been made under such circumstances, carried with it such a certain expectation of defeat, that our lay members could not consent to appear before the quarterly meeting conference. Moreover, it was and is our opinion that the subject in dispute was one which required special legislation, and after entering our protests, we intended to look to your body, for an act which would guarantee a better mode of procedure, should any instance of this kind, again occur. In the meantime, however, we were desirous of calling the attention of the annual conference to the illegality of the proceedings, and with that view, sent up to the conference the memorial marked B, (see page 327) and to which that body returned the document marked C. (see page 230,) of Mutual Rights.

If we have erred, it should be remembered, that it was at a time of great excitement, and under extraordinary circumstances. We feel confident, that the case was entirely new?

Who ever before heard of the organization of a prosecution committee in the Methodist Episcopal Church, consisting of seven persons? When was there ever a convocation of members of the church, for the purpose of arraying themselves as prosecutors, against another party of the church?

The measure was so new, and so inconsistent with all our former acquaintance with Methodism, that we were apprehensive, our prosecutors had been encouraged thereto, by some persons in high authority in the church.

When attacked in such a party manner, and under such new and fearful circumstances, we felt obliged to protest, and to publish our protest, that our friends and the public might know the highly im—

proper course of procedure against us; that we might not be injured to any very great extent, by the varied attempts of our prosecutors and their friends, until a fair and full investigation could be had.

We are much surprised at the resolutions of the Baltimore Annual Conference. In the first resolution the utmost scrupulosity as to the formalities of the discipline, is tenaciously observed in every point regarding the expelled, whilst not a word is said respecting the informalities, by which the prosecutions were characterised.

It appears from the second resolution, that a departure from the course prescribed, would be subversive of "wholesome discipline." That there is no general rule without some exception, is generally admitted, and we believe our cases furnish such an exception; having been prosecuted by those who had condemned us; and tried by those who had found us guilty and published it to the world, previously to their sitting on our trials, and acknowledging that they had so acted, even on the trials! Surely this was a course of things extremely out of place and character. In the fourth resolution, they state, that "if the local preachers, on the dissolution of the conference, had appeared before the quarterly meeting conference, and objected to the jurisdiction of that body, in such case, on an appeal, this conference would have fully considered and decided on the whole subject." This is a most surprising statement, in view of all the facts in the case. The local preachers did draw up a formal protest against the jurisdiction of the quarterly meeting conference, to try their cases, which they sent in, to the presiding elder, (the Rev. Joseph Frye,) as the document marked D, fully proves. With the most incontestible evidence before the local preachers, that a large majority of the quarterly meeting conference had prejudged their cases; that it was a party prosecution; that the presiding elder by favouring the dissolution of the district conference, was also on the side of the prosetion party; that Mr. Hanson was also on the same side; that the committee were also of the party; that almost all the members of the quarterly meeting conference had voted them "enemies to Methodism," &c. in view of these facts, they declined a personal attendance, trusting that the annual conference would defend them against such oppression; or that if the annual conference should sanction such procedure, the general conference would render them an impartial hearing, and decide only on the merits of the facts, and principles involved in the case.

Finally, brethren, your memorialists respectfully represent to the general conference, that as we have been expelled from the church, contrary, as we believe, to Scripture and Discipline, and which expulsion has been, and still is painful to our hearts, we do hereby request your highly respected body to take such measures, as in your wisdom, shall restore us to the church of our former fellowship, and receive with us those who have withdrawn on our account, on principles which shall secure to us and the church, the liberty of speech and of the press, without sanctioning the licentiousness of either; and may the great Head of the church have you in his holy keeping, and direct you in all your deliberations, to the praise of His glory, is the prayer of your memorialists.''

The reader will perceive that a reference is requested to a copy of our protest marked A. That document in addition to the other references served to make the memorial so completely develope the whole business, that the Conference were obliged to understand the iniquity of the prosecution.

CHAPTER XXIV.

Some strictures on the proceedings of the General Conference, in view of the memorial.

How obvious it is, that the General Conference ought to have interfered and shewn a disposition to wipe off the scandal of having expelled so many local preachers and lay members of the Methodist Episcopal Church, without a trial and without a just cause! Had they been the representatives of the Methodist people, and in course accountable to the people for their legislative and judicial acts, they would have felt the necessity of evincing their disapprobation of such arbitrary proceedings. So far from feeling any such accountability, they considered themselves bound in conscience to assert their high prerogatives, as of divine appointment; and to make plain their *conscientious* determination to maintain the whole amount of their power;—saying in terms, that cannot be misunderstood, that they can be "cordially happy in the society and fellowship" of such only, as are willing to be *peacefully submissive* to their absolute authority, and that to those who may be dissatisfied with holding such obedient relation to the church, as they the "divinely authorized expounders of moral discipline,'' &c. shall have prescribed, there remains no alternative, but to exercise "the right of ecclesiastical expatriation.'' A little attention to the report of the committee on petitions and memorials, as adopted by the General Conference at Pittsburg, will confirm this statement.

The first three paragraphs bring the reader to the conclusion, that in the estimation of the conference, "the claim of right to the representation contended for,'' the claimants are not entitled to demand, because the conference "believe it neither has been or *can be* shown,'' that the claimants have such a *right*, either *natural* or *acquired*. It can be no cause of surprise, after this, to find in the seventh paragraph, a declaration, that the itinerant preachers have been very condescending and gracious, in dispensing a participation of "privileges and advantages to the local preachers;'' and that they regret to perceive, that their bounty in the "addition of privilege to privilege,'' should be met with the ungrateful return from some of the local preachers; not only "of claiming more and more,'' but at length of "demanding them as matters of positive and inherent right.'' They felt this regret the more intensely, because in their opinion, the introduction of local men into the councils of the church, could not fail to endanger their itinerant economy.

Their sincerity in deciding against the right of laymen or local preachers to representation, is argued in the ninth paragraph. "It cannot but be well known, that our present economy bears with a peculiar severity upon the personal and domestic comforts of the itinerant ministry. And even an enemy could scarcely fail to admit, that, were we really ambitious of worldly interests, and of personal ease and domestic comfort, we might have the discernment to perceive, that the surest way to effect these objects would be to effect the changes proposed, and thus to prepare the way for the enjoyment of similar advantages, in these respects, to those now enjoyed by the settled ministry of other churches. And, indeed, were such a change effected, and should we even still continue itinerant, considering that, from the necessity of things, our wealthy and liberal friends would most generally be selected as delegates, we do not doubt that the change proposed, might probably tend to increase our temporal comforts. We think this the more probable, because, if such a direct representation of the laity were admitted, their constituents might ultimately become obliged, by some positive provisions, fully to make up and pay whatever allowances might be made to the ministry; which allowances, in this event, might also more properly acquire the nature of a civil obligation. At present our economy knows no such thing." In the opinion of the conference their motives soar far above considerations of personal interest, and the determination to hold their absolute power, is neither more nor less than an expression of obedience to the great Head of the church, by whose divine authority they hold and exercise that power. "The great Head of the church," say they, "himself has *imposed* on us the duty of preaching the gospel, of administering its ordinances, and of *maintaining its moral discipline* among those, over whom the Holy Ghost, in these respects, has made us overseers. Of these, also, viz. of gospel doctrines, ordinances, and MORAL DISCIPLINE, we *do believe*, that the *divinely instituted ministry* are the *divinely authorized expounders;* and that the *duty of maintaining* them in their purity, and of not *permitting* our ministrations, in these respects, to be authoritatively controlled by *others*, does rest upon us with the force of *a moral obligation;* in the due discharge of which our *consciences* are involved. It is on this ground, that we resist the temptations of temporal advantage which the proposed changes hold out to us." So that it is made as clear as a sunbeam, if the travelling ministers of the Methodist Episcopal Church were to admit of a lay delegation, it would be on their part, a very sinful act. They are the divinely authorized expounders of the MORAL DISCIPLINE of the church. They have expounded it accordingly; and the exposition is published in their book of Discipline. The book of Discipline, therefore, reports what is the result of their conscientious expounding, for the space of forty years. And when we compare this fact with the restrictive rules, we may safely conclude, that their resolution to hold fast their absolute power, is approximating to the principles which made the laws of the Medes and Persians unalterable.

In judging of the course pursued by the General Conference in respect to the expelled members, we must bear in mind the conscientious difficulties which stood in the way of a restoration of the Reformers. Our memorial called upon them to replace men who had declared a steady purpose to insist on an equitable representation of the church, in its legislative department;—of men, who in like manner, were *bound in conscience*, to assert their right to such representation. By an act of the laymen of the city of Baltimore, said to have been performed by themselves, "without any itinerant suggestion or influence whatever," the most troublesome friends of the representative principle had been expelled, and it would have cost the preachers a good deal of self-denial, to undo an act, which seemed to promise so much, and which so well accorded to the dictates of their consciences on the score of *moral discipline.* Our memorial called upon them to rescind proceedings, which the Baltimore Annual Conference had approved, as being consistent with *wholesome* and *sound discipline;* in course as having the sanction of so many who were "divinely authorized expounders." To have rescinded their decision, would have effected their reputation, as expounders of discipline. Our expulsion had been effected with the previous knowledge and approbation of Bishop George, and probably of the other Bishops.* The seven prosecutors and Mr. Hanson, and all their coadjutors, had done much in expectation to please the bishops and Conference. They probably had been assured that their proceedings would be sustained.

It was supposed too, that they had managed to bring about our expulsion, so as to conceal their purpose of ridding the church of the friends of representation, and by *an unanimous vote*, condemned us for speaking evil of ministers, and inveighing against the discipline. After their manner they had prepared themselves to say, it is of no consequence as it respects the accused, what may be the determination of the General Conference, in relation to lay and local representation. "It is not for advocating such a representation that we complained of the accused, but for the *means* they have employed to effect their object; if such indeed was their *only* object. Whatever else the General Conference may do, we are sure they will not acknoweldge the right of professing Christians to abuse and defame one another; and if, as some expect, they should make some rule of discipline, calculated more effectually to preserve the peace of the church, it is obvious, that such a rule could not have any retrospective operation;—any '*ex post facto*' application, and therefore could not be brought to bear on the circumstances under which the church now suffers. The peace of the church must be preserved, and the character of her ministers and members protected from unjust aspersions, *whatever be the*

---

* This fact is confirmed by other means than the former reference to it, when in view of the District Conference.

fate of the much agitated question of reform.'' (See Narrative and Defence, page 9.) But the friends of representation, expected their rights and privileges to be protected also. Vain expectation! The Conference did not believe their claim had been, or could be sustained;—that they had either a *"natural or acquired right"* to be represented. The preachers were bound in conscience to oppose representation. Therefore, the Reformers had no place in the conscientious obligations of the General Conference;—in the estimation of the Baltimore Annual Conference, they had no right to complain, much less to appeal.

CHAPTER XXV.

It is proved beyond the possibility of a doubt, that there was no misunderstanding between the Agent or the prosecutors, and the General Conference. The Agency, in course is established.

If the Narrative and Defence gives a correct account of the matter; if the prosecutors, or the Agent, possessed all the information which is implied in the above prediction of what the General Conference would do, and of which we have no doubt, then it follows, that the General Conference could not have reversed the decision of the Quarterly Meeting Conference of Baltimore. On the contrary, they were obliged to protect the reputation of Mr. Hanson, the Agent, the prosecutors and all concerned in our expulsion.—— These were to be protected, "whatever might be the fate of the much agitated question of reform.''

That the General Conference did pursue this course, and therefore, that the prediction of the prosecutors was not the work of chance, will appear from an examination of the terms or conditions, on which they were willing to permit *some* of the expelled brethren to return.

"Whereas, an unhappy excitement has existed in some parts of our work, in consequence of the organization of what have been called Union Societies, for purposes and under regulations, believed to be inconsistent with the peace and harmony of the church; and in relation to the character of much of the matter contained in a certain periodical publication, called "Mutual Rights,'' in regard to which, certain expulsions from the church have taken place: and whereas, this General Conference indulges a hope, that a *mutual* desire may exist, for conciliation and peace; and is desirous of leaving open a way for the accomplishment of so desirable an object, on safe and *equitable* principles; therefore resolved:

"1. That in view of the premises, and in the earnest hope, that this measure may tend to promote this object, this General Conference *affectionately advises*, that no further proceedings may be had in any part of our work, against any minister or member of the

11

Methodist Episcopal Church, on account of any *past* agency or concern in relation to the above named periodical (*Mutual Rights,*) or in relation to any Union Society as above mentioned."

This preamble with the first resolution, unequivocally expresses the approbation of the General Conference, in respect to the Baltimore proceedings. The proceedings and the alleged reasons for our expulsion, are all recognized and approved. And the "*affectionate advice*" that no further proceedings of the same kind may be had, proves, not only that what had been done, was right, in their estimation, but that the conference wished to have it understood, that they had neither the power nor the inclination to interdict a repetition of the same, whenever, or wherever any company of prosecutors might see fit, to imitate those of Baltimore. And in fact, a short time after the rising of the conference, similar expulsions were practised, in Cincinnati, in Lynchburg, and in other places. So that, whether the lay brethren in Baltimore acted with or without "any itinerant suggestion or influence whatever," the General Conference stamped the proceedings, with their most hearty approbation.

"2. If any persons expelled as aforesaid, feel free to concede, that publications have appeared in said "Mutual Rights," the nature and character of which were unjustifiably inflammatory, and do not admit of vindication; and that others, though for want of proper information, or unintentionally, have yet in fact, *misrepresented individuals* and *facts*, and that they regret these things:" That is to say, if the preachers and members who were expelled under the circumstances, and on account of the charges and specifications, as heretofore examined and exposed, can after all, go forward to Mr. Hanson and the prosecutors, and confess themselves guilty of the charges, and report themselves penitent, then, &c.

Moreover, "If it be voluntarily agreed also, that the Union Societies above alluded to, shall be abolished, and the periodical called the Mutual Rights, be discontinued at the close of the current volume, which shall be completed with due respect to the conciliatory and pacific design of this arrangement:" That is, if the Reformers on all hands, will agree to surrender the only effective means which they possess for maintaining their right to representation; in other words, if they will agree, without reserve, to give up their cause, altogether; "then this General Conference does hereby give authority for the restoration to their ministry or membership, respectively, in the Methodist Episcopal Church, of any person or persons so expelled, as aforesaid:" That is, until the Reformers shall first have thus humbled and disarmed themselves, to their own perpetual disgrace, and to the entire exculpation and consequent honour of the Baltimore station and the arbitrary ecclesiastical power under which they acted, in view of further proceedings, the conference *affectionately advises*, that they be suspended. But when the work of reform shall have been destroyed, the conference "*gives authority* for the restoration to their ministry or membership; provided the arrangement shall be *mu-*

tually assented to, by any individual or individuals, so expelled, and also by the *Quarterly Meeting Conference*, and *the minister or preacher* having the charge in any circuit or station, within which any such expulsion may have taken place." This provisory clause was calculated to prevent every one who had been expelled, from making the attempt, if they had felt ever so desirous to do so. And its conditions render it certain, that the General Conference intended to put it altogether in the power of the preacher having charge, &c. to reject any individuals who might have made themselves offensive. And should any one or more have happened to be successful, through sufficient confession and expression of *regret*, to move the commiseration of the preacher in charge, still, if those good people, so loyal that they expelled us "without any itinerant suggestion or influence whatever," should have thought the preacher might have been too compassionate towards any, they had power to interpose and forbid his lenity. Having without law, expelled us in our absence, and received the commendation of the Annual and General Conferences, how much more deserving they would have been, to have helped the consciences of the travelling preachers, by guarding their absolute power against a possible subsequent interruption;—by excluding any that they might have feared, would at some future time indulge their "*restless spirits*," or give way to their feelings of "disaffection." We hesitate not to say, that any body of men rightly understanding what are the perceptions and emotions which constitute honourable feelings, would never have made such terms, because they would have known, that no man of just pretensions to dignity, would ever accede to them. And so far from considering them expressive of a Christian disposition to "conciliate," we have always viewed them as the most domineering and insulting that could have been offered, by any man or body of men.

The preamble to the resolutions of the General Conference, concludes with, "and whereas, this General Conference indulges a hope, that a *mutual* desire may exist for *conciliation* and peace, and is desirous of leaving open a way for the accomplishment of so desirable an object, on safe and equitable principles; therefore resolved," &c.

That such a desire existed on the part of the Reformers, is in fact, too obvious;—they gave stronger evidence of its existence, than justice or propriety required. Their friends at Pittsburg were inclined to make concessions respecting the publications issued through the Mutual Rights, which implied too much; particularly, in consenting to discontinue the periodical, they went to great length, with the hope of conciliating the General Conference, and obtaining "peace, on *safe* and *equitable* principles."

But where is the evidence of a disposition to reciprocate this desire, on the part of the General Conference? The phraseology of the preamble, &c. is illusive. Had the instrument been worded according to its real intention and most obvious meaning, it would have read thus: viz. "Whereas, the General Conference indulges a hope, that the expelled and withdrawn members in Baltimore and elsewhere, are inclined to conciliate us and be at peace; and whereas, we also are desirous, that they may be permitted to follow this inclination, and therefore are willing to leave open a way for the accomplishment of an object, so *mutually* desirable to us all, on principles which shall be safe to us; which shall give us security against any further disturbance, in our possession of uncontrolled authority, and maintain to Mr. Hanson, the agent, the prosecutors, and the Quarterly Meeting Conference of Baltimore, the high standing which their late services have merited, and without which, no terms of conciliation can be considered by us to be *equitable;* therefore, be it resolved, that any individuals among them, who can feel free to go forward to Mr. Hanson and the prosecutors, &c. and confess that they have been altogether in the wrong; that their conduct admits of no vindication; that they regret their evil doings, and are ready to prove to the church their sincerity, by discontinuing their periodical, the Mutual Rights, and pledging themselves that no further attempt shall be made in that way;—after having thus humbled themselves, such individuals may be restored to their membership, if Mr. Hanson is willing, and the prosecutors and the Quarterly Meeting Conference have no objection." For such are the proposed terms of *"conciliation* and *peace,* on *safe* and *equitable* principles.' '!!

We cannot have erred in our views of this subject. Mr. Emory, in his remarks, says, it was the intention of the Conference "to leave open a door for the restoration of the expelled persons, "on certain conditions by *mutual consent.*" "It was never intended to force them upon the society in Baltimore *without consent.*" The word *"mutual,"* therefore, was to apply only the act of restoration.

That is, any individual Reformer, desirous to be restored, must make the prescribed concessions in proof of his desire to be at peace. But this alone would not do. Mr. Hanson, &c. in Baltimore, must also *"mutually"* consent to his restoration. This was necessary to make the restoration *equitable.* This same illusive word *"mutual,"* was applied by Mr. Emory in his *"remarks,"* to another subject. "The General Conference proposed, that by mutual consent, no periodical publication, to be devoted to the existing controversy, should be carried on by either side." This was a *mutuality* with a vengeance to Reformers, intended too, at the same time, to wear the appearance of *mutual pacification,* on *terms mutually safe* and *equitable!!* Suppose no periodical to be devoted to the existing controversy, to have been carried on by the Methodist Episcopal Church. This was precisely what they intended, and wished above all things to bring about, provided Reformers would be as silent on the subject, as the General Conference were willing to be. And how would the cause of reform have been affected by such a measure? Nothing could have been so fatal. And Mr. Emory and the Conference understood well the inevitable result. "The object," says Mr. Emory, "was to lay a ground for a sincere re-union, in affection and good feeling, as well as in form; which it was believed, in the existing excitement, could not be effected, if such a *periodical* controversy should be continued.

Here we have an admission of all that we have been labouring to establish, viz. That our periodical was the "monstrum horrendum" which gave the offence. That the destruction of it was the object, because they knew they could not resist its influence. That they would not have expelled us, after all our "speaking evil of ministers," had we consented to give up the periodical; and that having succeeded "without any itinerant suggestion or influence whatever," to obtain our expulsion, we could not be permitted to return, unless we would consent, first, to admit that we were expelled for having published defamatory papers in the Mutual Rights; and secondly, agree to give up the controversy forever. It is then an incontrovertible truth, that the terms which were peremptorily submitted by the prosecutors, when they sought their "friendly interview;"—the terms which were dictated by the agent, and repeated by his co-adjutor, doctor Green;—the terms again held out by Mr. Hanson, after he and his *constituted* court, had "defecated" the church as the agent had proposed;—and the terms prescribed by the General Conference, were the same, with only a slight variation in the phraseology of each, and some additional conditions appended to the terms prescribed by the General Conference. And such identity of purpose proves the existence of a concert.

But Mr. Emory says, "It was expressly stated that, individuals would be at liberty, even if the above *conciliatory* arrangement should be *mutually* agreed to, to publish what they might think proper, on their individual reponsibility." "It has been objected, continues he, that this meant on their individual peril. Be it so. And so it ought to be. And no man should be unwilling to bear his own burden." And this was liberty to publish;—but subject to the dangers of the gag law still!!

CHAPTER XXVI.

The terms or conditions made by the General Conference for our return, were deficient in probity;—they are more marked with cunning than honesty.

THE foregoing is a faithful account of what was required on the part of the General Conference, if Reformers wished to conciliate them and Mr. Hanson, and the prosecutors, &c.—of the brotherly conditions for "*conciliation* and *peace*, on *safe* and EQUITABLE principles." !!

The resolutions seem to propose an arrangement, which was about to be made between the Methodist Episcopal Church, as one of the parties, and the expelled and withdrawn members in Baltimore and elsewhere, as the other party;—of an arrangement which was to be based "on safe and EQUITABLE principles!!" And now we ask for the evidence of safety to us or our cause? Where do these "*equitable principles*" apply at all to the case of the Reformers? Terms of conciliation and peace on SAFE and EQUITABLE principles!! What insolent mockery! What did the Conference propose, for the purpose of conciliating the feelings of Reformers? What is the meaning of the word "conciliation?" It is the act of winning or gaining esteem, favour or affection;—or in general terms, it is the act of reconciliation. And is there any thing in the resolutions, intended to reconcile the Reformers? Every one must perceive, that the conditions of the General Conference were, in some respects more exceptionable than those proposed by the agent, or by Mr. Hanson and the Quarterly Meeting Conference of Baltimore; and we are compelled to believe, that there were many members of the General Conference, having too much understanding, to have entertained any expectation that we would accede to them. One thing is most certain. They were determined, if we were restored, that our restoration should cost us the whole amount of the value of our reputation, and of the work of reform. This was the only *mutuality*, the only *equity* contemplated by the General Conference.

The General Conference distinctly understood the subject as we now represent it. Mr. Emory, in his remarks, says, "the Reformers wished to be considered as the offend-*ed*, not the offend-*ing* party. And because the General Conference thought otherwise, it is now pretended to be considered a great insult. Their eye was fixed more upon doing the church service, by giving the General Conference opportunity to wipe off, not the disgrace of the Reformers, but the disgrace of the church." That is the truth; and the day will come when the honesty and propriety of the statements made in the letter to Mr. Shinn on this subject, will be duly appreciated by many, who now seem devoted to the wishes of the General Conference. But our views and publications, Mr. Emory says, have opened their eyes. "And so long," says he, "as such a spirit is perceived to exist, as those gentlemen continue to exhibit," the writer, Mr. E. is as well satisfied with our rejection of the resolutions for our return, as we who rejected them, can be. This last was an honest declaration. The affair had wound up as they intended, unless we were ready to sacrifice ourselves and our cause to *conciliate* them. As we had not seen fit to do this, they were glad to be rid of such troublesome "gentlemen." They knew full well, if we had been continued members of the Methodist Episcopal Church, with the liberty of speech and of the press, their people would ultimately have demanded and obtained, all the important changes in the form of their church government, for which we had been so arduously and disinterestedly labouring. But the report of the General Conference says, "we know that we have been charged with wishing to suppress free inquiry, and with denying to our ministers and members the liberty of speech and of the press,"—"the charge we wholly disavow."—"The rule in our discipline, page 88, new edition, never was intended to suppress such freedom of inquiry, or to deny such liberty of speech, and of the press, &c.—The design of the rule was, to guard the PEACE and UNION of the church, against any

mischievous, false brethren, who might be disposed to avail themselves of their place in the bosom of the church, to *endeavour* to
sow dissentions, by inveighing against our doctrines or discipline,
in the sense of unchristian railing and violence. Any other construction of it, we have never sanctioned; nor will we.—It is aimed against *licentiousness*, and not against liberty." The community will judge between us in respect to the construction given it, in
our expulsion. Mr. Emory echoes the declarations made on this
subject by the agent in his Narrative and Defence. He repeats the
unfeeling resolutions of the Annual Conference, and accuses us of
having held the church authorities in *"in stubborn and proud contempt,"* and therefore he says, we now have no right to complain.
It was our intention when we commenced this review, to try the
merits of the Narrative and Defence. It is now sufficiently clear,
not only that the Quarterly Meeting Conference, of the Baltimore
station, expelled us, calculating on being sustained by that work,
but that the Annual and General Conferences all relied on it for
their justification. We shall therefore pass in review the extracts
from the Mutual Rights, as they were published in the Narrative
and Defence; and then we shall see the value of the above declaration, respecting the construction which was given to their
"odious gag law" in our case, and which construction has now had
the sanction of the General Conference, that is of the whole Methodist Episcopal Church.

PART SECOND.

CHAPTER I.

Introduction to an examination of the extracts from the Mutual Rights;—or of the offensive papers, for the admission of which into our peribdical, we were expelled.

AT page 34 of the Narrative and Defence, under the heading "Remarks," following their extract from the constitution of the Union Society, the prosecutors state the principle, on which they held the members of the Baltimore Union Society, individually responsible for the *unfounded allegations* against the characters of their ministers, and the *"abusive epithets"* so liberally bestowed upon them in the Mutual Rights. For publishing these *"unfounded allegations and abusive epithets,"* as they have seen fit to call them, we were expelled, by virtue of the rule of discipline, which has been entitled the "gag law," found on page 88, of the new edition of the discipline of the Methodist Episcopal Church, the design of which rule, Mr. Emory, in the report, about the 18th paragraph, says, was to guard the peace and union of the church against any *mischievous false* brethren, who might be disposed to avail themselves of their place in the bosom of the church to endeavour to sow *dissentions,* by *inveighing* against our doctrines or discipline, *in the sense of unchristian railing.* "Any other construction of it, WE HAVE NEVER SANCTIONED, nor will we."

"Our complaint against the members of the Union Society," says Narrative and Defence, page 7, "is not on account of their opinions on the subject of church government, nor for the honest and candid expression of their opinions; but for the misrepresentation of the motives and conduct of our ministers, and for endeavouring to sow dissentions in the church, by inveighing against the discipline. Nor do we understand by 'inveighing' the temperate expression of opinion, or calm and dispassionate argument in favour of changing any part of our discipline—but we understand it to mean 'vehement railing,' abusive censure or reproach,'—The finding fault *with,* and proposing alterations *of,* our discipline are not considered as violations of our discipline," &c.—'It is not for being reformers themselves or for endeavouring to make reformers of others, nor for uttering and publishing their opinions on the subject of reform, that we complain of the members of the Baltimore Union Society, but we complain that they have employed against their brethren in the ministry, and against the discipline of the church, the *severest invectives, and the most vehement railing.* They

12

have impugned the motives of our venerable bishops, and our itinerant ministers, with unrelenting severity—and accused them WITH-
OUT THE SHADOW OF TRUTH, with conduct which would render men
odious in civil society, and how much more in the church of God.
They represent them to the world as usurpers—as tyrants and despots, 'lording it over God's heritage,' as exercising an arbitrary
authority, which was at first 'surreptitiously' obtained, and which
has been perpetuated by printing and publishing a falsehood in the
preface of our book of discipline, and by forbid-ling the people to
inquire into the truth of the affair. Nay, more, they are represented as holding opinions and exercising a 'domination' highly dangerous to the civil liberties of the country. As being wolves among
the lambs of the flock, and wolves too who openly shew their
'teeth and claws,' and to cap the climax, nearly one hundred of
these ministers, constituting the Baltimore Annual Conference, are
stigmatized as abandoned tyrants, 'as performing a laboured deed
of hard-earned infamy.' From the extracts which we shall give
from the "Mutual Rights' it will be shewn, that all this has been
said of our itinerant ministers, *and for these unjust accusations, for
these vehement railings*, we hold the Union Society accountable; because they have been uttered and published by an editorial committee, elected by the society, and who profess to act as its agents,
and under its supervision and control.'' See Narrative and Defence, pages 7, 8, 9. See a summary of the charges or accusations, preferred against the reformers of Baltimore!! "Unfounded allegations;—abusive epithets;—made and uttered by '*mischievous false* brethren,' who endeavoured to *sow dissentions* by '*unchristian railing;*'—*misrepresenting* the motives and conduct of their
ministers; '*vehement railing*, abusive censure or reproach;' 'the *severest* invectives and the *most vehement* railing;'—'impugning the
motives of the venerable bishops and the itinerant ministers with
unrelenting severity; and accusing them WITHOUT A SHADOW OF
TRUTH;—representing them as usurpers, as tyrants, and despots, as
lording it over God's heritage, as exercising an arbitrary authority
surreptitiously obtained and perpetuated by printing and publishing a
falsehood;—as holding opinions and exercising a domination highly
dangerous to the civil liberties of the country; as being wolves
among the lambs of the flock, who shew their teeth and their
claws;—abandoned tyrants, performing a deed of hard-earned infamy.'' These heavy accusations they attempted to shew in their
Narrative and Defence were supported by extracts from the Mutual
Rights. And admitting *their* comment, without correction, they
would seem in some sort to have sustained them. If however, it
shall turn out that their extracts are garbled, and much of their comment gratuitous and contrary to the spirit and design of the writers,
from which their extracts were taken;—if the statements made in
the papers which gave offence to the prosecutors shall be found to
have been true;—if an exposure of the necessity of reform, in the
system or the administration of the government of the Methodist
Episcopal Church, or of any instance of mal-administrat[...]
the faults of any of the ministers, was "apparently nece[...]

account of the great importance of the object which was pursued by the reformers; then the foregoing accusation will be considered MOST VIOLENT AND UNCHRISTIAN RAILING on the part of the prosecution, and the "evil speaking" with which they impugned the reformers, will most justly be chargeable upon themselves, and upon the Annual and General Conferences, who have identified themselves with the whole transaction, and made themselves equally responsible with the prosecutors of Baltimore.

At page 76, of Narrative and Defence, they say, "to speak that which is TRUE is not EVIL SPEAKING, however severe it may be"—"evil speaking means slander, defamation, calumny. The Doctor's (Jennings's) defence then ought to have been a very different thing from what we find it." "He should have set himself to prove the truth of the allegations made by him and his associates against our bishops and other ministers. If he had shewn them to be true, the charge of evil speaking could not have been sustained, although injuring the reputation of another by publishing his faults or failings, can only be justified by some *apparent necessity* for the disclosure."——"If the Doctor then can prove what has been alleged, both against the living and the dead, in the Mutual Rights, he will not only stand acquitted of *evil speaking*, but prove conclusively the necessity of a thorough reform, not only of our government, but of our morals."

In the sequel of the review this will be attempted, and it is believed we shall be able to satisfy the candid reader, that Reformers have been shamefully abused by the Agent and the Conferences. And that the Narrative and Defence is a most unwarrantable attempt to impose upon the people of the Methodist Episcopal Church, and the community, who it was believed, like the official men in Baltimore, would never "read the Mutual Rights at all."

CHAPTER II.

MR. SNETHEN ON CHURCH PROPERTY.

Church property altogether under the control of the Bishops.

"OUR church property as well as power are, in effect, in the hands or under the control of the superintendents, and should the constitutional test obtain, it will destroy all hopes of any legal or regular change for the better."* The "*constitutional test*" refers to the struggle, for several years maintained by many of the travelling preachers, for making the office of the presiding elders elective by the preachers who were to serve under them, and not leaving it to be an affair of episcopal patronage. If after all the laboured efforts to bring about this change, a majority of the General Conference shall determine to establish the appointment of the presiding elders

---

* Throughout this paper, the comments of the Reviewer are interspersed [i]n easy and familiar way; presenting the reflections which were produced [rea]ding it with a view to its publication. Mr. Snethen's work will be known [by] marks of quotation.

as a part of episcopal prerogative, then said Mr. Snethen, "all hopes for any legal or regular change for the better" will be destroyed.

Are not these statements perfectly consistent with truth and propriety? The bishops have the power of stationing all the preachers, and of appointing the presiding elders who shall exercise subordinate authority over them when so stationed. In view of these facts, Mr. Snethen says "our church property as well as power are in effect in the hands or under the control of the superintendents." And could he have said the contrary without a violation of truth? What is the difference "in effect," between placing "the property in the hands or under the control of the superintendents," and making it their prerogative to say, who shall occupy it? Why it should have given offence, because he said, "the power of the church is in effect under the control of the superintendents, we cannot see, without admitting the supposition that even a calm investigation of the principles of their government, was offensive.

"This controlling or disposing power over public property, in men who hold an office for life, is one of the essential principles of an absolute government, and by an extension of territory, must continue to increase indefinitely." And is not this a true sentiment? It is in fact one of the axioms of American statesmen. No sensible man doubts it; and its publication cannot give offence to any one, but the bishops of the Methodist Episcopal Church, and their devoted adherents. "The disclaiming all right or pretension to taxation by the General Conference, amounts to nothing like a check upon the power of the superintendents over property: but does in fact, tend to promote it. Were it in the power of the travelling preachers, by any means to secure an immediate support from the people, they might have the people's money to control the power of the Episcopacy; but in the present state of things, they can neither occupy the houses nor receive the people's voluntary contributions, without an official signification of the executive will." And is not all this likewise true, and perfectly inoffensive to all but those who are desirous to conceal this feature of the government of the Methodist Episcopal Church?

CHAPTER III.

All the Travelling Preachers at the disposal of the Bishops.

'ALL the travelling preachers are at the disposal of the superintendents." Nothing respecting the economy of what old side men call "Methodism," is more true than this. "So long as there shall be more preachers than there are places to support them;" that is, able stations and wealthy circuits;—and every body knows that the preachers are not sent to these *good places* by any order of rotation;—it is as the bishops please. "So long, then, as there shall be more preachers" than good places, "the surplus number must be dependent, and to make this dependence universal, no preacher has any security that his lot to '*turn out*' may not come next." We have attended the Virginia Annual Conference a few times, and in every instance there was a manifest anxiety prevailing in the bosoms of a number of the preachers. In fact, they could not conceal their fears, not knowing who and who, would be appointed to the circuit called "the Banks." And in the Baltimore Annual Conference, it has been said, if certain individuals were sent to particular circuits, it would make them friendly to the election of the presiding elders. It is the prerogative of the bishops to appoint whom they may see fit, to the good circuits and stations, and to say who shall "*turn out*" into the highways and hedges. "It avails nothing that the public property is in the keeping of trustees and stewards. If the houses cannot be taken from the preachers, the preachers may be taken from the houses." Then "the members of the church have in reality no church property," none that they have any ecclesiastical right to control. The bishops without consulting the members, have the exclusive right to say who shall be the occupants of the property. "And the travelling preachers have none in effect." They are all, at all times, "tenants at the will of the bishops; and at the end of each year may be removed." And surely all this is incontrovertibly TRUE. "Are we not virtually acting over again St. Peter's patrimony and Peter's pence?" The allusion here may not be perfectly appropriate. The question, however, is addressed to the Methodist people. If every house paid one penny to the pope, by way of acknowledging his claim to patrimony in England, do not the Methodist people, virtually make an acknowledgment of the bishops' patrimony in respect to their church property, as universal; and as to the worth of the acknowledgment, by far more valuable than a penny for each house? "In monarchies public property is vested in the crown, and of course, in him who wears it." And the church property in the Methodist Episcopal Church is at the disposal, as to its occupancy, of the bishops, and in course of them and their successors. "Hence we hear of his Majesty's arms and armies and kingdom, &c.—of 'we by the grace of God,' and of the 'pope's bull,' or seal affixed to his official acts. By the grace of God, is meant the Divine right," &c. All these are true, and admit of application according to the reader's understanding of the facts. If he can see any similitude to these badges and acts of monarchy, and the old hierarchy of Rome, in Methodist Episcopacy; or if he can perceive any features in the government of the Methodist Episcopal Church, which have a tendency, sooner or later, to imitate the church as it exists under such establishments, he has a right to his reflections, and will the bishops or preachers or people of the Methodist Episcopal Church, say openly, that Nr. Snethen, or the printing committee, had no right to think they can see signs of these dangerous tendencies? "The hundred successors of Mr. Wesley, who compose the British Conference, unite in themselves all the powers and functions that are exercised by our General Conference and superintendents. They are all bishops *de facto*. Our ordination conveys nothing which Mr. Wesley did not give to them. He was not a partial father, much less did he disinherit his first-born; we congratulate our British brethren in this thing, that they have good sense enough not to run after names and shadows." "There is neither divine nor human obligation binding on our General Conference, to confer a life office on any man. We know to a certainty, that Mr. Wesley never meant to confer any power for life, upon the superintendents, which he and doctor Coke ordained; for he actually had it in contemplation to recall Mr. Asbury. Of such an event Mr. Asbury, was so well aware, that he took special care to prevent it, by getting himself elected superintendent by the American preachers." Mr. Asbury has confirmed the truth of this himself, in his Journal. The reader will please to observe here, that this part of the argument is, that Mr. Wesley did not intend to confer on Mr. Asbury a life office. In proof of this, Mr. Wesley having appointed Mr. Asbury a superintendent for the United States, was about to recall him. Whether Mr. Asbury intended at the time to secure to himself a life office, by getting himself elected by the American preachers, cannot be known. By so doing, he placed himself out of the reach of Mr. Wesley's power. Had he not done this, we should have had the evidence which his recall to England would have afforded, that Mr. Wesley never meant to confer any power on him for life. The general argument is against life office. Mr. Snethen asserts, there is no obligation, human or divine, binding on the General Conference, to confer such office. By human obligations he obviously means, the authority of Mr. Wesley, which he says would have been expressed fully, by the recalling of Mr. Asbury. This was prevented by Mr. Asbury, for his own reasons, by taking special care to get himself elected by the American preachers. Is not this true? Are Mr. Wesley's or Mr. Asbury's *motives misrepresented!* Is there any *vehement railing* in this, or in any part of the foregoing quotations?

CHAPTER IV.

Mr. Snethen's papers on Church Property, were written for the benefit of the Travelling Preachers, in opposition to the unbalanced power of the Bishops.

MR. SNETHEN's essays on church property, were written for the benefit of those travelling preachers, who were friendly to the election of the presiding elders, and were intended, particularly, to call the attention of the itinerant ministers. The printing committee so understood them; and had no expectation, that the facts, or the manner of stating them, could give offence. "The consequence of exclusive proprietorship in public property, in the catholic church, is well known, and has long been seriously deplored; but it seems that we take no warning from the experience of others. We have fully set forth our determination, to participate with our elder brethren, in evangelizing the world. The General Conference, in their address, contemplate a meeting between the British missionaries and ours, somewhere on the eastern coast of Asia, or Japan. But when Methodism shall thus have encircled the globe, *will any regard be paid by the missionaries and their senders, to the mutual rights of the ministers and the people of the Methodist Episcopal Church?* No such thing. These senior and junior brethren, will divide the Methodist church property of the universe between them, without listening to any intimation, that the accumulation of so much wealth might *seem* to savour of monopoly or avarice, and *might possibly* be made to minister to ambition."

It had been published to the world, that the British Conference, and the General Conference of the Methodist Episcopal Church, were looking forward to the day, when they shall be able to extend a belt around the globe; and as this expectation accords well enough with a laudable emulation to evangelize the world, it by no means merited censure, nor was it noticed with a design to find fault with a purpose so commendable. But as the church property in England, pertaining to the Wesleyan Methodists, is held by the Conference, and as the church property pertaining to the Methodist Episcopal Church, is deeded to trustees, for the use of their General Conference, does it not follow, that when these two bodies of Methodists shall have encompassed the globe, they continuing to maintain the same principles in respect to church property, Mr. Snethen's prediction will be fulfilled? Will not these senior and junior brethren have divided the Methodist church property between them? And when we take into the account, the fact, that the Bishops and General Conference have sanctioned our excommunication for publishing this prediction of the course they will probably take, can any man of good sense, who is disinterested, say, that it was wrong for one, who knew Methodist preachers as well as Mr. Snethen did, to have thought he could foresee, and to have predicted, that, if the purpose of the two Conferences shall be accomplished, "they will not listen to any intimation, that the accumulation of so much wealth might *seem* to savour of monopoly or avarice, and *might possibly* be made to minister to ambition?" Good men, contemplating no ambitious designs, instead of being offended, would have thanked Mr. Snethen for the admonition;——would have regarded it as an evidence of his good wishes for the cause of truth, and profited by it, as there might be occasion.

Besides, Mr. Snethen had good reasons to suppose, that no inconsiderable number of the most intelligent travelling preachers, were ready to appreciate his essays on church property; and he had no reason to think, that any of them could imagine he intended to give just cause of offence. "The great defect in the government of the Methodist Episcopal Church," in his opinion, "is the want of an independent legislative department." He believed, most conscientiously, that "an independent General Conference never can exist, under the present organization." And it was his purpose to shew, that the irresponsible authority of the bishops over the church property, would serve, in aid of their appointing power as to the presiding elders, to give them an increasing influence over the General Conference. His desire to promote the election of the presiding elders, arose out of an expectation, that the independence of the General Conference would be promoted by that measure, for want of which, "a large proportion of the legislative body will inevitably be too much under executive patronage." In the opinion that the election of the presiding elders would serve to make the members of the General Conference feel themselves more independent, he consented with those travelling preachers who were once called reformers. And in broaching the subject of church property, he intended to make them feel the importance of admitting the introduction of a lay delegation into the General Conference. By this measure, any undue influence that the stationing power of the bishops might have over the preachers, would be still more effectually counteracted. But enough has been stated to shew, that Mr. Snethen wrote for the benefit of those travelling preachers who feared the increase of episcopal power, and the community will judge, how much reason the printing committee had to expect, that these same travelling preachers would be found amongst the most ready to sustain our excommunication for publishing Mr. Snethen's papers. "We have said that Mr. Wesley was rich in church property; and that he knew and felt he was so." Mr. Wesley wrote a letter to Mr. John Mason, dated, "near London, January 13th, 1790," a copy of which is published in the London Wesleyan Methodist Magazine for April, as follows:—"*My Dear Brother*,—As long as I live, the people shall have no share in choosing either stewards or leaders among the Methodists. We have not, and never had, any such custom. We are no republicans, and never intend to be. It would be better for those that are so minded, to go quietly away. I have been uniform, both in doctrine and discipline, for above these fifty years, and it is a little too late for me to turn into a new path, now I am old and grey-headed."[*] &c. Can any man believe that even Mr. Wesley, with all his firmness, would have written thus, if the chapels and church funds had not been under his absolute control? "We say the same of our superintendents; they too know and feel that they have a hold on the public property, in virtue of the absolute prerogatives of their office, sufficiently firm to enable them to dispossess any preacher, whenever they may think proper." A moment's reflection upon the fact, that Mr. Wesley's power was absolute, and that all the chapels were his, will prepare any man to see that what is said in respect to him, is *true*. And who that knows the extent of the power and patronage of the bishops of the Methodist Episcopal Church, can doubt the *truth* of what is said in respect to them. "It is to no purpose to say, they cannot convert this property to their own private use. There is no reason to suppose they would do so, if they had the title in fee. Kings are not wont to use the property of the crown for their own private benefit, or in other words to impoverish themselves as kings, in order to enrich them-

---

[*] Might not the Bishops and Conference reiterate the same, at this day? And if so, ought not republicans to be dissatisfied with their government?

selves as individuals. It is not to be supposed, that the holders of absolute power, will be less ambitious than prodigal or covetous monarchs. The glory of superintendents is proportionate to the amount of property they have in their possession. Every house that is built, and every collection that is made, adds to their consequence, by increasing their influence. *Poor* bishops of rich *diocesses are not common; and poor universal bishops are much less so.*" So far, all that has been stated by Mr. Snethen is *true.—True*, when considered abstractly in view of general principles and the well known and established laws of human nature. *True*, when applied to any denomination of people, if episcopal and granting to their bishops similar powers.

CHAPTER IV.

The Travelling Preachers not made better, by this disposition of the Church Property.

"THE travelling preachers also, while their imaginations are dazzled with the idea of their share in the title of property, secured by deed to the General Conference, feel rich and look down upon the poverty of local preachers; their exclusive right to seats in the Conferences, is indeed so flattering to their vanity, as in most instances to blind them to the actual state of things. Few of them can be brought to reflect steadily upon the fact, that they are little more than trustees for the bishops, who, as soon as they are elected and inducted into office, are no longer responsible to them." Universal experience and observation, make us know the effect of artificial and arbitray distinctions;—such distinction as is kept up in the Methodist Episcopal Church, between the travelling and local preachers. It has an irresistible tendency to generate an imaginary importance. Mr. Snethen, no doubt, in his day and time, had felt its influence. We believe that he and many other good men, Methodist preachers, have resisted the temptation to be vain on account of their superiority. But whatever may have been the modest resistance of the most worthy, every man of observation knows, the general statement made by Mr. Snethen in the foregoing paragraph, *is true.* As to their holding an interest, which in effect is little more than that of trustees for the bishops, this is proved to be *true,* by the foregoing statement of facts. It is a truth, however, which many of the travelling preachers are unwilling to hear. When men assume to themselves importance upon mistaken principles, they in course put a false estimate upon those principles, and are unwilling to be corrected. Truth in such a case is offensive. But it is as clear as a mid-day sun beam, that the deed to the General Conference is, in effect, a deed for the use of the bishops, who, have the right to say who shall occupy the property, and are not responsible to the General Conference for

13

their appointments. "The power or privilege of electing to an absolute office for life, is the most dangerous that can be vested in any body of men." It is "a power or privilege," which ought not to be held or exercised in a republican government. "The importance that such electors are prone to attach to themselves, is pleasantly ridiculed in the story of the cardinal and the pope. The cardinal when he wanted a favour, reminded his holiness, that he made him pope; who wearied at length with his importunity, replied, 'then let me be pope.' This piece of pleasantry, is very illustrative of the great folly of supposing, that men, when once put into office for life, will afterwards act like those who are made accountable to their constituents. It shews very clearly, the importance of the representative principle, which alone can make men know their dependence on their fellow men. "Our superintendents are not only chosen members of the Conferences, and presidents for life, with the power of choosing the presiding elders and stationing all the preachers; but to make them as independent as possible, they are pensioners on the book fund, to the full amount of all demands:" of "all demands" which they have a right to make. And what are the items "of all demands?" Their family expenses. It is stated in the Narrative and Defence, page 39—'It is *true* that the family expenses of the bishops are supplied from the book fund. The General Conference designate a committee of travelling preachers, to fix the amount which shall be allowed for the bishops' table expenses.' And did Mr. Snethen say or intend more, than the prosecutors have themselves admitted to be *true*. For their support, they are made as *independent as possible.* They are placed in a condition entirely different, in this respect, from other Methodist preachers. All, excepting the bishops, are supported by the contributions of the people; and their deficiencies may, or may not, be made up by the Conference collections and the annual dividend from the book fund, &c. The bishops have their salaries secured at the Annual Conferences, and their table expenses secured by the book fund, "to the full amount of all demands." What Mr. Snethen has written on this subject, then, is *true*, the flouncing of the Narrative and Defence, notwithstanding. "The discipline, by putting no check upon their power, presumes they can do no wrong." What power does Mr. Snethen mean?—Most clearly the appointing and stationing power. In what sense then does the *discipline* presume the bishops can do no wrong? In appointing the presiding elders, and in stationing the preachers. And is not this all *true?* "In one point of comparison it must be confessed that the American itinerant preacher seems to have the advantage of the British; but another view of their condition will convince any one, that none of these seeming advantages can be realized. In England, travelling preachers who have fulfilled their probation, are eligible to the vacancies in the Conference.—With us, they become members of the Annual Conferences, and are eligible to seats in the General Conference, and in course nominal proprietors of the church property. Here their glory ends. Innocence or neutrality gives no security to our preachers, to an equality of appointments. Every preacher, as well as the presiding elders, *may* become a minister to the episco- pacy. Probationers *may manifest* greater zeal for the prerogative, than men of long standing and experience. Offences must needs come, and do often come, in despite of the greatest prudence." All these things may and sometimes do come to pass, or Methodist bishops, and Methodist preachers, are exempted from the common infirmities of men. But of this, more in the sequel. "No travel- ling preacher can protect himself against episcopal suspicion, or jealousy, or displeasure; and however unjustifiable a bishop's feel- ings may be, he *may retain* them through life, and perhaps transfer them into the breasts of his colleagues." In such a government as that of the Methodist Episcopal Church, with an episcopacy holding such powers, any man acquainted with human nature, would be led, if there were occasion, to predict all these things. They have occurred and will recur, under existing circumstances, so long as bishops and travelling preachers are men. And when Mr. Snethen only exhibited them as men, and gave no intimation that he thought them worse than other men, in like circumstances, will any one say that the printing committee had any right to con- sider it libellous? Or was it the duty of the committee, to say one to another, this will not do? Bishops and travelling preachers are so puffed with vanity, that unless they shall be represented as being elevated above such human weaknesses, they will expel us for speaking evil of ministers! But what "great occasion" was there for exposing these weaknesses? The occasion was ample. What is the argument? That the government of the Methodist Episco- pal Church needs correction, in view of the well-being of the travelling preachers. Methodist preachers of Great Britain, are in more agreeable circumstances, than those of the United States. And the General Conference ought to see the impropriety of making bishops for life. They ought to elect their presiding elders. They ought to make their legislative body more independent, by introducing a lay-delegation into that department.

"It is possible indeed, that they cannot all be united in a pro- scription; but is it not infinitely more improbable, that fifty men will withhold their votes for a presidency, year after year, from every one who will not imbibe their prejudices. The chances, therefore, of being driven, or persecuted out of connexion in the two systems, bear no proportion. Though an hundred men may be as true to their common interests, as one or five, and a feeling of independence must be engendered in both instances, yet it is of the utmost importance to weaken and conceal the feeling as much as possible." In view of the premises how *true!* And upon the most cool and dispassionate review, we still think as we thought when the essays passed our board, they clearly prove that the writer understood his subject well, and that his arguments are much to the purpose.

CHAPTER V.

That part of Mr. Snethen's paper, which the agent says, can only find a parallel in the Romish Inquisitions.

"It is a maxim with some, and every four years of experience serves to confirm them in it, that if a preacher is not prepared to go all lengths in episcopal measures, he will do well to decline an election to a seat in the General Conference." The reader will please to keep it in recollection, that this paper was written for the travelling preachers, a number of whom, professed at that time to be friendly to reform. And was there any just cause of offence, in the fact, that Mr. Snethen understood it to be a maxim with *some* of the travelling preachers, that it was not quite safe, to appear in the General Conference, in opposition to episcopal measures?—or, in that it was his understanding, that every General Conference afforded experience to confirm them in their maxim? We were prepared to admit the statement without hesitation, by conversatons which happened at our house, whilst the General Conference of 1824 was in session, and which fairly intimated the same thing. It is well known in Baltimore, that much excitement prevailed. It was no secret, that a number of the preachers talked seriously of retiring *en masse*, so as to prevent those who might remain, from forming a constitutional majority. So anxious were they at the time to check the progress of episcopal power! Mr. Snethen, who had been a travelling preacher, had greater intimacy with the members of the General Conference than we, and had learned from them, that "it was a maxim with some" that it was safe not to go to the General Conference, if they foresaw that duty would compel them to oppose episcopal measures. "More than one travelling preacher, *might, perhaps*, feelingly repeat, in regard to Baltimore, with a member of the synod of Dort: O Dort, Dort! O Baltimore, Baltimore! would to God I never had seen thee! The hero of opposition may return to his work, complacent in the consciousness of his own integrity, unawed by the fear of man; but the eye of episcopal vigilance is upon him." Possibly Mr. Snethen, when he wrote this, was acquainted with one or more such cases. If he were not, then he supposed *"there might perhaps"* be found more than one, who had exercised their own judgment in the General Conference, and felt so firm as to think that no episcopal power or subsequent occurrence, would ever change their purpose. But at the same time that they might feel complacency in the consciousness of their own integrity, existing circumstances might at last weaken their integrity. Whenever they find it necessary to oppose episcopal measures, they must know that the eye of episcopal vigilance will descry them. The hero may at length find himself in such a situation, that he may not only cease to oppose, but yield to episcopal authority. Suppose, for instance, that "his health declines; the afflictions of his family, and cares and wants multiply upon him." In such a case it may become necessary for the comfort;—for the very existence of his family, that he shall have secured the commiseration, if not the favour of the bishops. If his family is sickly, then "he needs a house at hand; for he cannot move far off; he wants medicine and bread!" And to whom can he look in such extremity, but to the bishops? "To which of the saints" beside the bishops, "will he now turn, to which of his friends, say, pity me, O! my friend, for the hand of God hath touched me!" And is it possible that members of the General Conference, with all their imaginary rights to control the episcopacy, are so entirely dependent on the will of the bishops? "What? can he want a house and a home and the means of support, who inherits all houses and property, to the exclusion of local preachers and the laity? Can a member of that General Conference to whom so many thousands have been deeded, become a houseless wanderer, a pennyless stranger, among a strange people?" Whatever may have been his calculations upon his supposed interest in the common property of the church, if he should find himself thus overwhelmed with the afflictions and increasing wants of his family, it would be fruitless to look for aid, from any or all of his other companions in labours. He may ask for help from them, but in vain. He may be beloved of them all, and yet have occasion to say, "where now has the spirit of sympathy and fellow-feeling fled! O! where are his brethren whose turn may come next?" When all are alike liable to similar afflictions, will they not commiserate his case? However much they may be moved with compassion, the individual in distress may still have occasion to inquire, "is there no power in this heaven and earth?"—this whole body of Methodist preachers,—"to save him from the dread of starvation? None. How is this? Plainly thus: When all is given away, nothing remains. The General Conference have given the bishops a life power over that very property, which the donors vested in themselves. When they are made to know the worth of this property by the want of it, at that very juncture they may be made to feel, that they can enjoy no part of it." And is not this a strong argument against the propriety of conferring so much power for life, upon the episcopacy? With such views of the subject, was it not benevolent in Mr. Snethen, to admonish the travelling ministry of the temptations to which they have exposed themselves by the measure, the dangers of which, he has so effectually made evident? Who of them all when in distress, being heavily oppressed with forebodings of expected ills, will fail to cast about and say to himself, "and is there no remedy? Are bishops and presiding elders all past feeling? *Perhaps* there is one open door left." As a large majority of the clergy of England, in the days of Mary and Elizabeth, and Charles and Oliver Cromwell, found it convenient to accommodate themselves to the ruling powers, so also, *"perhaps,"* our hero might be induced, for the comfort of his family to accommodate himself to executive measures. And if such possible case should occur;—if the episcopacy should find it convenient to pursue one or more of such heroes to submission, *"what executive purpose can be so inflexible as not to relent, when executive measures have converted a poor and needy opponent?''* It is hoped that preachers, when made to see the pit which they themselves have digged, will shun it, by diminishing the episcopal prerogative. And it is hoped that bishops themselves will be wise to consent in the change, that they may escape the temptation on their part; especially when they' consider the obloquy to which such oppressive pursuit would expose them. Disinterested bye-standers would tauntingly say, "oh! we hope that none of these *elder brethren* will refuse to join the music and dancing, when one who was lost is thus found.''

The paragraph is now before the reader in all the fulness of its meaning. And where is there in it, any violation of *truth?* Or where the vehement railing or defamation, for proof which it was introduced into the Narrative and Defence? It appears to us in the same light in which it was viewed by the committee, when it was passed for publication. We then considered it an argument of great force, particularly addressed to members of the General Conference; and although it was calculated to rouse attention, yet in view of the nature of the subject, it was handled in a very delicate manner.

CHAPTER VI.

The Agent's comment, is a miserable distortion of Mr. Snethen's meaning.

THE reader shall now have an opportunity to judge of the fitness of our prosecutors for the high powers which they assumed, in expelling us for publishing Mr. Snethen's papers. "In the above quotation," say they, Narrative and Defence, page 41, "the picture which the writer has drawn in the last paragraph, of the intolerant persecuting spirit of our bishops, can only find a parallel in the Romish Inquisition. To starve the *healthy* dependent into submission to arbitrary power, would probably be considered sufficiently odious in a civilized, not to say Christian community: but to deprive the sick opponent of shelter, and food, and medicine, until he is forced into improper compliances with episcopal prerogative, is a hardihood of cruelty, at which the heart sickens, and at which the soul of an ordinary inquisitor would revolt. The wretch who would be guilty of such barbarity, ought to be deemed to have renounced all affinity with his species, and hunted down as the common enemy of mankind. Can any man believe, that such a monster is to be found among the venerable bishops of the Methodist Episcopal Church? If Mr. Snethen, or the Editorial Committee who published the accusation, know the man, and the facts, why not name the one, and point directly to the other. Why these cruel inuendoes, which may be ignorantly applied to the innocent." * * * * page 42. "It cannot be pretended, that the calumny we have quoted above, is not meant to describe what has occurred, but what may be anticipated. There are in the allusions of the author, a specification of *place* and *time*, and a circumstantiality of description, which necessarily point out an individuality of application, both as to the oppressor and the oppressed. And the sombre picture of the stern and inflexible tyranny of the episcopacy, which nothing but humble submission can appease, is only equalled by the profligacy of those "elder brethren," those panders to power and prerogative, who are represented by the author, as joining the music and dancing over the converted starvling—the broken hearted victim of episcopal cruelty and oppression!! It may be asked by the reader, how it was possible for the reverend author of the publication from which we have made the above extract, to be betrayed into such an indiscretion: as it will not be denied, that he had long been esteemed as an able minister, and a pious, amiable man." * * * * * * "The author was climbing the steep and slippery ascent, to revolutionary distinction."—"He was not only a partizan—but a leader of a party—and with reference to our church government and its administration, he looked upon every thing through the spectacles which party spirit had furnished him. Through this medium, every opponent and every measure of opposition is made to take the hue, with which party feeling discolours them, and the author mistook for realities, what were the mere visions of a disturbed and vivid imagination," page 43. "But what shall we say of those who published these ravings of a disordered fancy? Who with calm deliberation laid them before the public as sober realities? Reader, are you a Christian?—then shun party as an evil influence, which if indulged, will inevitably destroy the spirit of love and of meekness, and substitute for them, malice and revenge, and every evil work." Let the candid reader compare this coarse and strained comment with the true design of Mr. Snethen's paper, and he will be obliged to see the high pitch to which the prosecutors had wrought up their feelings, and the extravagant effort which the agent made to excite resentment in the feelings of the Methodist public against the friends of Mutual Rights:—and that they were partizans, who themselves furnished the most perfect instances of the want of "the spirit of love and meekness." In fact, their comment is such a complete caricature of Mr. Snethen's "picture," that one cannot well avoid the conclusion, when they said, "party spirit, for the spirit of love and meekness, substitutes malice and revenge and every evil work," they inadvertently published a report of their own experience.

CHAPTER VII.

The high and independent condition of the Bishops, naturally tends to produce an habitual practice of flattery.

"Our bishops must be flattered, or their power must be resisted." Considering the immense patronage of the bishops and their appointing power, Mr. Snethen was of the opinion, that the preachers generally, would be impelled, sooner or later, either to flatter them;—in course, from time to time to give them additional power; or to concert ways and means to check its growth. "But flattery is easier and more pleasant, than resistance to oppressive power." This is a *truth* confirmed by the experience of all ages;—and being true at all times, and under all circumstances;—"itinerant and local preachers, and members of the church, therefore will discover a proneness to flatter bishops. For the same reason, local preachers and members will feel disposed to flatter itinerant preachers." And was there any *vehement railing*, in supposing that Methodist itinerant and local preachers and members, would have a proneness to feel and act like other people in similar circumstances? Or was it requisite for the printing committee to believe, that the report of history could afford no assistance, when they were called on to judge of the character of Methodist people, and of the probable course they would pursue? "But can any reason be assigned, why the private members of the church should despise local preachers, or that they should manifest an indifference or aversion towards each other?" If this unhappy state of things exists, perhaps the cause of it can be developed. "Evidently, when the awe that the wealth and power of office inspire, is no longer felt or ceases to operate under the disguise of flattery, the mind experiences a re-action and seeks to revenge itself upon the name or form of the office deprived of its attributes." This sentence reports a law of human nature, and is therefore true: or if no such law obtains, it was at the worst, one of Mr. Snethen's *'visionary'* notions on the subject. We admitted its truth, and therefore published it: and would blush, if we were too ignorant of mankind, not to know it to be *true*. The prosecutors were at liberty to entertain a different opinion. "Let the property and power which are really in our bishops, and nominally in the itinerant preachers, be transferred to the local preachers, and the public feelings will also be transferred." And who that has made useful observation on men and things, does not know, that this sentiment is according to human experience? Men thus practice imposition upon themselves. Aaron and the children of Israel made a golden calf. They knew it was a creature of their own making, and yet they still consented to pay it homage. Men confer factitious honors upon their fellow-men, and then turn round and make themselves believe the elevation is a reality. In this way they flatter wealth and power, though known to be in the possession of men unworthy of notice. "The flatterer pleases himself by his flatteries, while he seeks to please those whom he flatters. And this pleasure proceeds from the relief which the mind experiences, from the uneasy or painful sensation of fear. Mankind are sparing of their flattery towards those of whom they have nothing to hope, and from whom they have nothing to fear. The president of the United States is not flattered as a king; but would be, if his power was as much feared." These sentences are all general *truths*, and need no comment. "We are aware, that an intimation, that our bishops and itinerant preachers are feared by the members and the local preachers, will be repelled with great indignation." In this prediction, Mr. Snethen, might be thought by some, to have been inspired with the spirit of prophecy. It was, however, a mere application of his theory, to the people upon whom his eye was turned. In respect to them "indeed our whole theory of feeling in this case, will be considered as visionary and erroneous. Our statement is nevertheless true, and admits of the clearest demonstration." The demonstration, to candid and disinterested men will be satisfactory, and will for ever stigmatize those who were so highly offended with truths, which ought to have instructed and reproved them. "Mr. Wesley, was greatly flattered, and so was Mr. Asbury. They, indeed, mistook these expressions for the marks of love, and so did those who made them. But though it is not to be doubted, that there was much sincere affection, this was to the men. Their property and power were feared; as was the fear, so was the flattery. Some of our bishops, we perceive, will be much flattered to the south and west of the Susquehanna, and *much* and *deservedly* loved too. But, it does not now seem probable, that they will receive much eulogy from the north and east. If this shall prove to be the fact, will not the limits of their praise be the limits within which their power will be feared?" These appeals to facts and circumstances, were made to the travelling preachers, with intention to shew them the inevitable tendencies of their episcopacy, unless they should take measures to limit the powers of the bishops. Mr. Snethen took pains to shew the secret workings of the mind and heart when brought into contact with power and wealth, and then presented explanatory facts of the highest grade, to confirm the truth, and shew the importance of his argument. His principles, he shewed them, would apply even to Mr. Wesley and Mr. Asbury, two of the best and most distinguished men, that had ever lived in the Methodist connexion. And he was informed by travelling preachers, some of whom, when he wrote, were inclined to resist the growing power of the bishops, but who since, have found it easier or more agreeable to run with the multitude;— he was informed, however, by some of these, not only that things were taking the usual course, but that some of the bishops would have an influence to the south and west, and others to the north and east;—an evil which he wished them to avoid. "We beg that these remarks may be attended to, and carefully kept in mind. These are the data, on which we have predicated the separation of the north and the east, from the south and the west. Where their power is not flattered, it will be resisted. This is not an unwarranted assertion; it is not a new case; it is the thing that hath already been. Leaving Mr. Wesley's name out of the minutes, is a parallel instance, and may be traced to a similar cause. The absence of the man, disclosed the workings of the fear: had he been present, flattery would have concealed it all."* This explanatory reference to a well known fact, tells in a language which cannot be misunderstood, what Mr. Snethen intended by the terms *"fear"* and *"flattery."* It also specifies the limits by which he intended

* This transaction will be noticed again in another place.

14

his meaning to be bounded. "Traces of a similar operation may be observed in doctor Coke's visits. His power was not half so much to be dreaded as Mr. Asbury's; and yet the conference required articles to curb it, while he was in England." So strangely does the human mind elude the observation of its own operations. "Of all the illusions which the human mind practises on itself, none is more wonderful, than that which takes place in the case of flattery. We always had occasion to notice, that Mr. Asbury placed his chief reliance for the ascendency of his influence, upon his presence. Where trouble was, there was he." His experience and observation had taught him to know how great the influence of his presence, and therefore wherever his presence was needed, like a faithful pastor, whatever pains it might cost him, there he would be found.

CHAPTER IX.

The misrepresentations of the Agent and the prosecutors conclusively demonstrated.

THE reader now has had an opportunity to see what were the views of the printing committee in publishing Mr. Snethen's papers on church property. And we fearlessly challenge any man to shew a departure from *truth*, or to specify any *vehement railing* or *evil speaking* in any part of them. We had no expectation that any other construction would be put upon them, than that which we have submitted in the preceding comments. Much less, that they would be subjected to such distortion, as the following remarks are intended to produce. See Narrative and Defence, p. 44. The Agent, for the prosecutors, says: "What a disgusting picture is here drawn of Mr. Wesley, our bishops and travelling preachers! The one catering for praise, the others fawning and cringing to power and prerogative, and flattering these tyrannical prelates as though they had places and offices of emolument, in their gift." Will the reader pause, and compare this account with what Mr. Snethen actually wrote? "Mr. Wesley was greatly *flattered*, and so was Mr. Asbury. They indeed *mistook* these expressions for the marks of love, and *so did those who made them*. There was much affection, this was to the *men*. Their property and power were feared; and as was the fear, so was the flattery." Mr. Snethen said, that Mr. Wesley and Mr. Asbury, and in like manner the bishops and travelling preachers, were all flattered, but it was the effect of the institution, insomuch, that neither those who flattered, in the sense in which Mr. Snethen used the term, nor those who were the subjects of the flatteries, were conscious of the act. But the prosecutors say, Mr. Snethen represented the one as *catering for praise*, the others as *fawning* and *cringing*, &c. Whether this barefaced misrepresentation, was intentional on the part of the Agent, or was unconsciously the effect of blinded bigotry, or of an honest misunderstanding of Mr. Snethen's meaning, we leave it with him to determine. In the mean time, we will only add, that so far are we from condemning Mr Snethen's papers, we consider it due to him, to say, that he is entitled to the gratitude of old side men and re- formers, for the very philosophical account he has given, of the deleterious effect of the government of the Methodist Episcopal Church.

Mr. Snethen, in the course of the foregoing argument against the life office of the bishops, says: "We know to a certainty, that Mr. Wesley never meant to confer any power for life, upon the superintendents which he and doctor Coke ordained; for he actu- ally had it in contemplation to recall Mr. Asbury. Of such an event Mr. Asbury was so well aware, that he took special care to. prevent it, by getting himself elected superintendent by the Ameri- can preachers." What was the object according to Mr. Snethen's view, which Mr. Asbury intended to accomplish by getting himself elected, &c.? To "prevent" his being recalled by Mr. Wesley. And was there any "vehement railing, any evil speaking," implied in the statement, that Mr. Asbury was apprehensive, that Mr. Wesley might recall him to England, but he greatly preferred staying in the United States, and therefore "took special care to get himself elected by the American preachers," that he might not be recalled? Was there any unkindness towards Mr. Asbury, implied in this? So far as we can judge, no disparagement was intended to Mr. As- bury's reputation. But the agent who made his selections and extracts with a view to their intended effect on the Methodist community, gives the following comment. "The allegation against Mr. Asbury, 'that *he took special* good *care to get himself elected, by the American preachers,*' is the 'unkindest cut of all.' Mr. As- bury refused to be superintendent of the Methodist Episcopal Church, unless he should be elected by the free suffrages of his brethren. And was it not praise-worthy to do so?" Did Mr. Snethen say it was not? "He might have been superintendent by Mr. Wesley's appointment, as doctor Coke was." True, and he might then have been subject to Mr. Wesley's recall. "But he would not exercise authority over any, but those who consented to confer it upon him, and this is called 'taking special good care to GET HIMSELF elected, by the American preachers.' " Mr. Snethen did not say Mr. Asbury took special good care to get himself elected, intending any reproach to Mr. Asbury, but that Mr. As- bury took *special care,* the word *good* he did not use at all; he took special care to get himself elected, in order to ensure his stay in the United States. What a detraction from Mr. Asbury's reputation!! Mr. Snethen said, in order to *prevent* his recall to England, which was to insure his stay in the United States, he took special care to get himself elected!! Had he not taken such special care, he would have been placed in a relation to the American preachers, similar to that of doctor Coke. He was apprized, however, that Mr. Wesley had thoughts of recalling him. He prudently took this step to prevent his recall. And for publishing this transaction, according to Mr. Snethen's view, the editors of the Mutual Rights,

were condemned. And the prosecutors have republished it with
their comment so managed, that with the old-side Methodists it
passes for *"vehement railing, bitter reviling* and *defamation."* "It
was in fact the unkindest cut of all." !! But we have dwelt on this
part particularly, to shew the reader, not only that the agent aimed
at the effect intended to be produced by the Narrative and Defence, but that he could misinterpret a sentence, and even add an
important word to the oblique interpretation, to make the effect
more certain. Mr. Snethen said, Mr. Asbury took special care to
get himself elected *to prevent his recall to England.* The agent
makes him say, Mr. Asbury took "special GOOD care to GET HIM-
SELF ELECTED." Admitting at the same time, that this was not
necessary for securing to him the distinction of being superintendent. This distinction already awaited him, by Mr. Wesley's appointment!

CHAPTER X.

EXTRACTS FROM NEHEMIAH ON THE EXPEDIENCY OF A REPRESEN-
TATION.

The paragraph extracted from a paper, with the signature of
Nehemiah, as it is made to read in the Narrative and Defence, is a
garbled fragment. Thus separated from its connexion, it was well
suited to their purpose. But when read in its place, so as to be
understood according to the true intent and meaning of the writer,
it is by no means offensive to any well informed reader.

So much of the essay as is printed in the Narrative and Defence, is
put in italics and restored to its place. When it shall be fairly examined, there is no doubt that it will be considered fully to justify itself.

"We now say, that it is *expedient* that the local ministry and
laity, should be represented in the General Conference. Their
right to be represented having been already proved, it is to the
question of expediency we now confine ourselves. When we say
it is expedient that representation should be allowed, we wish to
be understood as meaning that it is *fit, proper,* best upon the whole,
the present state of the connexion having been duly considered.
Respecting representation, for this is the point at issue, thousands
in the church, in the local ministry and among the laity, believe
they have a *right,* an *inalienable right,* to be represented; and that
as long as this right is withheld, they are unjustly deprived of that,
which according to scripture, reason and primitive Christian
usage, they ought to possess. Upon the other hand, those who
are opposed to representation, say, that the friends of reform have
no such rights as they now lay claim to. It must be remembered,
however, the right which is claimed is *common,* and therefore, when
they insist that the friends of reform have no such right, they admit *ipso facto* that they themselves have none. And if the reformers were permitted to exercise all the rights which they claim,
such an acquisition on their part, could bring no loss to their op-

ponents, inasmuch as they have no rights to lose. They would in such an event, be precisely where they are now, having none to lose, they could lose none.* But this is not the case in the judgment of those who wish a representation;—they think they have such rights. They know they have such rights. They think and say that their rights are unjustly withheld; and neither the language nor conduct of their opponents, can make them believe otherwise. To continue to be denied the enjoyment of these rights, will not convince them that they are not entitled to possess them. To withhold them, under the pretext of pleasing those who acknowledge that they themselves have no right to be represented, will not satisfy the reformers, nor silence their claims. We cannot see, then, how any one can reasonably, or consistently, oppose another man's enjoyment of a *right*, a privilege or a blessing, which he conscientiously believes he ought to possess, when that enjoyment will not encroach upon his own rights, or subtract from the sum of his own happiness.

As the friends of reform believe they have a right to be represented in the General Conference, is it to be supposed, that they will be satisfied with any thing short of a representation? As they have such clear grounds that they ought to be represented, and as their opponents can show nothing to the contrary, is it likely that they will be satisfied without it? It can neither be concealed nor denied, that an excitement of no ordinary character, at present exists throughout the connexion, and that this excitement so far from being lessened, is every day gaining strength and becoming more extended. The dissatisfaction which has long existed, has begun to show itself in a systematic opposition to the present form of church government. The principles of reform, are now beginning to shoot up, and it is weakness in the extreme, to suppose they will never come to maturity. Perhaps in some two or three places, they may be a little longer in the soil before they spring up, or they may be stifled in the growth; but even then, there will be no cordial assent or hearty good will to the present form of church government. And to us it is very evident, that there will be no peace in the church, unless representation be allowed, and believing that peace would follow, it is *expedient* that representation should be granted.

We are strengthened in the above opinion by considering the character, the number, and the influence of the men who make this demand. It will be asked, who are they that are dissatisfied with the present form of church government? And the question will be tauntingly answered, perhaps, as it has been done before; a few restless and backslidden local preachers. But is this the truth? We hope not. We believe not. The local preachers who are thus reproached, are not backsliders. They are men of God; ministers of the Lord Jesus Christ, who have borne the burden and

*Every sensible reader will perceive, that this is a mere argumentum ad hominem; intended ironically to throw back upon the power party their own sayings.

heat of the day. Many of them have spent the prime of their lives and the strength of their years in the cause of God, and although they have grown grey in the work of the ministry, they are still labouring, without fee or reward, to build up the walls of Zion. They are men of holy lives, whose moral and ministerial characters, stand as as fair now as they ever did, and would suffer nothing by being compared with the characters of those who traduce them;—by representing them in this unfavourable light. Nor is their number small, nor their influence inconsiderable. Hundreds in the ministry are dissatisfied with that feature of our church government, which gives to the travelling ministry the exclusive power to make laws for the church, whereby the local ministry and the laity, are excluded from a representation in the General Conference.

We would now, in the fear of God, put this question to the consciences of our readers. Is there no ground to doubt of the propriety of a system which will give dissatisfaction to so many ministers of Jesus Christ? Can it be supposed, that the course pursued by the opponents of Mutual Rights, can be of God, when that course will fill the hearts of so many of his old and tried servants with such deep distress; especially when it will be recollected, that the aggrieved would much rather, if possible, suffer than complain? Is it likely that a plan founded upon injustice and productive of so many exquisitely painful feelings, can meet with the approbation of righteous Heaven? We are grieved while we write;—we are pained while we contemplate the subject in its probable termination; for we honestly believe, that many of those degraded ministers, notwithstanding their attachment to the Methodist Episcopal Church, think it would be better for them to unite among themselves, to live under an equitable form of church government the remainder of their days, and leave such a precious legacy to their children after them, than to continue where they receive nothing but a denial of their rights upon the one hand, or abuse and reproach if they complain, upon the other. Nor is the discontentment confined to the local ministry. We believe thousand of the laity are dissatisfied also. And as the principles of the government of the church shall have been examined by them, their numbers will increase, and their complaints will become the louder. What can be expected under such circumstances, but that the intelligence, the piety, and the numbers of the discontented will have an influence upon the whole connexion. What then is to be done? Is it a proof of wisdom or goodness, to drive things to the extreme? We think not. We think it would be far better to take some steps, to adopt some measures which might conciliate the minds of those who are distressed and discontented, and thereby restore peace to the troubled, and preserve the integrity of the body. The last General Conference was the time for the adoption of such measures, but we hope it is yet not too late. Brethren seem still to manifest a wish to remain within the pale of the church, if they can do so consistently with their views of justice; and while they remain it will be much easier to propitiate them, than to bring them back if they once depart. O! that we could persuade those who have it in their power to go forward in this god-like work of reconciliation. We would beg and beseech them for God's sake not to turn their ear away from the admonitions of a brother;—not to delay to effect an object so good and so praiseworthy. We would entreat them to do something and do it speedily, to heal the wounds which have been inflicted upon our bleeding Zion. For the peace of the church it is *expedient* that something should be done; for we are well persuaded, that unless *peace* be restored, the day is not far distant, when many will depart and form a government for themselves. Can the present rulers of our church answer for the consequences? If they will not now take one single step to restore peace and preserve the unity of the church, will they be free from all blame in the eyes of our sister churches? Yea, will they be able to answer to God for the refusal or neglect? These we know are solemn and weighty considerations. We trust they will have a proper effect upon some, though we are free to confess, we fear they will not upon all of our travelling brethren.

But let them go, say some, this is the very thing we wish, and the sooner they go the better. They are only troublesome men, and as long as they remain in connexion with us, the church will have no peace. This seems to be the opinion, at least this is the language of some who are opposed to representation. But does this opinion, or this language, afford evidence of piety or policy? If it could be made to harmonize with the spirit of christianity, which we are sure it cannot, is it consistent with sound policy? The advocates for representation are right, or they are wrong. If they are right, their opponents must be wrong in denying their requests, and cannot censure them for withdrawing from the connexion, in case they should do so. Nor would the sin of schism, (if a separation from a church, whose government is founded upon injustice, can be called schism,) lie at their door but at the door of those who would force them to such a measure. We shall suppose, however, at present, for the sake of argument, that the reformers are wrong; that their views of church government are erroneous, and their demands unreasonable. What results are likely to take place, according to the judgment and statement of those who are opposed to representation? Why, they say, if the reformers leave the church, they will certainly leave the Lord, go back into the world and sin, and finally lose their souls.* Although we are far from believing that the grace of God is confined to the Methodist Episcopal Church, or that the Lord would not hear the prayers of those who would call upon him, and keep them from sin, though they might not be of that body of religious professors, yet, assuming their statement with all its alarming features, it will bear upon themselves, and not upon the reformers. Merciful God, is it the case that these men can believe what they say, and yet not strive to prevent it. Is it possible that the opponents of representation, would rather souls should depart

* This was said by many of the anti-reformers.

from the Lord, than that they themselves should depart a hair's
breadth from their legislative prerogatives? Is it a fact, that they
would rather souls should be damned by thousands, than that a representation from the local ministry and laity, should be admitted
into the General Conference? God of love, can these men possess
thy spirit, enter into thy benevolent designs of saving souls, or
imitate thy gracious example, who would not change a feature of
the government of our church, which is *merely human*, to prevent
souls from going to the bottomless pit? This is the amount of the
argument in its application to themselves. But we hope better
things of them though we thus write. What have they done to prevent these dreadful evils which they portray in such vivid colours,
in order to prevent the members of our church from becoming reformers? We fancy we hear one say, I fail not wherever I go, to
warn the people against reading the Mutual Rights. I fail not to
inform the people, that the men who edit that work are "all burning with a schismatical and fanatical zeal," and that "their plans
are held in *sovereign contempt*" by some of those who fill the *highest*
offices in our church.* This, to be sure, is a short way of answering an argument. But is it the way to remove error? Is it the way
to set us right if we are wrong? Is it the gospel way of converting
a soul from the error of his ways? Or, is it not rather the very
principle upon which the *inquisition* has been established;— first call
the man heretic, and then it is right and lawful to put him on the
wheel, or burn him at the stake!!

In this last statement we have proceeded upon the supposition,
that the reformers are wrong. * * * But, let us suppose, for a moment, the reformers are right; that, in asking for a representation,
they ask for nothing but what is reasonable and just; that the humble attitude they assume, evinces their love of order, their respect
for their itinerant brethren, and their attachment to the Methodist
institutions; that the length of time they have borne their privations, affords indubitable evidence that they are unwilling to leave
the pale of the church. We ask, notwithstanding their long suffering and patience, is it likely that they will always remain in the
connexion?"

"*Convinced, as they [the Reformers] are, that they have everything
on their side that would justify them in the sight of God, in the eyes
of the world, and in the demands of their own consciences, to withdraw, is it to be expected that they will continue to submit to those who
withhold their rights? To remain would be hopeless. To remain in
the connexion, would be to remain to be made the butt of the contumely,
and insult of every one opposed to reform. If nothing be done in favour of the reformation, it will be construed into a total defeat, and
will so inflame their opponents, as to induce them to add farther inju-
ries to the grievances already felt. What, then, can the Reformers
promise themselves by continuing in the connexion, in the event of a
total denial of their claims? Can they promise themselves peace?
Peace, they will have none. Can they hope that, by continuing to*

* This was said or written, by one of the Bishops.

suffer, justice will be done them in the end. Alas! injustice like death, has neither eyes to see the miseries of its subjects, nor a heart to feel for the wounds which it inflicts. Every symptom of patience, and every returning period, will only encourage their oppressors to be firmer in their denial, and will induce them to augment the distresses of the distressed. Can they, under this view of the subject, calculate upon the common courtesies and civilities of life? They cannot. For, at the present, and while the cause is depending, the shafts of reproach are frequently hurled at them, even from the pulpit:

"We will now suppose that the General Conference, rigidly adhering to the present system, with all its features of injustice, reject the petitions which may be presented for a representation. We will suppose, that those friendly to an equitable church government, based upon representation, will then proceed to take such measures as will be deemed necessary to form themselves into a church; will not many of our best and oldest local preachers be of that number? Will not many of the most intelligent and respectable laymen and their families be of the number? Will not some who are at present in the travelling connexion, and who are ground, as it were, between the upper and nether millstones,* on account of their liberal sentiments, be of that number? We have no doubt of these things. How whole districts of country may be affected by the formation of a new connexion, we cannot tell;—but, we shall neither be surprised nor mistaken in our calculation, if societies were to withdraw by scores from a church, whose ministers, if they speak the truth, would rather see them go into sin, and finally go to hell, than allow a representation in the law-making department of the church."

"If then, the *unity* of the body in the bonds of peace be at all desirable, we say it is *expedient* that representation should be granted."

This paper was considered one of the most offensive; and the extract in italics was quoted with uncommon interest. Their *"remarks"* in the Narrative and Defence are, "we have here, a plain, unequivocal developement, of the ulterior views of the Union Society. They are determined to carry their measures, whether with, or without the consent of the majority, or leave the church." Nehemiah had said no such thing. The paper in no shape justifies such a remark. It says, *"we honestly believe*, that many * * * think it would be better for them to unite among themselves, to live under an equitable form of government, the remainder of their days, and leave such a precious legacy to their children after them, than to continue, where they receive nothing but denial of their rights, upon the one hand, and abuse and reproach, if they complain, on the other." And again, *"we are well persuaded,* that unless peace is restored, the day is not distant, when *many* will depart and form a government for themselves." This expression of his *belief* respecting the *thoughts of many,* and his *persuasion* respecting the *departure of many,* are presented as arguments, which, in his opin-

* Witness, Messrs. D. B. Dorsey, and W. C. Pool, &c.

15

ion, go to prove, that it would be expedient to grant to the people a representation in the legislative department of the church. No candid man of sound judgment, will admit that any thing more was intended. It should be kept in mind too, that it was well known to us all, that many had seceded and arrangements were making by the Methodist Societies, to organize themselves. To this we were opposed, because we were persuaded, that by means of our periodical and Union Societies, we should be able in due time, to effect the necessary reform in the Methodist Episcopal Church, *by the consent of the majority, and not leave the church.* The power party were so apprehensive of this, that they determined to prevent us, by effecting the destruction of the Mutual Rights and Union Societies, Nehemiah says, "convinced that they," (not the Union Societies; these were opposed to a secession,) but the many would be justified in the sight of God, in the eyes of the world, and in the demands of their own consciences, to withdraw, is it to be expected, that they will continue to submit to those who withhold their rights? To remain would be hopeless * * * * would be, to be made the butt of the contumely and insult of every one opposed to reform, &c. &c. In the event of a total denial of their claims, can they promise themselves peace? Peace, they will have none. Can they hope that by continuing to suffer, justice will be done them in the end?" &c. All this was argument, to prove the *expediency* of granting a delegation to the people.

This paper was published about three years before we were expelled for publishing it. Surely Nehemiah was a prophet; and all his prophecies about *injustice* and want of *eyes to see* or *hearts to feel,* were but too soon, literally fulfilled. We were unjustly expelled, and the Annual Conference deliberately resolved that we had no right to complain. We were determined to remain, and continue our labours to convince the power party, of the expediency of granting a lay representation. But they determined to expel us;—a very conclusive argument in proof of their opinion to the contrary!!

The writer of the Narrative and Defence, thinking himself hidden behind his extract, makes the comment for the introduction of which, this paper was "indicated." "They call," says he, "travelling preachers oppressors of their brethren, and declare that these oppressors have neither eyes to see the "miseries" of their flocks, nor hearts to feel for their "wounds," nay, that they would rather see their flocks go into "SIN" and finally into "HELL," than accord them their rights." We deny the truth of this comment. It is in fact, an impudent attempt at imposition. Nehemiah had qualified every strong statement contained in his paper. In respect to that above referred to, by the Agent, the following is the qualification. "In the event of a *total denial of their claims,*" &c. can they, (the reformers,) hope, that by continuing to suffer, justice will be done them in the end? He had argued the justice of their claim to representation. He was endeavouring to convince old side men, that it would be best, safest upon the whole, to do the reformers justice. But supposing they should refuse to the last, how would their conduct be viewed by reformers? They would then conclude them unjust. When would they come to this conclusion? "In the event of a total denial of their claims." In that event, he asks, can reformers hope that by continuing to suffer, justice will be done them in the end? If the *total denial*, the proper test of their injustice be pronounced, then reformers need expect no more. For *alas!* injustice like death, has neither eyes to see the miseries of its subjects, nor a heart to feel for the wounds which it inflicts. And therefore, when the reformers meet a total denial, &c. they will surely withdraw. Now says Nehimiah's argument, brethren do not meet them with a total denial—do not give this evidence of injustice to provoke to such a course. Rather admit the *"expediency"* of granting their petition; rather do them justice and prevent all these evils.

How different this, which is the true view of the writer's design, from the interpretation of the Agent? He first gives a caricature of Nehemiah's argument;—a total misrepresentation of his design, and then in view of his own distorted picture he cries out, "gracious Heaven! are these men Methodists? and are they speaking of the whole body of itinerant Methodist preachers? * * * if this is the language of love, what is the language of hatred?" &c.

We ask the candid reader, who is the caluminator in this case? Nehemiah, or doctor Bond? He has accused the editorial committee of publishing a certain writer's remarks, "knowing that they were unfounded," and yet says he, "they allege that they have not been charged with any immorality. They must excuse us if we entertain a different opinion!" We give him back this gratuity, as very fitly applicable to his comment on Nehemiah, and in the sequel shall find other occasions to restore to him similar bounties, for which we have no use, and which can be stored most conveniently, in the depot from which they were originally taken.

CHAPTER XI.

Extract of a letter from the Union Society of Baltimore, to a member of the Union Society at Bedford, Tennessee.—Mutual Rights, Vol. 1. p. 90, 91.

"We have for a long time, been sufficiently well informed respecting the great dissatisfaction of many intelligent brethren, who, at the same time that they are fast friends to the doctrine of holiness, [according to the peculiar manner of inculcating that doctrine,] which we have received as a common legacy from the great founders of Methodism, are nevertheless unwilling to be tributary to the *perpetuation of a system of government*, which, in their opinion, is forging fetters for themselves and their posterity." Narrative and Defence, page 47.

The reader will perceive at once, that it was considered treasonable to publish an opinion, that the government of the Methodist Episcopal Church, if perpetuated, has a tendency to endanger the liberties of the people under its authority. The publications were charged with inveighing against the discipline;—with being abusive or speaking evil of a part, if not most of the ministers of that church. That the above extract contains nothing personal; that it has no reference to the moral discipline of the church, is very obvious. The writer ventures an opinion, that a church Government which has placed all the legislative, executive and judicial power, in the hands of the ministry, if perpetuated, will eventually be dangerous to the liberties of the people. For publishing this opinion, we were expelled, and our prosecutors cover themselves behind doctor Bond's Narrative and Defence, which says it is vehement railing; it is *slander and misrepresentation."* The true cause of their objection to the extract, will be better understood by a reference to the paper itself from which it was garbled.

Copy of a letter addressed to a member of the Bedford Union Society, Tennessee.

DEAR BROTHER,
Your highly important communication, bearing date 14th September, has been received and submitted to the consideration of the Union Society of Methodists in this place. The manner of its reception, and the interest which was manifested by the Society, will appear upon a perusal of the extract from the journal of proceedings, which is enclosed for your information.

It was thought to be every way consistent with propriety and mutual confidence, that you should have calculated upon the paternal sympathy and support of the Union Society of Baltimore; since it is well known to us all, that we advised the measure which has brought you into difficulty. And if there were any doubts respecting the necessity or morality of the measure, the consequences which have followed would have a tendency to produce in us very painful regret. The fact however is very far otherwise. At the same time, that we are deeply sorrowful on account of the transaction which so materially concerns the brethren who are involved in its "exterminating" design, our sorrow has reference also to other highly momentous considerations. We are indeed grieved at the affliction of our brethren, but much more at being informed that a tribunal has been found in the Methodist Episcopal Church, where some of her members have been subjected to trial and expulsion, for doing that, which they consider to be an imperious duty; which no existing power or authority had any shadow of right to forbid, and which must have the approbation of the wisest and best men in these United States. And so momentous is this expression of high-handed measures, that if no other instance or occasion could be found to give strength and confirmation to our opinion respecting the necessity of reform in our ecclesiastical government, this one would be sufficient. But we were fully satisfied upon this point, before we heard of your case, which is one instance only of the manner in which men in power can put in force their influence and authority, when occasion and inclination concur. Of course, we add it to the account of those facts and circumstances which in our opinion most clearly show, that the time has arrived when the friends of religious liberty in the Methodist Episcopal Church, are called upon to make a firm stand, and declare their sentiments openly. If this be not admitted, it follows, that the Methodist people are bound silently and submissively to acknowledge, that it is the right of the itinerant preachers, not only to have and to hold all power and authority, but to expel any who dare to think and speak otherwise; and thus to stop the mouths of all who may be inclined to put a check to the growing power, or to recommend any measures of security against its maladministration. In a word, it will follow, that the itinerant preachers have a right to prevent all inquiry into the subject. We have for a long time, been sufficiently well informed respecting the great dissatisfaction of many intelligent brethren, who at the same time that they are fast friends to the doctrine of holiness, which we have received as a common legacy from the great founders of Methodism, are nevertheless unwilling to be tributary to the perpetuation of a system of government, which in their opinion is forging fetters for themselves and their posterity. And we have admired the manner in which many of them have published their arguments, intended to prove that the existing monopoly of the legislative and executive power of the church, has had an injurious effect upon the connexion, and threatens eventually, to produce ruinous consequences. We have seen this necessary enterprize again and again repeated by travelling preachers as well as others, and no step has been taken to accuse or condemn any one, as having committed a breach upon the rule, which is found in the Book of Discipline, chap. 2, sec. vii, article 3d; and which it appears has been arbitrarily enforced in your section of the country. Indeed, we have had no fear upon this subject; and now that we have the information furnished us by your letter, we are at a loss to conceive of the conduct of the presiding elder and assistant preachers, who have so rashly and extensively acted upon it. Our surprise is not a little increased, when we perceive by your communication, that the court which sat upon your case, made special objections against that part of your preamble, which was as follows, viz:——"And that this amendment should introduce an equilibrium into said church, by admitting a representation from the local ministers and laymen, equal to that of the itinerant ministers, into all assemblies convened for the purpose of making laws and regulations for government." We cannot see how the discipline or doctrines of the church are censured or reproached by the publication of a desire or intention to obtain, if it can be obtained, such a change in the government of the Methodist Episcopal Church as may constitute it a representative government. Is it indeed a truth, that the discipline is reproached and scandalized by making the fact notorious, that it does not recognize this principle which is so essential to the liberties of the people? Then let those whose duty it is, put away this reproach, not by compelling men to keep silence, but by admitting the principle. For who could condemn a freeman in this land of liberty, for making an open and manly declaration concerning the importance or the necessity of general representation, especially, when the discipline not only does not recognize, but in fact makes no mention of it; or who can so effectually be guilty of scandalizing the church, as those who sit in judgment and expel her members for making such a declaration?

Surely such proceedings cannot be justified by the decision of the Annual Conference. At any event we have no hesitation in giving it as our opinion, that if the conference act a becoming part, they will reinstate the brethren.

This letter needs no comment. It was published in November, 1825. No papers were "indicated" of earlier date, except Mr. Snethen's on church property, and Nehemiah's on the expediency of representation. They had already expelled fourteen of the friends of reform, in the state of Tennessee, for having taken measures preparatory to the formation of an Union Society, that is, for being about to be guilty of that great offence. That too was WHOLESOME and SOUND discipline!!

CHAPTER XII.

Extract from an answer to Querist by Bartimeus—alias Mr. Shinn.

"IF they (the travelling preachers) go on, and enslave the people, the consequence will be, that they will ultimately and inevitably enslave themselves and their children after them." Narrative and Defence, page 47. That this extract was garbled with intention to produce effect upon the minds of men, "who had not read the Mutual Rights at all," will be obvious, as soon as it shall be read in its proper connexion with the clause from which it is taken.*

3. *If the members of our church have heretofore neglected to consider the principles of church government, it is the more necessary for them to consider them now; especially as it is assumed in the argument, "that a particular rule which has been in the book of discipline a great number of years, constituted a particular engagement on the part of each probationer, to remain silent in this matter." Is the embargo taken off, when this probation is out? Or is he bound to remain silent, by virtue of the long standing of this rule? If the rule was wrong and unjust at first, will it grow into justice and goodness by age? Was it the duty of the members to examine the principles of government at first? And because they neglected their duty then, must they still neglect it? If the age of a wrong principle has already nearly taken away their right to do their duty, how necessary for them to rouse themselves to examinaton, before it shall become still older, and get entirely out of their reach. If its age has already taken away part of their rights, there appears to be danger that it may at last become old enough to take away the whole*

*We have put the whole clause in italics, and beg the reader to mark well how true it is in all its parts.

of them. Most of the churches in christendom have the advantage of the Methodists, in this argument; for several of them are hundreds of years old: does it follow then, that whatever may be "the fundamental principle of their church polity," all their members are bound under "a particular engagement, to remain silent in this matter?" Then Luther, Calvin, and Erasmus—Wesley, Fletcher, and Whitefield, were each under "a particular engagement," and this engagement was "constituted" by the long standing of the principles which they opposed, "to remain silent in this matter."

"Complete and absolute authority on the part of the itinerancy," it is said, "has never been departed from," and is the "fundamental principle of our church polity." We think our church ought to have better "fundamental principles." But suppose Mr. Asbury had succeeded in his council plan—then a bishop's council would have been the fundamental principle of our church polity, and we should have had no general conference. And how was the fundamental principle altered, when that conference was made representative? If we enlarge the sphere of representation, and establish a better constitution, will this destroy the fundamental principle? or, will it not rather exchange one very defective principle, for several valuable axioms in church government, that are truly and scripturally fundamental?

Having thus, we think, refuted the argument, the following short reflections may be added.

For the people to examine the principles of church government, and to assist each other in the examination, is, first, their duty: for God has made them rational creatures; church government is instituted for their sake, and for the sake of displaying the divine glory, therefore they are under obligation to examine, and see whether these ends are effectually answered by the government. The argument we have been examining, supposes it to have been the duty of all the members, to make themselves acquainted with the government, when they first joined society: well, if they then neglected their duty, let them not neglect it eternally. Secondly, it is their wisdom: for what but folly can it be, for any people to remain in stupid unconcern and ignorance of the government under which they live? Is this to act the part of rational creatures? Thirdly, it is essential to their safety: for if a people leave to others, to manage the affairs of government over their heads, while they themselves remain ignorant and unconcerned about the whole matter, in the name of common sense, what security have they for their liberty or happiness a single hour? In the argument we have considered, we see it assumed that a government acquires authority by age; and nothing but ignorance or thoughtlessness can hinder the Methodist people from perceiving, that they are liable to lose the dearest rights of humanity, by absolute principles in the church, as well as in the state. Who, but a people that are tamely willing to be slaves, are willing to remain ig-

*norant of their own government, or to leave the whole matter to the
management of others?   Fourthly, it is essential to the welfare of the
church: for if her principles are sound, they will shine the brighter
by being examined, and will be the more firmly established in the confidence of the people; if any of them are unsound, the removal of
those which are so, will be a real benefit and an honour to the whole
church.   Fifthly, it is essential to the welfare and happiness of the
travelling ministry: for if they go on, and enslave the people, the
consequence will be, that they will ultimately and inevitably enslave
themselves and their children after them: therefore, a wholesome
authority of "check and control" in the body, is essential to the
real interest and happiness of "the ruling power."*

*To conclude: the persevering efforts and struggles we have beheld,
to enjoin silence on preachers and people, furnish a strong presump-
tion of something unsound at bottom, and would be really alarming,
were it not for the protection afforded by the civil government under
which we live: and every day's experience tends to increase the conviction, that no persons among us, but those who resolve, in the name
of God, to act upon principle, will be found qualified to act as persevering reformers.*

BARTIMEUS.

Pittsburg, June 14, 1826.

CHAPTER XIII.

*Extract from a letter to the Editors of the Mutual Rights, forwarded
from Alexandria, District Columbia.*

"Is it not a possible case, that some of our rulers may be looking forward to an establishment, especially as they claim a divine
right to absolute government over those whom they have been the
instruments of converting from the error of their ways; and truly,
if they have this divine right, they should have it established by law,
to keep the restless spirits down." Narrative and Defence, page 47.
This extract is taken from a paper which is sufficiently explained
by a reference to the provocation which gave it birth and justified
it.   See Mutual Rights, page 46, vol. III.   "I take the liberty
of enclosing you a paper in the form of a remonstrance, said
to have been drawn up by George Mason, of Virginia, and
presented to the legislature, shortly after the revolution; thereby
defeating a bill, then before the house, intended to establish some
religious sect.   Although the present controversy is not, whether
we shall have an establishment or not, yet there are some things,
that may be drawn from the remonstrance, that may be rendered
useful to the cause of reform.   "*Is it not a possible case, that some
of our rulers may be looking forward to an establishment, especially
as they claim a divine right to absolute government, over those whom*

they have been the instruments of converting from the error of their ways: and truly, if they have this divine right, they should have it established by law, to keep the restless spirits down." The preachers here, are not mealy mouthed in saying, *that they are invested with the high authority of making laws for the church, and they ask nothing of the people, because they are not accountable to them for any of their acts.* If such principles are to be silently instilled into the minds of men, until the Methodists shall have members sufficient; with the present form of church government, what are we to expect from them, but to enforce obedience to the laws of the holy church? Even now, they endeavour to deter us from reading the Mutual Rights, by saying it is wicked, and that the reformers have lost their religion. Our preacher and our presiding elder, strongly intimated, and that from the pulpit, that "the reformers are influenced by the devil." After a public assault of this sort, the brother at Alexandria, reacted, so far only, as to forward to the editors of the Mutual Rights, the paper above referred to, said to have been written by Mr. Mason, of Virginia, accompanying it with this brief account of the occasion which had induced him to request its publication. We thought it a sufficiently mild rebuke for the preacher and presiding elder. The occasion seemed to the editorial committee, to call for it; not so much to protect reform from such rude assaults, as to save the church from the scandal of being subjected to the instruction and rule of men, who appeared to have so little regard to their own dignity, and still less respect to the feelings of those, who honestly differed from them in opinion upon the subject of church government. If we were not at liberty to publish such a rebuke, in reply to an accusation of being influenced by the devil and destitute of religion, surely we "had fallen upon evil times."

CHAPTER XIV.

Mr. Joseph Walker's letter to the Editorial Committee.

ALABAMA, DALLAS COUNTY, MAY 10TH, 1826.

Dear Brethren,

"A few days ago, a friend put five or six numbers of the Mutual Rights into my hand, to read. It gave me heartfelt satisfaction to know, that the spirit of reformation is at work in our favoured country, and especially, that it has begun in the Methodist Episcopal Church, where it is so much needed. When we look back and think of the privations, and sufferings, and fightings, through which our fathers struggled in the revolutionary war, for the attainment of civil liberty, and religious mutual rights, and then turn round and see all the principles of liberty trampled upon, by our travelling preachers, in the conferences and in their administration of church government, it is enough to grieve a heart of stone." We

16

ean see nothing in Mr. Walker's letter from its commencement to this place, to which any body ought to object. But the agent expected his readers to "mark well" the imputation "that *all the principles of liberty are trampled upon by the travelling preachers of the Methodist Episcopal Church in their conferences, and in their administration of church government.* But is this not true? The people and local preachers have no participation in the deliberative or legislative acts of the conferences; and the legislative, judicial and executive powers, are all in the hands of the travelling preachers. When it is considered that the great and fundamental principles of civil liberty, are well understood by the people of the United States, whilst at the same time the travelling preachers appear totally to disregard them, in their conferences and in the administration of church government; we cannot perceive that Mr. Walker's statement is at all inconsistent with *truth*, or that his language is too strong, when he says the principles of liberty are *trampled* upon by the travelling preachers. This however was a very conspicuous part of the alleged slander for the publication of which we were expelled.

"I can but weep to see our Zion *so oppressed*." The old patriot seems to have understood the subject upon which he wrote. He had read the paper on church rights. He had learned "that christian freedom is as truly the right of the *church*, as it is the right of the *state*,"—that "an association of millions of christians, under a civil government of their own choice, would not constitute a free christian community." That no community could be free, whilst it is controlled by absolute rules;—that it could not "be safe, should those rules intentionally or otherwise, give a wrong direction to the multitude." He knew, that it was asserted by many, in and out of the Methodist Episcopal Church, that the principles and actual powers of that system of church government, may be compressed into one short sentence. *"All power must be in the hands of the preachers; none in those of the members of the church."* He knew, "that the powers of the travelling preachers in the Methodist Episcopal Church, are as plenary as it is possible for them to be;—that they can, not only legislate for the church without the consent of the people or of the local preachers, but according to their discipline, and their latest report on the subject of their powers, they can make and unmake a constitution. He considered it a very serious concern, that such amazing prerogatives should be lodged in the hands of a few travelling preachers. He was informed, that a vast amount of suffering and discontent were annually generated under the existing regime, and that there was cause to fear, that the minds of many, would become impatient of the irritating cause. Therefore said he, "I can but weep to see our Zion *so oppressed*." I am the son of an old patriot of Pennsylvania. I have been a preacher in the Methodist Episcopal Church for more than twenty years; have been ordained, Deacon and Elder. My house has been all that time, a place of retreat and rest for the travelling preachers, and of constant resort for the brethren. Having, therefore, had frequent opportunities, I have intimated to bishops, presiding elders and travelling preachers, the propriety and necessity of reform. They have commonly replied, it might be right, perhaps, and *that those who wished reform, could withdraw, whenever they might see proper.* I was led to pause! I pondered within myself! Oh, the depth of spiritual wickedness, apparently, in high places! Oh, the curse of ingratitude! Good Heavens! thought I, filled with astonishment! How many hundreds of dollars have I and many others spent, for the exclusive use of the Methodist Episcopal Church. She has been our constant care, and for her we have laboured twenty years and more, and never have received one dollar of reward. Indeed, some of us, like the Apostle Paul, would rather have died, than have been deprived of this our glorying in the cross of Christ, And after all, if we object to our condition of living under continual oppression and privation, *we may go out of society,* in search of relief! And if we should take them at their word and go, then our characters would be destroyed. Nothing would save us from reproach, if we cease to be called by this name." Who that is at all acquainted with the Methodist preachers and the late expulsions and subsequent treatment of reformers, can doubt the *truth* of any part of Mr. Walker's statement? Indeed the whole is too true, and accords exactly with what occurred here in Baltimore. And can any man of dignified feelings be surprised or offended at the good old man's soliloquy. He felt himself an American citizen. He felt his right as a member and minister of the church of Christ, and as one of Christ's freemen, to suggest to the members of the legislature;—the "bishops, presiding elders, and travelling preachers," the propriety of making some improvement in their code of laws. Instead of treating him with common decency, they let him know, if he did not cease to trouble them, he might have leave to withdraw. "Oh!" said he to himself, "Oh, the depth of spiritual wickedness, &c!" Oh, the curse of ingratitude, &c. &c. Notwithstanding all his beneficence, care and toil for the promotion of the interests of the church, he must not open his mouth. If he dare to complain, he must withdraw. And because we had the effrontery to publish the old oppressed brother's letter, as if to give a thundering confirmation of the truth of the whole matter, the agents of the Methodist Episcopal Church expelled us, here in Baltimore, and in other places, and to *destroy our characters* tell the world they only exercised *wholesome* discipline, with design to "defecate the church" of the authors and abetters of slander, "of speaking evil of ministers!!"

"I was personally acquainted with Bishop Asbury. I have heard him converse with the Rev. Hope Hull, who was a friend to reform; and I easily collected the information, that our church government was framed chiefly by subjects of Great Britain. Of course, I never wondered much, that such men should have shaped their code, and made their ecclesiastical laws, according to their own model. But when I consider, that nearly all our present preachers are Americans; when I consider how excellent and powerful is the republican spirit, which prevails in these United States, and how equal the civil laws under which we live. When I see how carefully our civil and religious liberties are secured to the people of every possible variety of denominations, I am compelled to ask the question, is not the form of our church government and the manner in which it is administered, an open insult to the constitution of the United States? It surely is, and were it fully investigated and exposed to public view, such a despotic institution would make a bad appearance before the observation of a religious republic." We consider the condemnation of this truly patriotic paper, as one of the strongest evidences of the necessity of reform in the Methodist Episcopal Church. The publication of this plain and true exposition of the principles of Methodist Episcopal Church government constituted an offence of the first magnitude. And who will wonder at this, when it shall be understood, that some of the same men who were engaged in the prosecution, have devoted themselves to the service of the same government, and engaged in conducting a periodical to prove "that in constituting this Methodist Episcopal Church government, for the citizens of our free republican country, the preachers from England had a right, and were solemnly enjoined by the Scriptures, and the actual condition of things, to give all power to an itinerant ministry;—that bishops ought to have absolute power to appoint the preachers to their labours, and to change them every year, or not, as the bishops may please;—that these bishops have also a right to make sub-bishops over the preachers, and remove these sub-bishops when they choose;—that itinerant preachers alone ought to compose Annual Conferences;—that they alone ought to be represented and be the representatives of one another, in composing the General Conference:—and that this general representative body, composed of itinerant preachers only, representing one another after this manner, ought to make and administer the rules of moral discipline, and hold the titles to all church property;—that the itinerants ought to appoint to all offices, or authorize and prescribe the mode of all appointments; select all committees for the trial of alleged immoralities, and preside at the trials. In a word, that itinerant preachers ought to be absolute in power, and the people be in absolute subjection." Surely all wise and candid men will admit, that an honest and blunt man of the days of seventy-six, said truly, that such an institution, set up in these United States, is "an open insult to the constitution."

"The power of the Itinerancy in this part of the country, is already in a trembling condition." This certainly was true as far as Mr. Walker's acquaintance extended: "all that is necessary, is, for the people to be freed from the terrors of the gag-law." This was a very offensive sentence. It calumniates the discipline by calling one of its provisions the gag-law. It is nevertheless true. And the expulsion of reformers in Baltimore, Cincinnati, North Carolina, Tennessee, and Lynchburg, &c. &c. will remain a perpetual memorial of the true spirit and intention of the rule against inveighing, &c.——that it is intended to stop the mouths of all members of the Methodist Episcopal Church, who may chance to feel any objection to the absolute power of the itinerant preachers.

"The people generally, think rightly if they only dare speak out. For my part, I was born in the year 1776, and a warm current of the blood of freemen, runs through my veins. I delight to entertain a just sense of man's equal rights in church and state." This sentence we will presume, led the Agent to insinuate that Mr. Walker wanted good *"manners."* To talk about the blood of freemen and equal rights in church and state! what clownish insolence! "My son-in-law, Ebenezer Hern, is now and for several years has been, a presiding elder in the Mississippi Conference; and my oldest son, R. L. Walker, is a travelling preacher in the same conference. These facts serve with other considerations, as you may suppose, to make me more solicitous for a change in our church government. For I do not wish to see any of my family, have a part in holding the reins of a *government*, which is administered in unrighteousness." That is, in violation of the plain principles of justice and equal rights. The objection is specifically against the government. His son-in-law, a presiding elder, his oldest son a travelling preacher. Both participating in holding the reins of the government, which in his opinion, is administered in unrighteousness, because its powers and privileges are *unequally* distributed;— because the power of the travelling preachers is absolute, and the people and local preachers are made subject to their power; and by the law against inveighing are forbidden to complain.

"There are many things which I would be glad to communicate. But I am aware, that my zeal in so good a cause, after having been so long suppressed, may be in danger of rising too high. I must, therefore, come to a close."

"I send you ten dollars. You will be so good as to send me one copy of your first volume;—if convenient, send it bound. Also, six copies of your second volume. I have procured no subscribers for them, as yet; but I will see to it, that they shall be well circulated." This last clause, we conclude, was particularly offensive. It told of a contribution of ten dollars, towards the extension of Mutual Rights. It promised diligence, in giving a good circulation to the volumes which he had ordered to be forwarded. He was in earnest, and his spirit was too independent, to escape the notice and resentment of the Agent and prosecuting committee. But what is so offensive to these friends of clerical power, our printing committee considered every way commendable in a good citizen;—a proper expression of the feelings of Christ's freemen, who in obedience to their Lord, refuse to call any man master.

"Any use you may think fit to make of these, my remarks, will have my approbation. I try to live before God, independent of the frowns or smiles of men. My name is Joseph Walker, my place of residence is Dallas county, state of Alabama." Too independent to be an acceptable member of the Methodist Episcopal Church!

"I will conclude with saying, that in the whole extent of my reading, in ancient or modern history, I have not met with any notice of a single order of people, except the Roman Catholics and Methodists, whose preachers convene without the consent of the

people, make laws for the government of the people, and afterwards turn round and execute those laws. I have been wide awake
to the cause of reform, fifteen years or more. But the subject not
being popular, I have been compelled to speak of it, only in confidence. Men of the best minds in our itinerancy, are of the same
opinion. How can it be otherwise? But supremacy and self-pre-
servation keep most of them silent. Let us be faithful to God, and
the cause of equal rights in the world, will be secured without firing
a gun or shedding of blood.''

CHAPTER XV.

*The minutes of the Methodist Episcopal Church, prove, that the pre-
paratory measures which served to establish the power of the bishops
and travelling preachers in the United States, were tainted with
acts of usurpation.*

IN Mr. Walker's letter, a reference is made to the origin of the
government of the Methodist Episcopal Church. We will, therefore, present to our readers, a few things not generally known, or
if known, now generally forgotten, which will prove, that Mr. Walker's remarks are true and justifiable. They will serve, moreover,
to prepare for the reading of Luther, in his turn, whose paper is
represented by the writer of the Narrative and Defence, to consist
of the ravings of a madman.

We learn from the general minutes, that the first Methodist Conference in America, was held in Philadelphia, in the year 1773.
The minute says, this Conference consisted of ten travelling
preachers. A careful examination of the subject, has convinced us
that six only, and these all Englishmen, were the acting members
of the Conference; Thomas Rankin, George Shadford, John King,
Francis Asbury, Richard Wright and Robert Williams. Lee's history says, this conference consisted of six or seven travelling
preachers. The apparent uncertainty, about six or seven, grew
out of the fact, that the name of Robert Strawbridge, an Irishman,
and successful local preacher, of Pipe Creek, Frederick county,
Maryland, is placed on the minute, as if one of their body. In the
minute of 1774, his name is not found. In the year 1775, he appears to have been stationed in his own county. After that date,
his name is no more to be seen. With Mr. Lee, therefore, we
doubt the propriety of reckoning more than six. The remaining
three, William Waters, Abraham Whitworth, and Joseph Yearby,
were young men received that year on trial, and admitted into the
connexion the following year. The six English preachers, with
Robert Strawbridge, the local preacher, including the three young
men, make up the account of ten, as constituting the conference.
Before this conference of six, or seven British subjects, three great
questions were proposed and answered;—answered, it would seem,
by the six Englishmen It would have been useless for Mr. Straw-

bridge, to have objected to their views: and it is not probable, that any one of the three young men, just received on trial, was prepared to look forward to ultimate consequences, or to make objections to the resolutions of those, from whom they were ready to receive instruction.

The first question was, "ought not the authority of Mr. Wesley, and that Conference, to extend to the *preachers* and *people* in America, as well as in Great Britain and Ireland.* In couse, the English preachers answered, yes. And the remaining four thought of no other answer.

The societies at that time amounted to eleven hundred and sixty. But they had no part in the transaction. The six, or seven, or ten preachers determined for them and all others who might afterwards be disposed to unite with them, that the whole of them should be subject to "the authority of Mr. Wesley, and that Conference."

The second great question proposed was: "ought not the doctrine and discipline of the Methodists, as contained in the minutes, to be the SOLE RULE OF OUR CONDUCT, who labour in the connexion with Mr. Wesley, in America?" To this question they all answered, "yes." Reformers think, the word of God ought to have been the SOLE RULE OF THEIR CONDUCT, and not "the commandments of men." By the first question and answer, they had "*assumed*" the prerogative, to subject all the American preachers and people, who had associated as Methodists, and all who might be inclined to unite with them, to "the authority of Mr. Wesley, and that conference." By the second question and answer, they "*assumed*" the high prerogative of prescribing to all American Methodist preachers the "SOLE RULE OF THEIR CONDUCT."

The third great question, which was proposed as being inferable from the two preceding, evinces their *despotic* character and design; and reads as follows, viz: "If so, does it not follow, that if any preachers deviate from the minutes, we can have no fellowship with them till they change their conduct?" To this again they answered, "yes." Now to place these proceedings in their proper light, let it be recollected, that the Methodist Societies under the authority of Mr. Wesley, in England, &c. did not constitute a church, separate and distinct from the estsblished church of England, they were generally made up of members of the church. Mr. Wesley, was a regularly ordained presbyter of the national establishment. It was, therefore, a very large "*assumption*" of authority in the case of Mr. Wesley himself, in Great Britain, to require the submission of a people, under the pastoral care of other ministers. But when these six Englishmen crossed the Atlantic, assembled themselves in Philadelphia, and placing themselves under the ban of Mr. Wesley's authority in England, asserted their intention to rule over all the Methodist preachers and societies then existing, or that might ever afterwards have an existence in America;—this was "framing a church government, it was shaping

* This was the first formal assumption of these high prerogatives.

a code and making ecclesiastical laws, according to their own model," sure enough. Our brother Walker's view is correct.

The authority of this first conference, commenced as above stated, and the dictatorial attitude which these six Englishmen then assumed, was so continued and made efficient in the training and management of the young preachers raised up in America, and in the formation and drilling of the societies through their instrumentality, that within the term of little more than twelve years, things were in readiness for the formation of an establishment, by which all power is placed in the hands of the travelling preachers, and through which, they have gained a degree of ascendency over the people, sufficient to induce them, "without any itinerant suggestion or influence whatever," to expel from their communion, faithful servants of Jesus Christ, for having the boldness to call in question, the legitimacy or reasonableness, of a system of church government which still retains the powers so "*assumed.*"

The mighty influence of these English preachers, and their manner of exercising it in view of its ultimate object, will be more satisfactorily understood by attending to an additional sketch or two from the history of those early times.

From the date 1773, the revolutionary troubles interrupted the progress of the work for several years; and we read in the preface of Lee's History of the Methodists, &c. page 5, "there have been, in general, very many errors and imperfections in the minutes of the Annual Conferences." We shall therefore take no notice of them from the year 1773 till 1779. In this year, 1779, two conferences were held. One at Mr. F. White's in Delaware, the place of Mr. Asbury's retirement;—the other at the Broken Back church, in Fluvanna County, Virginia. According to the large minutes which were published in 1813, it appears that on the 28th April, 1779, sixteen preachers attended the conference at Mr. White's; and thirty-two at the Broken-back church, on the 18th of May following;—twenty-two days only, after the conference at Mr. White's. The number of preachers reckoned for the two conferences is forty-nine.* We have been told, however, that the conference at Mr. White's, was attended by Freeborn Garretson, Joseph Hartly, William Glendenning, Daniel Ruff, Joseph Cromwell, Thomas S. Chew, Thomas McClure, Caleb B. Peddicord, John Cooper, William Gill, and William Waters, who, together with Mr. Asbury, made up twelve in number. If this communication was erroneous, and the true number was sixteen, it will not materially change the view which we propose to take of these two conferences.

The conference at Mr. White's, was convoked by Mr. Asbury, and if sixteen in number, it consisted of less than one third of all the preachers who ought to have been present, in order to do the weighty business which was done by them.

One of the questions proposed and answered, was as follows, viz:
"Ought not brother Asbury to act as General Assistant in America?

* There must have been one absent, whose name was afterwards inserted.

Ans. He ought. 1st. On account of his age. 2d. Because originally appointed by Mr. Wesley. 3d. Being joined with Messrs. Rankin and Shadford, by express order from Mr. Wesley."

Another question proposed and answered by the same conference, was as follows, viz:

"How far shall his (brother Asbury's) power extend?

Ans. On hearing every preacher for and against what is in debate; the right of determination shall rest with him, according to the minutes." That is, his power in America, shall be equal to Mr. Wesley's, in England.

The appointment of a General Assistant, and the adoption of a resolution conferring upon him such plenary power, was an act of the greatest importance. At the time when this was done by eleven, or if we admit it, by fifteen, there were thirty-two other preachers, all absent. But the eleven, or say fifteen, "*assumed*" the prerogative to say for the whole forty-nine, that Mr. Asbury "*ought*" to rule over them all, after the manner above stated. To judge rightly of the extent of this "ASSUMPTION" it must be recollected, that the regular conference* was expected to meet in about twenty days, in Fluvanna County, Virginia, where, in fact, thirty-two did meet, and passed resolutions and adopted measures, promising to be more consistent with independent American views of church government. To make this measure plausible, Mr. Asbury held out this conference as one preparatory to the conference at Broken-back church, and appealed to a similar 'instance in Mr. Wesley's administration, in England:—not seeming to have perceived, that his appeal implicated his assumption of a standing parallel with that of Mr. Wesley. And it is the assumption of which we complain.

In 1780, 24th April, a part of the preachers met in Baltimore, it would seem at the instance and under the special influence of Mr. Asbury. Shall not this conference be considered to have been a preparatory one, as well as that which met the year preceding, at Mr. White's? The regularly appointed conference, was expected to meet at the Manakin town, in Virginia, on the 8th day of the next month, two weeks from that time. This second preparatory conference, was composed of about fourteen or fifteen young men, nine of whom attended the conference at Mr. White's. To these nine were added Messrs. John Hagerty, Richard Garretson, Micajah Debruler, Joshua Dudley, Philip Cox, perhaps, and John Tunnell. The large minutes would lead to the supposition that the conference consisted of twenty-four. But there were at least five young men received on trial, which would make the number of acting members to be nineteen. The minute seems to be marked with uncertainty. It is obvious, however, that the whole number of the preachers as stated for the year 1780, is forty-two. In course that nineteen of them met in Baltimore;—we will say nine-

---

*Freeborn Garretson, in his last letter, recognizes this as the regular conference.

17

teen, in order to conform to the minute, and these nineteen *"assumed"* the power to "nullify" the proceedings of the regular conference;—of the thirty-two who met the preceding year, at the Broken-back church, in Virginia.

Three questions were proposed and answered in accomplishing this nullification, viz:

"*Quest.* 20. Does this whole conference," [all these nineteen preachers,] disapprove the step our brethren have taken in Virginia?

Ans. Yes.

Quest. 21. Do we look upon them no longer as Methodists, in connexion with Mr. Wesley and us, till they come back?

Ans. Agreed.

Quest. 26. What must be the conditions of our union with our Virginia brethren?

Ans. To suspend all their administrations for one year, and all meet together in Baltimore."

And was not this, the most absolute dictation? To us it has that appearance.

Mr. Asbury's influence must have been very considerable, or he could not have succeeded in carrying into effect, measures so inconsistent with the rights of the preachers. Under that influence a few of them *"assumed"* the right to act for the whole, in declaring him the general assistant and in awarding to him a degree of power, totally incompatible with American views of government of any kind. Under the same influence, another *preparatory* conference "assumed" the right to nullify the proceedings of a majority, and actually to declare the majority excluded from the fellowship of Mr. Wesley and themselves, unless they would submit to the dictation of the minority, and show their obedience by a strict regard of that dictation for one year, and then present themselves at Baltimore, ready for further orders.

The Virginians, although they had some disposition to assert their rights, were not able to resist the influence of Mr. Asbury, whose authority was already admitted by the preachers to the North. We read in Lee's history, page 73, that Mr. Asbury "met with the preachers in Conference at Baltimore, as has been already mentioned. He then visited his brethren in Virginia, and attended the Conference at the "Manakin town," * * * and "had to exert all his powers, and to use all possible prudence, in order to bring about a settled peace and union among all the preachers." He might have said *in order to bring all the preachers into the* state of submission, proposed and established by the eleven, at Mr. Whites. It would seem, that the Virginians could not perceive at first sight, the weight of the reasons assigned for making Mr. Asbury general assistant, and clothing him with absolute power. The eleven had said he "OUGHT" to act in that capacity, because of his age. And how old was he? In 1771, when he came to America, he was twenty-six. In 1779, he was thirty-four. Virginians could not feel sufficient weight in thirty-four years, to justify the appointment. But the eleven had two additional reasons, or at the least, one additional reason, twice told, so as to seem to have had three. They said he *ought* to act as general assistant, because he "was originally appointed by Mr. Wesley." Virginians knew, that Mr. Wesley, did not originally appoint him to act as general assistant, but as an assistant only, and as inferior to Mr. Rankin. But to guard against this exception, which appears to have been anticipated by them, they state the reason over again, and admit the truth of the case, as if it were a third reason, and say, "he *ought* to act as general assistant, *because he was joined* with Messrs. Rankin and Shadford, by express order from Mr. Wesley." Virginians knew, that Mr. Wesley appointed one general assistant, and no more;—Mr. Rankin; and that Messrs. Shadford and Asbury, were assistants to Mr. Rankin. They were not misinformed in respect to this matter. Mr. Rankin travelled at large himself, and appointed to Messrs. Shadford and Asbury, from year to year, their respective circuits and stations. As to the motive of Mr. Asbury, and those entering into his views, in aiding and sustaining him in these measures, by which he was daily gaining new accessions of power, we shall say nothing to the disparagement of his reputation. Mr. Wesley, had set the dictatorial example. Mr. Asbury, thought it best to follow on in his footsteps;—and, that he considered his course to be *apostolical*, his own journal bears ample testimony. But in view of the principles of government, it is undeniably true, that he had not any other than an *"assumed"* authority, to convoke and organize a conference of twelve of the preachers, when the whole number of them was forty-nine. And when it is considered, that this *"assumption"* was intended to forestall the regular conference, that was so soon to meet at Broken-back church, we are compelled to feel toward the measure, the greater objection. This unauthorized conference, had no right to appoint Mr. Asbury, general assistant. The writer of the minute seems to have been conscious of this, and the questions which were proposed and answered by the Englishmen in 1773, as well as those which were proposed and answered at Mr. Asbury's conference, at Mr. White's, were framed accordingly. When they had respect to the authority of the preachers, in the instance of 1773, and to the appointment of Mr. Asbury, in the instance of the Delaware conference; they were made to read thus. "Ought not the authority, &c?" "Ought not the doctrine," &c. And "ought not brother Asbury, to act as general assistant in America?" As if it were a matter of doubt. And yet their decisions were acts of legislative purpose; and the question, which was intended to mark the extent of Mr. Asbury's power, is obviously imperative; as thus: "How far SHALL his power extend? The conference which was convened at Baltimore, consisting only of a part of the preachers, and obviously intended to forestall the depending conference at the Manakin town, had none other than an *"assumed"* authority to nullify the proceedings of the majority at Broken-back church. Nevertheless, things went on after this manner, and Mr. Asbury continued to gain such an ascendency over the South, as well as over the North, that as early as the year 1782, he had pretty well secured all that was necessary. "The conference in the North, says Mr. Lee "was of the longest standing, composed of the oldest preachers; it was allowed greater privileges than that in the South; especially in making rules and forming regulations for the societies. Accordingly, when any thing was agreed to, in the Virginia conference, and afterwards disapproved of, in the Baltimore conference, it was dropped. But if any rule was fixed on at the Baltimore conference, the preachers in the South were under the necessity of abiding by it." With these things in view, WE cannot be surprized, that the preachers were prepared by the year 1784, for the adoption of an episcopal form of church government so constructed, as to exclude the people and local preachers from their conferences, and secure to themselves and their successors, all power to legislate, and all authority to execute the discipline of their church.

It is due to the lay brethren, to state, that all these matters were conducted by the preachers alone. The people had no part or lot in the matter. And we have no desire to bring them into view at this time. But the bare insinuation, that the powers of the preachers had been "*assumed*," seems to have provoked the Agent to accuse us with having alleged things against the "*fathers*" which we ourselves did not believe to be true;—we have, therefore, given this sketch, in order to shew to him and others, that the kind of "intrepedity" with which he has attempted to impugn us, will not apply quite as well as he expected. Besides, a recollection of these things, as they occurred at the commencement of the establishment of the Methodist Episcopal Church, will be useful, as we pass on through the remainder of our work.

This account of early times, will justify many of the remaining extracts, for the publication of which we were expelled, and which have been thought offensive by some well meaning people, because they were unacquainted with the considerations which induced us to give them admission into the periodical. Such was the case with many in respect to the paper which will be the subject of the following chapter. The writer who took the signature of Luther, resided in North Carolina. His paper was printed in the October number of the Mutual Rights, 1826. Reformers had then been expelled in Tennessee, and in North Carolina, in the neighbourhood of Luther. The preachers in authority there, were inclined to deal very roughly with the friends of reform. The reader, therefore, will expect to meet with warmth;—with signs of excitement, corresponding to such lofty proceedings on the part of the men in power. And it is important that it should be understood, that Reformers, even in the judgment of the prosecutors, had at that time done nothing worse than publish and read the papers on church property by Mr. Snethen, and on the expediency of representation by Nehemiah,* and they were beginning to form Union Societies. And for these, the authority-men began to expel us. This subject will be resumed in another place.

Those two papers are all that were indicated of earlier date than Luthers.

CHAPTER XV.

*Luther on Representation;—the paper which the Agent considered to
contain "denunciations and invectives, which might have been taken
for the ravings of a madman."*

THIS chapter presents not only the parts of Luther, which were
"indicated," but the paper very nearly entire. A few comments are
interspersed to aid the reader in perceiving the grounds of its justification.

"With much interest I have perused several numbers of your
Mutual Rights. The friends of reform speak very intelligibly the
language of the American family. They reiterate the theme of
those who gloriously repose in the stillness of Thermopylæ, Mar-
athon, Chæronæa, Pharsalia, Monmoth. They resist the same principle which slew the Martyrs, slaughtered Poland, assailed America, and was vanquished. "That principle is despotism." And is
not this assertion true? What is despotism? It is *absolute power;
it is authority unlimited and uncontrolled by men, constitution or laws.*
This *principle*, reformers resist. In resisting this principle, they
"speak very intelligibly the language of the American people;—
they resist the same principle, which slew the Martyrs," &c. &c.
Dare any man say, these propositions are not true? And who
could have believed, when this paper was published, that we would
be expelled for publishing such *true* propositions. "At this plain
word some will cry out treason; or what is tantamount, *apostacy.*"
The writer of the Narrative and Defence, says, "we learn from this
writer, that the Methodist Episcopal Church is, such a despotism
as was resisted by the Greeks and Romans, and by the Americans
at Monmoth. This declaration grossly misrepresents Luther. Dr.
Bond identifies the Methodist Episcopal Church with the principle—or at the least, he accuses Luther with saying that the Methodist Episcopal Church "is predicated on *the same principle, &c.*
The candid reader cannot fail to perceive, that Luther intended to
keep up a marked distinction between the Methodist Episcopal
Church, as a body of christians, and the government or church
polity, by which its moral discipline is administered, and its powers and prerogatives dispensed. Nay more, he intended a further
and very satisfactory distinction, between the government in view
of its commendable principles as well as such of its operations as
are proper for the purpose of spreading religion, and this one objectionable principle which very much mars its beauty, in the opinion of all lovers of liberty. He says in effect, that the principle of
despotism, by some means has been permitted to find a place in the
government of the Methodist Episcopal Church, and this despotic principle in the government, the reformers oppose. And is
this slander? Is this an offence for which it was right to excommunicate reformers out of the church? Let Luther, now speak for
himself. "Oh Messrs. Editors! how profoundly I regret, that truth
will apply this hateful characteristic to any part of Methodistical

polity, the searcher of hearts alone can tell." Can any thing be more clear, than that he intends to refer the imputation, specifically and exclusively to the *"polity"* of the church? But Dr. Bond tells the people, who "never have read the Mutual Rights at all," that the imputation is charged upon the church. "For sixteen years have the sympathies of my heart, and the energies of my mind been deeply interested in behalf of our Zion. During that time, I have lingered, with fond solicitude about the outer courts, (not having shared in her councils, though of her priesthood;) I have willingly hewn her wood and drawn her water; all the while hoping, that her leading chieftains would roll away this reproach from her *honour*, banish this cloud from her *beauty*, purge this poison from her vitals, * * * * and enable her to walk forth in all her *native beauty*, fair as the moon, clear as the sun, and terrible as an army with banners; the praise of the whole earth." Very differently from the unjust distortions of doctor Bond, the printing committee learned from the foregoing clause, that in Luther's opinion, the Methodist Episcopal Church had honour and native beauty sufficient to make her the praise of the whole earth. But that her honour was sullied and her beauty defaced, by having admitted the principle of despotism into her polity. And was it the duty of the printing committee to consider this to be vehement railing?" Until the last General Conference, I viewed this despotic trait in her polity, as the offspring of casualties; a sort of wild exotic, which by some mishap had sprung up in the *garden of the Lord:* a wandering demon, which had insinuated himself into our *paradise*, unobserved; and like Milton's toad at the ear of Eve, infused into the genius of our church, portentous dreams and dreary visions.* I looked to that General Conference, for an achievement worthy of primitive christianity and American Methodists. My fond imagination displayed to my view, an august assembly of holy men, hurling this monster (despotism) from the heights of their Salem, a spectacle to an admiring nation. But oh! cruel disappointment! Methodism has lost one of her richest laurels. Never did an epoch of her history, give to her rulers, so distinguished an opportunity of shedding an immortal lustre upon *her own* name and *their own* memories. But that circular, the ominous offspring of her labour, too barren to merit citicism, serves only to mortify the best friends of Methodism, and legalize oppression." Here the extract takes a leap over a page and a half of matter, which did not suit the purpose of the agent. We will supply it, as furnishing the most satisfactory explanation of the justifiableness of the paper. "It, (the circular of the General Conference,) finds a suitable helpmate, a sort of counter part, in the barren speculations of doctor Armistead, with this difference;—in the former, we have a skeleton or a pile of bones in plain attire; in the latter, we have the same thing in meretricious ornaments. But neither

---

*For a more perfect understanding of all these figures, and of the previous imputation of despotism, we refer the reader to his recollections of 1773, and 1779, &c. &c.

the simplicities of the one, nor the frivolities of the other, I trust, will ever reconcile any well informed American, to that monster, (despotism) which for so many ages, has fattened the fowls of the air with the flesh of fallen mortals, and drenched the earth with their blood. Think not Messrs. Editors, *that I identify the men with the principle, or the* CHURCH *with* either, (the principle or the men.) For the men, I have a heart full of brotherly charities;—for the principle, a lash of scorpions;—for the CHURCH, my best affections. By the church, I mean Christ's Eccleisa, or *called out* of which, HE is the only HEAD; and to which bishops, elders, deacons and private members, bear subordinate relations, for the work of the ministry, for the perfecting of the saints, for the edifying of the body of Christ. I admit that a church is a visible Theocracy, and in this particular, it differs from all other associated communities;—that its divine founder and supreme head, holds in his own hand, all that is necessary to its real being;—such as the principle of life, by which it is sustained;—the principle of love, by which it is united;—the power by which it is defended;—and the sanctity by which it is made worthy of himself. Bishops or elders, and deacons, are properly servants (not lords) of this body, more or less obligated, in proportion to the qualifications conferred on them, by the Supreme Head. On each of those, power is conferred for the duties required. This, I presume, is pleasant doctrine; be it so. The duty required of every christian minister is, to help his fellow men to Heaven; and his obligations are in proportion to his ability. The most effectual help in this great matter is, to use those efforts which will most effectually produce heavenly mindedness, purity of heart, and a likeness to God, in others. And among the various qualifications of a christian minister, no one will be found more potent for this purpose, than a luminous exemplification in his own life, of the heavenly simplicity he inculcates on others; while but few things can more effectually thwart his usefulness, than an arbitrary dictatorial manner, or domineering attitude towards others. There is a nameless something in our nature, depraved as it is, which feels the potent allurement of heavenly suavity and christian condescention; and in the same proportion, *that something*, feels an unconquerable repugnance to all that is dictatorial and lording. That domination which is odious and injurious in one man, is more so in a multitude;—unless we admit that numbers sanctify enormities. The church is the family of Christ; the more freely the members of this spiritual household commingle in domestic consultations and enterprizes, the more peaceably, harmoniously and safely, will they glide along the stream of time to endless rest.

Invidious distinctions are especially dangerous to christian communities, because self denial, heavenly simplicity and brotherly equality, are prominent features of the christian religion; and the opposites of these, wherever they occur, destroy christian confidence and sever the bonds of union and love." Here we pause to ask what part of this paper so far as we have gone over it, as an editorial committee, we could have found cause to reject. Our periodical was open for the investigation of church polity, and particularly for the admission of suitable essays in favour of mutual rights and a lay-delegation to the General Conference of the Methodist Episcopal Church. And if we were not at liberty to admit such a paper as this one by Luther, it is obvious we were not at liberty to investigate the subject at all. And, by the by, it was the object of the prosecutions, to prevent the further publication of papers like this. If permitted, they would inevitably have been fatal to clerical ambition.

"Upon what principle the General Conference, the great legislative council of our church, pretend to imagine, that the final exclusion of a vast majority of the ministry, and all the laity from their deliberations, can subserve the cause of godliness in the United States, I cannot conjecture. The General Conference is composed of men, selected from the itinerancy, headed by an episcopacy for life. They are only accountable for their acts, to the authority which clothed them with representative power, that is the itinerancy: if their legislative acts had an exclusive reference to the itinerants, their only constituents, their authority would claim the sanctions of liberality and justice. But this is not the case, and when those representatives of the itinerants, who alone elect them, presume to legislate for all the locality and laity of the Methodist Church, what assumption can be more unwarrantable, what system more oppressive? In case of grievance, where shall the locality and laity look for redress? They have no check upon their law-givers. The members of the General Conference are all pledged to their itinerant brethren, who send them there; and the itinerancy in mass, are all indirectly pledged to the episcopacy: hence the episcopacy is frequently strengthened and the itinerancy is always guarded; but the rights of the laity and locality are trampled upon." This is TRUE. Witness the report of the General Conference, 1824, which in view of a claim to the rights of the laity and locality says, *"pardon us if we know no such Rights."* "The truth is, the laity and locality have no representation on that floor (the General Conference) no advocates to plead their cause. THESE REMARKS HAVE NO REFERENCE TO THE MORAL CHARACTER OF THE GENERAL CONFERENCE; for, however holy that body may be, it is no impeachment of thir goodness to suppose, that men so entirely divested of the cares of life, as they are, cannot be qualified to legislate usefully, for those who are variously related to civil and religious society, as the locality and laity are. To legislate usefully for others, we must not only see, but feel; we must not only know, what will be fit, but what will be pleasant or painful, pernicious or profitable. But all this, by some will be thought irrelevant. We disclaim, say they, any interference with your civil rights, and our clerical authority we derive from God. * * * But Messrs. Editors, who shall draw the discriminating line between civil and religious rights; and after it is drawn, what layman of an enlightened mind and heavenly soul, will suffer any band of legislative volunteers, to regulate the policy of his eternal state, at their own discretion, while he stands ready to be immolated on the altar of freedom, rather than suffer an officious despot to point his course through this transient vale of tears? Oh! is the religion of Jesus, with all its enrapturing joys; the soul with all its indescribable powers; heaven with all its inconceivable glories; and hell with all its unutterable horrors; are these matters so trivial, that we leave them to the winds;—to the speculations of self-created conclaves, while we guard the sanctuary of our civil rights, so inviolably? Illustrious prophets and martyrs, had you been thus pliant, instead of sailing through the bloody storms of time to endless rest, you had smoothly glided down to hell; instead of leaving your track to glory a living galaxy of heavenly light, the heavy clouds of the second death, would now fling their thunders upon your weather beaten spirits; instead of handing down to posterity the word of life, pure and undefiled, you had bequeathed to the world, a darkness more dreary than that which fell on ancient Egypt. But, ye reverend spirits of Europe and Asia, you have fought the good fight, and laid hold upon eternal life. It is for us, American Methodists, to prostrate ourselves at the foot of a spiritual aristocracy, and say, let us eat our own bread, and wear our own apparel; but let us be called by your name. It is for us to cower at the foot of that *principle* in ecclesiastics, which was chastised by our our forefathers upon the agents of a civil despot. It is for us Methodists, to take the humiliating responsibility, of shamelessly encouraging a spiritual domination, in the face of free Americans! It is for us, the emancipated sons of conquering chieftains, to rivet those chains upon our descendants, which were torn from our hands;—if we only give them the name of religion. Names, Messrs. Editors, are very influential with many; and but for the name, this despotic trait in our church polity, had long since waked up the solicitude of every friend of Methodism in the United States. It is called "MINISTERIAL AUTHORITY." "The RIGHT of the ITINERANCY," &c. A despotism is not virtually changed, in my estimation, because it falls into the hands of ecclesiastics; neither will the goodness of the ecclesiastics change its nature. This may restrain its violence. Despotism in the hands of a good man, is like a sword in the hands of a son of peace: while it rests there, it is not felt, but when he hands it over to a warlike successor, it wastes the earth. The irresponsible authority of the General Conference, to say the least of it, is a dangerous precedent under a free government. It may be equally injurious to the morals of those who hold it, as to the rights of those who are to suffer by its exercise. The moderation of former conferences, is no security against the abuses of those to come. The bishops of Rome were anciently moderate, good men; in succeeding ages, they became the pests of the earth, and the scourges of mankind. The plea of goodness in behalf of the itinerants, is one of the most powerful arguments used in favour of their authority. With all the goodness of the itinerants, to which I would gladly subscribe, abuses already exist, which loudly call for a check or balance, from some other department of the church. * * * * Power to *serve* the church, and power

18

to *command* it, are different things. The delegates of the church, would be really her servants, because she could control them. The delegates of the itinerancy may be her lords, because in matters of legislation, under the present state of things, they may bid her defiance.

What extent of power is absolutely necessary to the ambassador of Christ? As the legate of heaven, he can only make known to men, the terms of reconciliation with their God, and urge motives to induce a compliance. As the servant of the church, he should preach the word, administer the sacraments, receive the worthy to her communion, pronounce her sentence on the refractory, and in all things, present in his own life, a sample of piety to his flock; *and he who craves more power than this, is unworthy of any in the church of Christ.* In all matters of vital importance, the scriptures of truth are sufficiently explicit, and beyond them in such matters, no one should dare presume to go. In business of mere economy, and such we consider the business of the General Conference, it certainly would be for the honour and interest of the church, to have all her departments represented upon a fair ratio. Then men of the 'same grade would be eligible to the same rights, and the joint deliberations of all the departments, would abundantly strengthen the bonds of union in the church." What candid man will say that Luther's paper ought to have been rejected on account of any thing it contains to the end of the above quotation? The garbled fragments extracted by the agent, needed only to be replaced in their proper connexions, to render them perfectly inoffensive to any, but those who were morbidly sensative on the subject of the Methodist Episcopal Church government, and even to those we cannot see why they were offensive, except only, that the *truths* they contain, were improperly disagreeable.

"But Messrs. Editors, valuable as your paper is, the friends of reform must appeal to the public through other mediums, in union with that. You encounter a well organized, artful, enterprizing opposition, which spreads through almost every city, village and neighbourhood, from Maine to Georgia." That this statement is true, let the Narrative and Defence and this Review be two witnesses. "Their first effort is to conceal to the utmost, the disquietudes and grievances which exist in our church, and to lull a spirit of inquiry to rest." Every careful observer of their conduct, knows this likewise to be true. "Where this is impracticable, they arraign the motives of the reformers with uncharitable, with uncivil severity." Considering that they affect to have expelled the reformers here and elsewhere, for evil speaking, this last sentence is a truth calculated to excite astonishment. "Your own paper, if I have not been sadly misinformed, having been branded as a sort of libel upon the church, published by deperate designers, has been kept out of the hands of valuable men to whom it was addressed, and left to linger in post offices. Oh! how I regret to know the men, and the character they sustain in society, who are employed in this midnight stabbing." This figure is strong, but its meaning is defined, and its application specified. We looked at it with attention before it was published. We thought it severe, but knew it was true. In too many instances our paper was "left to linger in post offices," and one post master told us, he had burned or otherwise destroyed some of our papers, which had to pass through his hands, alleging as his apology, that he did not wish to see the peace of the church disturbed, by the introduction of the Mutual Rights into that neighbourhood. This was the kind of secret operations, which Luther intended to rebuke, and which the committee, for the reasons above stated, thought it right to permit him to rebuke in the figurative language of *midnight stabbing*." "Could I believe in transmigration, I might imagine that some of the Jesuits expelled from Europe, had taken up their residence in the bodies of some I . . . . in the United States." Dr. Bond spells out the I . . . . and nine points, and makes them read *Itinerants*. But as the abuse refers to wilful delays or other misconduct in post offices, &c. it is as sensibly spelled out, *interested*. It is a point of no importance now, who did it; and it is obvious, that the post master to whom we allude above, and who was once an itinerant, thought he had a sufficient interest in the issue of the transaction, to practice this malfeasance of office, that his imaginary good might come of it to the church. And Luther had a special reference to the imputation commonly fixed upon the Jesuits, that *"the end sanctifies the means."* "Parsimony is a strong hold to which very successful appeals are made. *The local preachers want salaries, city settlements, &c. &c."* This imputation has been charged upon the reforming local preachers in every direction. "And the great men (in common style) want to send the little men home, who serve cheaply, &c. To the last of these charges, I plead guilty with all my heart; for I have long believed, that if the church could exercise the right of suffrage, she would sift the talents of her ministry, and secure the best for her service. But the fallacy of the other subterfuges of the anti-reformers bears its own characteristic. The majority of suffrages will always be among the laity, they will therefore have it in their power to check abuses, and under a well balanced form of government, those presumers, who grasp so greedily after power would sink into merited contempt, while modest worth would be duly promoted. I say you must appeal to the public through other mediums. You have past the Rubicon; there is no returning without a sacrifice of principle, without abandoning your church to her degraded destiny. If you suffer another General Conference to legislate for you, I am ready to say, prepare for tame submission or banishment." The committee considered this prediction rather extravagant, but the event has confirmed the accuracy of the calculation. We were expelled before the General Conference met. "Your missionaries should now be on the high ways of the nation, and in the pulpits of your churches; and the friends of reform should send their private communications every where. You have the prejudices of many years arrayed against you, and that still inglorious repose, which undisturbed power artfully administered, gives, refuses to part with its slumbers. In a word, you are

about a great work, and to accomplish it successfully, requires all
the wisdom and enterprise of christians, and a permanent reliance
upon God. * * * *

If I understand the general object of the reformers, it is, to dif-
fuse through your *paper*, the light and warmth of liberal principles
throughout the Methodist church, in America, so luminously and
feelingly, that the anti-reformers illumined by their rays and cheer-
ed with their beams, will be constrained to say to their reforming
brethren; come into our sanctuary, ye blessed of the Lord. Your
motives and spirit are such as good men must admire, and I doubt
not but Heaven approves. But the signs of the times too clearly
evince *their* utter insufficiency to accomplish the objects of reform.
As well may you expect the pacific spirit of friends, to be a barrier
to the strife of nations, as that the mild spirit and conclusive reasonings of the Mutual Rights alone, shall reform your church.
When the order of nature is reversed, and the streams "which rush
to the Atlantic, shall smoothly glide to the submit of the Allegha-
nies, then expect such an effect, from such a cause. In a word,
when men become what they should be, your present plans will be
all sufficient to accomplish your laudable object. I repeat, the
signs of the times are against you. Your paper which seems to be
the only engine of the reformers, is branded with heresy, so far as
the laws of the country will allow;—that travelling preacher, who
ventures to peruse it, risks his reputation, and if he patronize it, in
all probability, his office." How exactly this opinion was soon
verified by the two cases of Messrs. Dorsey and Poole. "The better half of your members have never heard of it, and many of
those who have, are detered from its perusal, from the horrid character given it by those whose itinerant career gives them every
possible opportunity to defame it and its authors." That they
availed themselves of these ample opportunities, is sufficiently
evinced by the facts which have made this review necessary. "Who
among the opposing host, deigns to read your publications, much
less to investigate the points of difference? * * * What conciliatory advances have the memorials and remonstrances of the last
twelve years procured? That healing breviat, that knell of charity,
the General Conference circular, is the bonus of so many prayers
and tears! Oh! Messrs. Editors, is your Mutual Rights a sufficient barrier to restrain the proud waves of this mighty ocean?
Never did Leo X. treat Luther, with such utter contempt, as you
receive at the hands of your anti-reforming brethren; and I doubt
whether the history of the christian church, can furnish a parallel.
If the reformers feel the subject at heart, why not talk about it? If
it is of immense importance, why not publish it on the house top?
But, if it be a bad cause, why not abandon it! Those temporizing
measures serve to irritate without healing; to fatigue the church
without giving her rest. I am neither a prophet nor the son of a
prophet, and I hope, I may not be deemed a visionary when I tell
you, that the reformers must do more than write for those who will not
deign to read, or they never will do much for the benefit of their
suffering church. But what is to be done? This I confess brings

my mind to a sort of *ne plus ultra*. I have no disposition, could I do it at a word, to decamp, as one said, and set up for ourselves, and thereby add another petty sect to the numbers which already disturb the christian church and distract society. Nor am I willing to continue to mourn and pipe for those who will neither lament nor dance, until another General Conference may strip me of my little Osier shield, and compel me by another legislative colossus to cringe or fly. In all systems, animate and inanimate, with which we are acquainted, there must be a centre of union for the associated parts. That centre is now imperiously necessary, for the harmony and energy of the republican Methodist reformers. There should be some definite characteristic by which the monarchy and anti-monarchy men of our church should be identified;—should be compelled to feel their responsibility to civil and religious society, and to account for it. Here I entreat the aid of my brethren, and here I naturally look round the United States for a Moses, who has goodness, wisdom and firmness, to erect a standard, around which, the dispersed reformers may gather, and under which, their emancipated church shall march up to freedom, prosperity and happiness? Oh! under such a state of things, my enraptured mind beholds her bright spires rise above the blue waves of time, and her massy battlements lose themselves in the mists of far distant ages, crowned with rejoicing millions. A reform in this way, will for a moment resemble an imperium in imperio, but the strife will be of short duration. The claims of the respective parties being once clearly understood, the spirit of freedom would *leaven the whole lump*, and the genius of liberty would sit enthroned, in the bosom of every American Methodist. Who could dare deny the right of suffrage? Who would claim the odium of blindly submitting to an ecclesiastical domination? I for one say, form associations, send out missionaries; you will thereby inform the ignorant, strengthen the week, give energy to the labours of the resolute, retain many who will shortly seek repose in other churches, and rescue your own church from disunion, anarchy and perhaps ruin. Speedily organize your plans with wisdom and goodness, and carry them into operation with all the violence of ingenuity and love; and those who are now securely enthroned on the submit of the cloudy Olympus of power, when they shall feel the mount quake and tremble beneath them, will become solicitous to know what is the matter, and not before. Pelopides, the famous Theban General, when met in a defile by a powerful band of Lacædemonians, and informed by an officer of the advance, "we are betrayed into the hands of the enemy," replied why not say, *they* are betrayed into *our* hands?—and so the event in part proved. The Reformers and anti-reformers must try the strength of their respective claims. Oh! that the issue may be for the furtherance of love, the prosperity of the church, and the glory of God?"

Instead of presenting this paper, as having been published at a time when there were so many causes of excitement, and when there was an expectation that the writer would be called on, to answer for his attachment to the good work of reform;—instead of presenting the paper in its true spirit and design, doctor Bond collected out of it a garble of short sentences and disjointed words, and exhibited it as if an honest epitome of the essay; telling the community, that Luther called the Methodist Episcopal Church a despotism,—predicated on the same principles which slaughtered Poland, and slew the Martyrs. That he had represented the church to be an assumption;—an usurpation;—an unwarrantable and oppressive assumption;—that he had said the rights of the laity and locality are trampled upon;—that the conferences are self-created conclaves;—that the members of that church, prostrate themselves at the feet of a spiritual Aristocracy. Spiritual domination, &c. &c. Luther habitually deals extensively in metaphorical language. No sensible reader can fail to discover this on perusing his paper. Persons uninformed of this fact or unacquainted with the circumstances which attended the establishment of the Methodist Episcopal Church in her mighty power, could readily be induced to think, the language of the extracts too strong and perhaps quite reprehensible. But the printing committee saw the subject in its proper light, and felt confident, that Luther's paper would be read with interest, and be particularly useful at that time of threatened "defecation" of the church both south and west. As to the imputation of a tyrannical trampling upon the rights of the laity, the locality, and of the *itinerant ministry,* when it pleased the men in power to think it expedient or necessary to do so, we had been compelled to view the subject, very nearly in the light in which it is exhibited in the Methodist Correspondent, page 132. It appears, that old side men have accused some of the ministers who have left their fellowship and come to us, of retaining the old leaven. The paper will make the following short chapter.

CHAPTER XVI.

Tyranny appears to be inevitable in the administration of the Methodist Episcopal Church.

MR. EDITOR,—It is frequently said of Reformers, they were arbitrary, and tyrants, in the administration of discipline, in the Methodist E. Church. This is held up as an argument, against their being what they profess; and the people are to view them as tyrants, deceivers and false pretenders. Therefore, the statement merits attention: though it can have no application, but to those, who have been in the itinerancy of the Methodist E. Church.

We acknowledge that this may have been the fact, at least in some instances: our astonishment is not, that this was the fact, but that under the circumstances in which they stood, the voice of reason and revelation, should have brought them to yield and surrender participation and emoluments in the citadel of POWER, and become the advocates of religious liberty. While the sacrifice they have made, is proof of the soundness of their reformation; it must be evident, the source from which a man obtains official power, the principle on which he is held accountable for exercising it, and the tribunal to which he is amenable for official action, together with the manner in which he is prepared for office, and the mode of inducting him into it; will each and all have great influence on his official character and operations. And if it shall be evident on examination, that those features in the Episcopal itinerant system, necessarily tend to make men arbitrary and tyrannical, it will follow, that the *system* is to blame, and not the men; and should be abandoned as ruinous in its tendency to civil and religious liberty.

The priest, pope, or bishop who claims a divine right to his official power, &c. independent of the people, will be regardless of their rights, interest, and will; only so far as suits his will, power and pretensions. He places every thing at the control of his whims, notions, and WILL, which he holds to be superior wisdom, holiness and inspiration. He says, he is only accountable to God in his official character and administration. He brings himself to believe, the Almighty pledged to sustain him, and that no weapon formed against him shall prosper; however, virtuously or righteously raised.—The love of power charms him till it becomes his idol. His confidence in power, renders him imperious. He asks, who is this 'Moses;' who is this 'Luther;' *who asks my negative, &c.* It also renders him blind to danger, till it overtakes him; and then his proud heart will not yield. This delirium is desparately fatal, when it becomes prevalent, in a body of men professing to be ministers of Christ. Such maniacs, however, are not irresponsible to the public and the Great Head of the church, for their pretensions, assumptions, actions, and the fatal effects thereof. The eighth section, Chapter 1, of Methodist Episcopal Church discipline, of the method of receiving *travelling* preachers, and of their duty, presents the following facts, viz. 1st. The discipline is specially called to view, seven or eight times. 2d. Conscience is called on twice, to enforce obededience to it. 3d. Each candidate must give up his own will, and submit entirely to the will of others. 4th. He receives two disciplines; the first, the only book given to him, when he is to call sinners to repentance, make full proof of his ministry, and be careful to weigh what the discipline contains. The second;—he is freely to consent to, and earnestly endeavour to walk by; and these are the terms on which others shall rejoice to acknowledge him as a fellow labourer. 5th. All this is to be regarded by every preacher in charge from the time he is admitted to join the itinerancy. And in section 12, chapter 1, as a special thing to fit him for his *charge;* he is to understand, and love discipline, particularly ours, (that is episcopal.) Not a word, so far, about his weighing, keeping for conscience sake, understanding, desiring to walk by, or loving the bible.—All this training to fit each candidate for office, *when he may be entrusted with the exercise of power.* In ordination this is still more imposingly forced on his understanding and conscience;—and unless he pledges himself, he will not be ordained. All this not to make a better man or minister; but to shackle his mind, and secure submission to Episcopal power. Now he must *follow with* a glad mind, and will *their Godly* admonitions, *and submit* to their *Godly judgments?* His failure, or refusal, in course is construed into rebellion on his part, and an impeachment of their godliness and judgment. Hence, he is deemed a rebel, and an enemy. To get on with all this, we are obliged to think he must be fully prepared to believe the discipline, and the Episcopal power, with all its auxiliaries to be scriptural, apostolic and right; and therefore, feel himself, in understanding and conscience bound, to submit to such authorities.

Take two elders; all they hold as ministers, or by scriptural ordination must be equal. But in the Methodist Episcopal Church all official authority, to elders and deacons, in administration is by the *bishop's word.* Therefore, local deacons and elders, have no lot or part in the matter. The bishop in placing two elders on a circuit, gives the power to which he pleases. He may place the lad of eighteen or twenty, or comparatively young, over the minister of gray hairs, long experience, good talents and established reputation.

The youngster, (perhaps a probationer only,) wields this power because the bishop says so; while the venerable, talented minister, *bows to the episcopacy,* in the boy.——This is ruinous to one, and degrading to the other.

Look at presiding elders; see how youth reigns over those who are *elders indeed.* The time was, when the episcopacy, thought gray hairs necessary, before a man was raised to be presiding elder. But now, the young men who rally round the episcopal chair, with the greatest zeal for high episcopal prerogative, are the stuff of which to make presiding elders; that they may be brought up to the episcopal hand. The episcopacy having breathed official life into them, and made them in their own likeness, have a right, to take the life they gave, when they please. Thus situated, the presiding elder goes by the episcopal will, in all his acts. Therefore cannot see, or feel the rights, interests, or will of preachers, or people, only as he views them connected with, and subservient to, the interest of the office of which he is the deputy.

The man, old or young, put in charge of a circuit, is placed at the will and direction of the presiding elder, and still liable to the primary episcopacy.

We see then, that the *tuition, induction* into itinerancy, and the several gradations and ordinations, as performed and in such cases made and provided, are all calculated to make men tyrants; especially in the administration of a system of such construction. Each one, in the several grades of advancement, having believed and felt himself in conscience bound, to submit to such *authority* and *government,* he now thinks all others equally bound to submit. Hence he is prepared to wield the episcopal sceptre, as far as it is committed to him;——to wield it 'in all good conscience' as did 'SAUL' of Tarsus to wield the power committed to him by the Jewish High Priest. And equally, as intelligently: that is, "to do it ignorantly." It is evident, the only way a man thus situated can be saved, or redeemed from being a tyrant, is to have the light of history, reason, truth and scripture, to irradiate his mind, show him the error with which he is surrounded, and bring him to a sense of the duplicity that has been practised on him; and discover to his mind the various forms of church polity the world has witnessed;—the dire effects of corrupt systems, priests, and power set forth in the history of the church. Then if a love of power, or some of its auxiliaries has not gained the ascendency in his heart; he trembles at the ruin which stares him in the face, and he honestly inquires, *"What wilt thou have me to do?"* Otherwise he must recede from the *light*, and convinced of error, persist in his course, and be the willing vassal of priestly power, which neither reason, the history of the church, scripture, nor his own conscience can approve.

ANTI-EPISCOPAL.

CHAPTER XVII.

Persecutions of reformers for joining Union Societies, most inconsistent with propriety or benevolence. The real design of those Societies.

THAT the agent and prosecutors were altogether reckless of the cause or fate of reformers; that they had no thought of justice, but with undeviating purpose laboured to make an impression on the Methodist public, favourable to their course of cruel and unprincipled persecution, will be more clearly seen by turning attention to the following remarks, introductory to this paper. The travelling preachers in different places, had expelled reformers for having joined Union Societies a considerable length of time before the commencement of similar proceedings in Baltimore. In Bedford county, Tennessee, the friends of reform had a meeting in February, 1825, preparatory to the formation of a Union Society.—Nothing more was done, than to subscribe a paper and appoint a committee to prepare a constitution to be presented at a meeting in the month of May, following.

In April, Mr. James Gwinn, their presiding elder, for this offence, proceeded at a quarterly meeting to read out the names of fourteen members, who lived in different circuits. They may say in truth, that these brethren were not expelled for being members of the Union Society; it was not yet formed;—but they were willing to be members, and were making preparation to organize, and for that willingness, in the opinion of Mr. James Gwinn, they merited expulsion.

In September, 1826, we were informed of the expulsion of brethren in North Carolina, for being members of the Granville Union Society. A few days after learning that such a society had been organized, Benton Field sent to each of the several individuals, a letter of reproof, "for their UNSCRIPTURAL and peace destroying conduct,"—and said he, "if you see proper to yield to re-

19

proof, so far as to engage in future to leave off such pernicious conduct, I shall rejoice to hear the same; but if you refuse, you will thereby bring me under the necessity of calling you to account before the church, to answer for your conduct."

The brethren felt no obligation to obey such a tyrannical mandate; and according to Mr. Field's threat, they were cited to trial, having been charged with "uniting to sow dissentions, by inveighing against the discipline of the Methodist Episcopal Church." Mr. Field endeavoured to substantiate the charge; but failing, he put the question in the following words. "All you who think their conduct will have a bad effect, will signify it by rising up." A majority arose—and the brethren were expelled. A short time afterwards, the preacher in charge of the Tar River circuit, had three or four brethren expelled, for joining the Union Society.—— These acts of violence were practised first in February, 1825, in Tennessee; and before October, 1826, in North Carolina. For having been accessary to the formation of a Union Society in the former, and for having joined such societies in the latter, reformers were expelled. The reader is requested to take particular notice of these facts, of the dates of their occurrence, and of the nature of the offence with which they were charged by the preacher, viz: *"uniting to sow dissentions, by inveighing against the discipline of the Methodist Episcopal Church."*——When our prosecutors were gathering extracts, to justify the expulsion of reformers for being members of Union Societies, they ought to have selected some such as the following, which is printed in the Mutual Rights for February, 1826, vol. II. with the signature of Paul. It reports the real design for which Union Societies were formed.

"It is a just remark, that without system, nothing of importance can be effected. System is as essential to all the studies and operations of men, as light is to their labours. It matters not how complex the subject, if it be reduced to system, order immediately arises out of confusion, light beams through the darkness, and the whole becomes intelligible to the mind at a glance. Nor is it of material consequence how difficult the enterprize, if those who engage in it, reduce their operations to system, and proceed on a wisely organized plan. If their object be lawful and their cause righteous, they must succeed in the very nature of things. Reflecting on the cause of reform in the Methodist Episcopal Church, we have been highly gratified, to witness the judicious and systematical plan of operations adopted by the reformers:—Their grand object appears to be, the introduction of a well balanced form of government into their church. This is certainly an object worthy of the men who have engaged in its pursuit; and if effected, will reflect honour upon their memories, and confer a blessing on the church, the benefits of which, will be felt to the end of time. The means they are using to effect this desirable end, are at once simple and efficient.

"The first means employed by them, is the press with its powerful energies. This is an engine, which, when guided by the unerring light of truth, is mighty in pulling down the strong holds of error, and in establishing the civil and religious liberties of man, on a basis not easily to be shaken. It was with this engine, guided by the light of reason and revelation, that Luther made the papal power, which had subjugated all Europe to its domain, tremble to its centre; and gave priestly domination a defeat, from which it can never recover. And it is by this engine, at no distant day, that every species of usurpation and superstition is destined to be overthrown, to rise no more forever.

"Another means employed by the reformers to effect their purpose, is, that of associating in companies, called "Union Societies." These are composed of pious, decided reformers; are regularly organized, and correspond with each other on all subjects of importance to the cause of reform. The advantages attendant on these associations, are numerous.

"1. They are productive of much good to all the members of each society, respectively. They introduce the reformers of several states and counties to a personal acquaintance with each other, and to a knowledge of their respective views and wishes; and mutually edify and strengthen all the members of the association. In the discussion of topics, the warmth of one member is corrected by the cool deliberation of another. And the fears and despondency of one man are removed by the encouraging arguments and stimulating hopes of his brother. While the information received from all quarters, gives to every member a comprehensive view of the progress of reforming principles in the church.

"2. Union Societies are mutually beneficial to each other. By corresponding with each other, they keep all the reformers advised of every important transaction within the bounds of their respective districts. No reformer can be *persecuted*, even in a corner, without its being speedily known to all the reformers in the United States. They furnish a mutual support; for if the members of one Union Society are persecuted or maltreated, they make common cause with the sufferers, and use their utmost effort to obtain for them redress of grievances.*

"3. They are beneficial to the church. They prevent many persons from withdrawing, who otherwise, are fully prepared to leave her communion; and some who had actually departed, have been induced to return, and are now united with their brethren in the good cause of reform.

"4. Union Societies will greatly promote the cause of reform, by concentrating the views of the whole; and presenting to the General Conference, petitions from all parts of the United States, which shall speak the same language and breathe the same spirit. This last particular is a very important one; the want of it was severely felt at the last General Conference; for there was a great want of uniformity in the multitude of petitions presented to that body.

"It has been said, by certain persons, that "Union Societies favour separations." Those brethren will permit us to say, that we know

*This was one of the chief reasons wherefore the men in power desired their destruction.

the contrary to be the fact, and that had it not been for the institution of Union Societies, there would have been, long ere this, separations in more places than one. It has been said a by travelling preacher, in the north, who opposes the formation of Union Societies, that, "when the reformers are all organized, have ascertained their strength, and petitioned the General Conference for a redress of their grievances, and the General Conference refuse to listen to them, they will *naturally* break off, and form themselves into a separate church."

"Now we would ask, does this good brother suppose, that the *mere circumstance* of the reformers being organized into Union Societies, will, in the event of the General Conference refusing to listen to them, necessarily induce them "to break off, and form themselves into a separate church?" Or does he mean to say, if they shall not be organized, they will have neither sense nor spirit enough to come to an understanding among themselves on the question "of breaking off," if breaking off be absolutely necessary? If the former be his meaning, we are inclined to think, it will be neither *naturally* nor *necessarily* the case. What will prevent the Union Societies from remaining within the pale of the Methodist Episcopal Church? Might they not still cleave to her with as much tenacity as they do now? We admit, that a refusal on the part of the General Conference, to listen to the reasonable requests of the reformers, would be a serious trial to all of them and would produce some important additions to the plan of operations; but it by no means follows, that, therefore, they will *naturally* or *necessarily* leave the church, and organize a new one.

"If the latter be his meaning, we will take the liberty to say, he is much mistaken; for if there were no Union Societies in the United States, and it were made manifest, that the proper time was come to raise up a new church, there would neither be men nor means wanting to effect the object.

"But why all these foreboding fears of separation? And why make this a ground of opposition to Union Societies? If we are to believe our brethren, which we really do, they wish us to depart. Yea, some of their leading men have requested us to do so, again and again. Why then will they clamour against us for adopting a measure, which *they say*, will "naturally" take us off? If our "principles are pernicious," and if "the reformers are like tares among the wheat," the more carefully and effectually we collect them together, with intention to remove them, the better it will be for the church. Indeed, to be consistent, our old-side brethren should furnish us with every facility to collect those noxious weeds, and to remove them hence. But we will assure our brethren, that we have no desire to leave the church; but if we are to go out, then, "verily, let them come themselves and fetch us out." PAUL.

The foregoing paper could not have been misunderstood. It most explicitly makes known the objects contemplated by reformers, in organizing the Union Societies. It as clearly makes known the fact, that these societies were intended to secure the integrity of the Methodist Episcopal Church, at the same time that they were expected to ensure reform. It also must satisfy any candid reader, that as certainly as we had a right to call the attention of the Methodist public to the subject of a reform in their church government, we also had a right to do so in a systematic way. It follows that any attempt to hinder the formation of Union Societies, or to break them up, when formed, was in every instance a direct act of opposition to the labours of reformers, as well as a violation of our rights.

If however there should still remain a doubt on the mind of the reader, respecting the objects of these Union Societies, his attention is requested to the following occurrence.

The different seceders were invited by a circular sent in every direction, to meet in New York, and form a constitution for a new Methodist Church. An application was made through a special messenger to the Union Society of Baltimore, to send up a delegation, to co-operate with them. The application was met in a manner consistent with our public declarations on the subject, as will be seen by a perusal of the letter sent in reply, with the signature of brother John Chappell, the president of the society.

Baltimore, February 15th, 1826.

DEAR BRETHREN,

Your communication upon the subject of a convention for the purpose of uniting and consolidating the different societies of Dissenting Methodists, was received by the hand of the Rev'd. Samuel Budd. The respectful manner of your application to us, to unite with you for the accomplishment of this object, is duly appreciated, and a suitable acknowledgement is hereby respectfully tendered to you in return.

It must be obvious, however, to every intelligent member of your association, as well as to us, that such a measure, if effectual, would produce in regard of us, a result the reverse of the object which we have in view. In the number of the Mutual Rights, for August, 1825, page 2, we have made the declaration to the world, that we have no design to separate from the church, much less to divide it; but on the contrary, that we are labouring to prevent secessions and divisions. Our Union Society has organized itself, and instituted the publication, called the Mutual Rights, with intention to show to dissatisfied brethren, that a struggle is making, and will be continued, for the accomplishment of a better state of things, in the Methodist Episcopal Church. In doing this thing, we intended to *prevent secessions*, and consequently, any participation in the measures which you propose, would be inconsistent with our avowed intentions.

JOHN CHAPPELL, *President.*

With the foregoing exposition of the true character and design of Union Societies, the friends of truth and equal rights, will be prepared to perceive the amount of the injury done to reformers, by the expulsions in Tennessee and North Carolina. And it ought

not to be considered to have been improper on our part to have
rebuked such tyrannical proceedings with suitable pungency. In
the notices that will be taken of the remaining extracts, as they
appear in the Narrative and Defence, references will be made to
the occasions which were in view of the printing committee, when
the papers which have been "*indicated*" were severally admitted
for publication.

CHAPTER XVII.

*Timothy, alias Rev. George Brown's Defence of himself, on account
of extracts from his address to the junior Bishop. This paper was
written in the year 1827. It was recently revised, by request, and
forwarded for insertion in this review.*

IN all cases of controversy, there is danger of an undue excitement of the passions. This fact may receive a practicable illustration, by an appeal to the history of all the controversies that have
ever been carried on in *church* or *state. Man* is but *man*, in whatever
condition he may be placed; and to engage him in controversy, is
to surround him with circumstances, calculated to enlist his passions; this point must be evident to all candid men, of the least
observation.

Our passions generally, become enlisted, in proportion as we
conceive the subject of discussion to involve important interests.
We, our friends, the church, the world, are all concerned, it may
be in the decision. Multitudes yet unborn may have a heavy stake
in this affair.——Human happiness may be affected by it in this
world, and in the world to come, to an extent not easily known.
It will, therefore, be found extremely difficulty, if not impossible,
to make a subject, on which so much appears to hang, a mere
question of intellectual investigation, from which all feeling is to
be entirely excluded. Were men turned into angels, this thing
might be expected. We conclude, therefore, that candid allowances should be mutually made, for the frailties of our common
nature; and that we should labour diligently and prayerfully to rule
our own spirits in such a manner, as to allow the present controversy in the Methodist Episcopal Church to be carried on, as fully
as possible, under the influence of reason, and in strict accordance
with the holy word of God.

In the course of this controversy, our minds are sometimes struck
with a kind of *superstitious fear*, and we feel ourselves considera-
bly embarrassed. If the subject were of a different character, if it
were some philosophical or political question, if it were some
question of science, not so intimately associated with religion, if
it did not draw around it, so much apparent *sacredness*; we could
proceed with more *firmness*, and should consider our church government, as legitimate a subject of intellectual investigation, and
as open to the public eye, as any other in the world. Aye, and
many of our people, who still remain silent, would come forth to
our help, and render important service to our cause. Now, why is

it, that we attach all this *sacredness* to church government? **Why**
does the tongue *faulter*, the head become *giddy*, and the heart
faint, when we enter upon an investigation of the high claims of
the itinerant clergy of our church? Is it because the polity of the
Methodist Episcopal Church in all its details is actually from heaven, and was revealed to doctor Coke and Francis Asbury, on the
holy mount? No man will pretend this. The fact is, all *ecclesiastical establishments*, as well as *civil*, are of an *earthly growth*. They
are alike the offspring of *human reason*, and of *human weakness too*.
All such establishments are fit subjects for rational investigation,
and no *superstitious sacredness*, drawn around them by the craft of
either *kings* or *priests*, should save their *arbitrary principles*, from a
just exposure to the light of open day.

If reformers are not continually on their guard, "the fear of
man," that always "bringeth a snare" may prove injurious to our
cause. The church authorities are beginning to array themselves
against us, not to argue, but to punish. It will require no little
mental and *moral energy*, to look these men in the face and not fear.
No matter how good our cause may be;—no matter how ably
it has been, or can be supported by arguments of stirling worth;—
our opponents have the power to punish, and are beginning to employ their punitive power against us. To write arguments with
becoming *independence*, or examine them *impartially*, will be no
easy matter, while men in power are holding over us, all the terrors
of an unjust excommunication from the church of God. We will,
however, quiet our fears the best way we can, and address ourselves to the task of making replication to the "Narrative and Defence," so far as we are concerned.

My present undertaking is extremely delicate. Two of our
bishops will be concerned in my remarks, both of whom I really
wish to honour, on the account of their *age, talents* and *great moral
worth*. I cannot, however, forsake the high ground of *free* and *independent inquiry* on their account. This I trust, they do not wish.
In my observations I desire to move forward, with *cautious* and *un-
wavering steps*, and with an *unfaultering voice*, speaking the *truth*
in *love*.

I shall commence with the case of our senior bishop, noticed in
the Narrative and Defence, p. 56. It would have been better, if
my meaning had been more fully *explained* and *guarded*, in the address to the junior bishop, where it is said, "*and our senior bishop
is arched over the whole*." It never entered into my mind, that any
one acquainted with the arrangement of matters among the bishops,
at the General Conference, of 1824, would misunderstand me on
that point. In this matter, it seems, I was mistaken. I owe to
bishop McKendree for whom I entertain the highest respect, I owe
it to myself, and to the community at large, to say definitely, what
I did mean. This thing, for which the seven prosecators "were
not prepared"*—"this accusation of usurping an arch episcopal
authority"—this taunting appellation"—"this biting sarcasm"—

* He was not informed, respecting the Agent.

"this unfeeling insult"—"this bitter phillipic," as these very amiable brethren, in the overflowings of their christian charity have seen proper to call it,* can, I hope, be so explained, as to do no one any harm; and that too without any, the slightest departure from the truth, as it is in Jesus.

I did not intend to convey the idea, that our senior bishop had "*usurped* an arch-episcopal authority," or that in any sense he was "legally superior" to his colleagues. I only meant that on the part of the General Conference, or the other bishops, perhaps both; on the principles of *courtesy*, not of *law* or *usurpation*, a relation was now given to Mr. McKendree, which might, in the very nature of things, eventuate in the establishment of an arch-episcopal or a patriarchal authority, over the Methodist Episcopal Church.——In other words, I meant that by an arrangement entered into at the last general conference, not in strict accordance with *former usage*, or the *rule of our discipline* (p. 25.) which requires our bishops severally, "*to travel through the connexion at large*," bishops Roberts and Soule, were restricted to the *south*, as to *labour* and *support*. Bishops George and Hedding to the *north*, as to *labour* and *support*. And that our senior bishop, without any notice of *superannuation* at all, had the whole connexion for his field; and as to *labour* and *support* was at home in the *north*, and at home in the *south*, or in the language of the address, on the score of *courtesy*, not of *legality*, or of *usurpation*, he was "arched over the whole."

Full credit is here intended to be given to our senior bishop for "his faithful labours"—"his devoted life"—"his long and valuable services to the church," but to me it did appear, that in the above arrangement a bad precedent had been set. I calculated that each succeeding *senior bishop*, might claim to be similarly situated, until this thing would grow into a regular *usage* in the church, and finally be established by the General Conference as a law in our Israel. All history will attest the fact, that, in *all ages*, and in *all countries*, *civil* and *ecclesiastical power*, has maintained its *onward march*, from less to more, in this *silent*, and almost unnoticed manner. May I not hope that this explanation will be deemed satisfactory by all men of candour; and that even the seven prosecutors themselves, will admit my explanations, and that in future, they will no more, in an ill natured way, take the very worst meaning they can, out of a brother's words, and then fall on him in an unmerciful manner, with their "taunting appellations"—"biting sarcasms"—"unfeeling insults,"—and "bitter phillipics?" How their "Narrative and Defence," blooms with these ungodly flowers, which send forth an ill savour! I have understood from as high authority as any in the church, that this matter, respecting the "*arch over the whole*," is pretty generally understood to the north, as I have now explained it, and since the members of our conference said nothing to me on this subject, I infer, that they generally understood it in this way. In all probability, it would have been interpreted *thus*, by the pro-

---

* These pithy sentences are to be placed to the credit of the writer of the Narrative and Defence, not of the seven prosecutors.

secuting committee themselves; but for "the infelicity of the times," and the great work to be accomplished. "Carthage must be destroyed."—In other words, by whatever means, *radicalism must be put down.*

The Rev. Jesse Lee, in his "History of the Methodists," observes in reference to the title "bishop," that, "this was the first time (1787,) that our superintendents ever gave themselves the title of bishops in the minutes. They *changed the title themselves,* without the consent of the conference; and then at the next conference, they asked the preachers, if the word bishop might stand in the minutes, seeing it was a Scripture name, and the meaning of the word *bishop,* was the same with that of *superintendent.* Some of the preachers *opposed the alteration,* and wished to retain the former title, but a majority of the preachers agreed to let the word bishop remain," p. 128.—On this piece of our history we remark, 1st. That to all human appearance, the motive for taking the "title bishop" was a good one. "It was a Scripture name." And certainly all christians should be allowed to cleave close to the Scriptures. 2d. No man at that time, would have thought of charging doctor Coke and Mr. Asbury, with ambition in effecting this change of title. All allowed as the word *"bishop,* meant the same as the word *superintendent,"* that no increase of power could be expected by the change. How great the disappointment! The change once effected, Methodist episcopacy became independent of Mr. Wesley, and an increase of power did follow. 3d. But suppose no increase of power had followed this change of title, Messrs. Coke and Asbury, were to *blame,* for taking the *responsibility* on them, of "changing the title *themselves,* without the consent of the conference." Aye, and contrary to the directions of Mr. Wesley, under whose authority they acted. 4th. I think it is pretty clear, that "our fathers" did feel themselves a little to blame in this matter. That in fact, they had gone entirely too far, or why did they humble themselves, and "ask the preachers at the next conference, if the word bishop might stand on the minutes." 5th. So it appears, that the *"title bishop"* was first taken without *law* or *consent,* and "printed in the minutes," according to the sovereign pleasure of *two Englishmen,* and at the next conference, what was thus taken by *illegal seizure,* these gentlemen had the address, by *crouching* a little, to *get confirmed to them by law*—"a majority of the preachers agreed to let the word bishop remain." "But some opposed," to their honour be it spoken.

We shall only trouble the reader with one other passage from this author;—it has respect to the origin of presiding elders. Mr. Lee informs us, p. 183: "That such an order has never been regularly established before. They had been appointed by the bishop for several years; but it was a doubt in the minds of the preachers, whether such power belonged to him. The General Conference now (1792,) determined that there should be presiding elders; and that they should be *chosen, stationed,* and *changed* by the bishops." On this portion of our history we remark: 1st. Our bishops may

20

have sincerely thought, for aught we know, that the prosperity of
the work required them to appoint presiding elders, "for several
years" before any "such an order" had been "regularly established,"
by any law in our church. 2d. This power, great as it was, the
preachers conceded to them, for a time. Probably they deemed
such officers necessary to the welfare of the church, and for peace
sake, declined laying in their objections to the arbitrary manner of
appointing them, by *the single will of the bishop alone*, uncontrolled by any law of the church on that subject. 3d. Even then it
seems, there were "restless spirits" in the ministry, who disapproved of our bishops using more power than had been given them by
the laws of the church. "It was a doubt in the minds of the
preachers, whether such power belonged to them." 4th. This
power, so *taken, conceded* and *employed* "for several years," was
finally, (as in the other case noticed,) confirmed to our bishops by
law. "The General Conference now determined that there should
be presiding elders," &c. 5th. From both of these quotations from
our own history, and from many others that might be made, may
we not conclude without giving offence to our present bishops or
to the General Conference that probably concurred in the arrangement mentioned in my explanation, that there is at least a call for
caution. What has been, may be again. "The best of men, are but
men at the best." Our present bishops are made out of the same
kind of materials, that "our fathers" were. *These* are good men
upon the whole. So were *those.* But all fallible like ourselves. A
concession made by the juniors to the senior bishop, and accorded to him by the General Conference, may really terminate in something very little expected or desired by any of us. "A prudent
man foreseeth the evil and hideth himself; but the simple pass on
and are punished."

The prosecuting committee are volunteers, it seems, and act
wholly on their own responsibility; I shall regard them accordingly.
I will not complain of their calling me to answer at the *bar* of the
entire community for what I have written;—for there, it gives me
pleasure to stand with permission to speak for myself. I will not
complain, that I stand charged by these brethren, in company with
many other valiant friends of christian liberty, with "evil speaking"—"slander,"—"defamation" and "calumny." To prove these
against me, the extracts have been taken from my "address to the
junior bishop," and published to the world. Vain effort! But I
will complain that I was not called before this tribunal sooner, so
that my *explanations, arguments, &c.* might have saved the editorial
committee, and the Union Society in Baltimore, an unjust expulsion from the church of the Lord. I will complain, that after my
name was officially demanded, and given up to Bishop Hedding;
after I had on the principles of pacification conceded to him all I
could, at our last conference;—still my supposed offences are visited on men who are not responsible for them. If any further sufferings were due for my offences, I alone deserved to suffer. I was
always ready for my fate, and never dreamed that after my name
was delivered up, the editorial committee or Union Society, were

any longer endangered by what I had written. If this is justice, I am persuaded it is not current every where. It is not civil justice. It is not the justice of the New Testament. It can only be the justice of *inflamed party zeal*, from which may heaven deliver, *even* our prosecutors themselves!

These brethren have the goodness to assert, with all the confidence of popes, that my *"premises are false,"* p. 56, respecting the "arch," &c. and that they "cannot doubt the fallacy of my conclusions," in reference to the *"march of power,"* in the *Methodist E. Church.* But waiving for the present, any notice of their pontifical manner, let us suppose, that my premises as I have explained them, should turn out to be true. May it not follow, that my conclusions respecting the "march of power," are equally true? My explanations are submitted to men of *candour*, and my conclusion shall be defended in due time. All I ask is an impartial hearing.

The seven prosecutors [the Agent,] represent me as "accusing" bishop McKendree, of "usurping an arch-episcopal authority," &c. and then on the next page they say, "this author well knew there existed no legal superiority among the bishops," &c. Meaning to be understood, I suppose, that with all my knowledge to the contrary, I had ventured to state, that there was a legal superiority of the senior bishop over his colleagues. Unless this is meant, their observation is without point, as their object was to convict me of slander. But they must be favoured with uncommon penetration indeed, to be able to find both of these meanings in the words used by me. If I meant Mr. McKendree was an arch-bishop by *usurpation*, I could not have meant, that he had attained to that great dignity and authority, in a *"legal"* way, unless some rare genius among the *seven*, will be pleased to convince the community at large, that *usurpation* and *legality* mean precisely the same thing!

For Mr. McKendree, to become *legally superior* to his episcopal colleagues, it would be necessary for him to be advanced to that eminence according to some *law* in the church. But as no such law exists, and as I have not intimated its existence, nor yet, said one word about his *"legal superiority"* to the other bishops, it cannot, therefore, be fairly inferred, that legal superiority was my meaning. As to the *"usurpation,"* of which our prosecutors say I have "accused" Mr. McKendree, that word conveys a stronger idea, than any thing said in my address will justify. My words, *"and our senior bishop is arched over the whole,"* can hardly be so interpreted with *fairness*, as to mean *"forcible, unjust, illegal, seizure or possession,"* which is the definition of the word *usurpation*, according to Walker. It is true, no *law* or *usage* of the church, has made any provision for seniors in the episcopacy, to occupy the ground now assigned to Mr. McKendree. Yet as he did not *force* himself into that situation, but on the contrary, was perhaps *passive* in relation to it, or as some say, was *importuned* by his *colleagues* and the *General Conference* to accept of it, I was, therefore, never disposed to consider "the good old man" as an *usurper.* Still, I blamed the entire arrangement, and am of the *opinion now*, and expect to continue of the *opinion*, that in his case a precedent has

been fixed, the tendency of which cannot fail to be injurious. Let
this arrangement stand, and an arch-episcopal or patriarchal government over the Methodist Episcopal Church, may be looked for
in due time. On this I calculate, not from any pretensions to the
spirit of prophecy; but from the natural tendency of the well known
principles of human nature.

Since the prosecuting committee have voluntarily taken upon
them, to involve my brethren and myself in the accusation of "wilful slander," and thus to fix on us this foul *disgrace*, before the
whole community, let us inquire a little into the accuracy of *their*
statements.——They very gravely tell us, with a view no doubt, to
magnify my supposed offences, "We had considered Mr. McKendree as *superannuated.*"——"We believe, moreover, that this exemp-
tion from the burden and cares of office, were *asked* and *obtained*
from the General Conference." p. 56. That bishop McKendree
is *naturally* "*superannuated*," I most cheerfully allow, but that he
"asked and obtained" an *official* "superannuation from the General
Conference," does not appear from any document now before the
public. If the journals of the General Conference contain any
account of this fact, why were they not made public? And how
was I, or any other person, to regard him as officially superannuated
without any information to that effect? May we not conclude,
that his superannuation is quite problematical; seeing we have no
information of it any where, save in the "Narrative and Defence."
a publication most extraordinary for inconsistencies, and for severity far exceeding the Mutual Rights.——Perhaps it will be said, they
do not *positively* assert that Mr. McKendree was *officially* superannuated. They only say, "we *believe* moreover, that this exemp-
tion was asked and obtained."

But let me ask, to what does all this amount? Why plainly to
this, namely, that our prosecutors have attained to the great perfection of being able to *believe*, what will benefit themselves and
injure their opponents, without any evidence at all!! This is no
"new thing under the sun." If the General Conference do not
superannuate our senior bishop, which I hold to be pretty certain, is
it not strange that the prosecuting committee would take upon
them to do it? Do they intend to *expel reformers, superannuate bishops,
publish "Narratives,"* and like Jehu, *drive on furiously?*——if so, let
them declare it openly, in the face of the sun, that we may all be
prepared for the hard times to come.

So far as the *junior bishop is concerned*, I really did intend, in
writing that address, to speak in respectful terms of bishop Hedding's *person, piety*, and *talents*. It is a matter of deep regret, that
in writing to a person of his age, my language should have savour-
ed, in the least degree, of *familiar disrespect.*——I here beg the
bishop to be assured, that I only intended with manly and becoming firmness, to address him, on the subject of his opposition to
the cause of reform, as manifested at the close of the Annual Conference, in Washington, Pennsylvania. Had it it not been for this
opposition, I should probably have remained in silence during this
ecclesiastical war, beholding the mustering forces on the field of

conflict, listening to the increasing clangor of arms, and trembling with solicitude for the success of liberal principles. Bishop Hedding chose his own *time, place, and method* of opposition. I did sincerely believe, that I had a right to ward off the blow, if no one else did. And since he did not ask reformers, what plan he should pursue, in his efforts against our cause;—so neither was I bound to ask him, in what way I should make my reply. His opposition being open, and public, and intended to have a paralyzing effect on the investigation of an entire conference of preachers and people, I did believe that no *private explanations* that could be given, by letter or otherwise, to me or any other aggrieved brother, would justify our passing over in silence, his opposition to *public discussions*. The maxim that *"the doings of the clergy are to be kept from the eyes of the people,"* I did believe to be a disgrace to any reformed church. I think so still. It savours so strongly of the old Roman Harlot, and opens the way for every ecclesiastical abomination—unless some one will *prove* church history *false*, and that human nature is *purer* than I have hitherto supposed it to be, my views on this subject will probably remain unchanged to the end of my life.

It was under the influence of such views and sentiments, the address to bishop Hedding was prepared, and sent to the editorial committee in Baltimore, for publication. When it came from the press I read it with care, and corresponded with my brethren, and found their sentiments in unison with my own, as to its being *correct in matters of fact*, but somewhat severe in language. It was with sentiments and feelings of profound astonishment that I read Mr. Hedding's note to doctor Jennings, demanding my name, and calling the address *"unjust, a misrepresentation throughout*, and a *vile slander* on his *character."* My name was forthwith surrendered to bishop Hedding, under an unshaken conviction, founded on the maturest reflection, that I had not treated him in the manner reported in his note.[*] After reflecting awhile, and consulting with faithful friends, selected by bishop George and myself, from both sides of this controversy, I offered of my own accord, to the conference in Steubenville, the following concessions, to be presented to Mr. Hedding by bishop George. I am obliged to publish this document, for the purpose of correcting erroneous impressions, which some of our own preachers have taken much pains to make; and lest it should be supposed by any, that in my "explanations and apologies," mentioned by the prosecuting committee, p. 58, I had acknowledged myself guilty of all they charged me with.

"Having understood that some of my brethren, are dissatisfied with me as the author of an address to the junior bishop, signed Timothy, I cheerfully avail myself of an opportunity to offer a few remarks to the conference, on that subject. My object in doing so, is to assure my brethren, that for peace sake, I am willing to enter

[*] We hold many certificates from men of standing, several of which were published in the Mutual Rights, confirming the truth of Mr. Brown's statements in his address to the Bishop.　　　　　S. K. J.

into measures of pacification. And that I may not be misled by
my feelings, and to prevent any future misunderstanding on this
subject, I have thought proper to place my present views and sentiments on paper."

"Peace is my object. I concede therefore, that in two particulars in relation to bishop Hedding, I have erred, and failed to select
the most excellent way. In the first place, considering the age
and standing of bishop Hedding, and my own youth and relation
to the church, I think it would have been more proper for me to
have conversed with the bishop, or written to him for the purpose
of explanation, before I published. This seems to have been required by the law of brotherly love and christian usage. I admit
and regret my error in this particular. Secondly, I also concede
that in some reflections and inferences in my address, I was un-
necessarily severe, and that the asperity should have been evaded
as tending to disagreeable results and unpleasant excitements.—
This I also regret: for although I thought at the time, that my severity was justified by the circumstances, yet I now believe a more
mild and cautious manner would have been preferable.

"I will farther concede, that I have misconceived the meaning of
bishop Hedding in some instances, and hence may have made an application of his positions, beyond what he intended; but if this was
the case, it was an inadvertency, no unfairness of construction
was intended by me, and no departure from *principle*, *truth*, and
justice. Nevertheless, I do not admit the charge by bishop Hedding, of *"injustice," "misrepresentation,"* and *"slander."*

"After mature reflection, I offer these explanations to the conference, as due to bishop Hedding, to them, and to myself: and as
required by the ties of our common brotherhood, christian courtesy, and the pacific principles of our holy religion.

GEORGE BROWN."

The foregoing concessions were deemed by my *advisers* and
myself, sufficient; and as the conference, the members of which
had heard the bishop's address, and had read my reply in the paper
signed "Timothy," asked nothing further, I felt myself to be toler-
ably safe, and so the matter rested.*

*At the General Conference in Pittsburg, in 1828, being very desirous of a
good understanding with bishop Hedding, I went before the committee on
episcopacy, at the request of the bishop, and two of the members of
that conference, as I understood it, for the purpose of a *friendly explanation.*
When there, I found that great stress was laid by Mr. Hedding on *two words*,
viz: *"reform,"* and *"discussion,"* which he said I had used, in a sense far too
broad and *undefined.* He insisted that from the manner of my using these
words, an idea might be taken up, that he was opposed to all manner of *"reform,"* and all manner of *"discussion,"* whereas, in his address he had admitted of *reform,* so far as the election of presiding elders was concerned,
and he had admitted of *discussion* among the preachers *privately.* My great
desire for an *amicable adjustment* of this affair, which the bishop's note to the
editorial committee, demanding my name, had made by far, too *personal,* led
me to go as far as possible in the way of *concessions.* I therefore conceded,
that I had not been sufficiently *careful,* in *distinguishing* the *precise sense,* in

The Baltimore prosecutors have been pleased to say—"There does not appear even from the writer's own showing, that there was any thing *amiss* in the junior bishop's valedictory address to the Pittsburg Confererence," p. 57. That there was nothing *morally* "*amiss* in the bishop's address," is most cheerfully admitted by me. In what I have written, his *piety, talents,* and *personal respectabili-ty,* have been spoken of in a favourable manner; but that there was something "amiss" in the *principles* and *policy* of the bishop's address according to my "own showing," I think is very clear. In order that the reader may judge for himself in this matter, I will not quote the *paraphrase* on my "showing," given by the prose-cutors in the "Narrative and Defence;" but I will quote from the Mutual Rights, vol. 3. p. 109, where my "showing" of the princi-pal facts of his address may be found. "You opposed our preach-ers taking any part in the discussions of Mutual Rights: You op-posed our members in church fellowship, having any thing to do with that work: You supported your opposition by two arguments, viz: that the Mutual Rights would agitate the church; that the change called for by reformers, would never be brought about, be-cause it was not desired by one in twenty of our people: You then gave us an advice to *be still,* and say nothing, until we got upon the floor of the General Conference, for there, and there alone, was the proper place to discuss such subjects." Now as the Pittsburg Conference has sustained me, in refusing to admit the charge by bishop Hedding, of "*injustice, misrepresentation* and *slander*," of course, the prosecutors had to take this thing according to my "own showing," and make the very best they could of it; or com-mence an open attack on our entire conference. They prudently chose the former of these alternatives.

I have shown bishop Hedding to be opposed to *all public discus-sions* of *ecclesiastical matters*, by our *preachers* and *people, any,* and *every* where, save "on the floor of the General Conference," and I feel perfectly able to prove from the "Narrative and Defence" itself, that our prosecutors in their *coolest* and most *dispassionate* mo-ments, did see a *great deal* "*amiss*" in my "showing" of his ad-dress to the conference in Washington. They say, "we have never wished to prevent our brethren who differ from us in opinion, from *fully* and *fairly discussing* the subject of church government in general, or of our's in particular," p. 7. These prosecutors did

which I used the words "*reform*" and "*discussion;*" and that possibly, *infer-ences* might have been drawn, &c. which were incorrect.

But on the most mature reflection, I incline to the opinion, that *my con-cessions were hardly called for by truth.* All cool-headed, impartial men, would understand me to represent the bishop as opposing the kind of "*reform*" contended for in the Mutual Rights, and not all manner of reform;—as op-posing "discussion," as carried on in that periodical, and not *private* "discus-sion."—The very periodical then, in which my piece was published, limited the meaning of the words *reform* and *discussion, so* as to leave the bishop un-troubled about the *little reform* he *befriended,* and the *private discussion* he *allowed.* See a statement of this whole affair in the 4th vol. of the Mutual Rights, p. 380.

GEORGE BROWN.

Pittsburg, June 28th, 1831.

certainly see something "amiss" in the bishop's opposition to public discussion, when they made the above declaration. Again they
say, "we are not aware that any *injury* would arise from such
a *controversy*, if it were carried on with *proper temper;*—with a *strict
regard to truth*, and to the *feelings* and *characters* of all concerned," *ibid.*—Here the seven prosecutors are in *direct opposition to
the bishop.* He was afraid of "agitating" the church to its "injury."
They are "not aware that any *injury* would arise from this controversy;"—of course in their cool moments, they allowed such efforts
as his to be altogether "amiss." As to "proper temper"—"a strict
regard to truth, and the characters of all concerned;" we do not
desire liberty to *violate these* with *impunity*, and we will count that
man our friend, who, in a *christian like manner*, will point out our
errors in these respects; but would respectfully suggest to the prosecuting committee the propriety of a strict attention to *"truth,
feeling,* and *character,"* on their own part, before they lecture
others, less deeply involved than themselves. Our prosecutors
farther say—"In these declarations we believe we speak the language of our brethren generally," *ibid.* Now what is this but to
tell us plainly, that bishop Hedding in his opposition to public discussion, stands pretty much *alone*, and that they, and the Methodists generally, are against him, and why against him so pointedly
unless his efforts were "amiss?" "We are prepared," they say,
"to follow the leadings of providence;"—"and to adapt our economy to the circumstances of *time* and *place*, in such a way as may
be deemed best calculated, to promote the glory of God, and the
salvation of mankind," *ibid.* Now in all of this, the committee
seem to see something "amiss," in such efforts as we have *shown*
Mr. Hedding to have made. He was favourable to the election of
presiding elders, it is true. So far he went for reform, but no
further, and for this much, *little as it is,* I should have given him
credit in my address. But the prosecutors are disposed to "adapt
our economy to time, place and circumstances," as *providence may
open the way.* This is all we ask. Let us all agree to discuss the
subject calmly, and follow providence. If this is done, our church
government will certainly be *altered* for the *better*, because we shall
then be qualified as a people to enjoy a better. But should the
right of public discussion be denied us, and our people be *thereby
involved* in *profound* and *perpetual* darkness on this subject; a
despotism will be the very best kind of government that they will
be qualified to bear, and of course, providence will give them no
other. Our brethren wind up on this page by telling us, that neither
they, the *preachers*, nor our *members*, have any *"wish* or *desire"*
to *"suppress inquiry,"* or to *"prevent discussion."* Nothing could
have been more opposite to Mr. Hedding's address, according to
my "own showing," and yet strange to tell, in my "own showing"
of that address, *they can see nothing "amiss"!!!* They very gravely tell us, in their *sage* and *weighty* remarks, that bishop Hedding
"very properly advised them (the conference) to postpone the discussion until by themselves or their representatives, they should
have an opportunity *calmly* and *deliberately* to consider it on the
floor of the General Conference," p. 57. Now is it not clear that

at page 57, they go all lengths with reformers, as to the *right* and *utility* of *free discussion?* And is it not equally clear, that in their unguarded moments, they have *contradicted* themselves, by going the whole way with the bishop in his opposition to public discussion? And we are to consider the bishop's opposition, &c. under the notion of very "proper advice," are we? Why now, how hard things are softened!—What a *white washing committee is this!*—I shall leave them to reconcile their own contradictions in the best way they can, and shall conclude this part with two observations.— 1. If, according to my "own showing," there was nothing "amiss" in the bishop's address, then surely I have not *slandered* him, unless these *seven wise men* can make it appear, that it is slander in reformers to state nothing "amiss" of brethren in the opposition. This is not the first time that speaking nothing "amiss" has been considered slander, by the supporters of the enormous claims of our itinerant clergy. 2. Nothing *morally "amiss,"* is pretended in this case, but we do think there was something "amiss" in the *principles* indicated by Mr. Hedding's address, in opposition to public discussion. His motives may have been good. He wanted, no doubt, to preserve the church from "agitation," and to keep peace within all our borders. But to attempt to preserve a community *unagitated* and *peaceful*, by obstructing or withholding the right of *free* and *fair discussion*, I contend is *arbitrary* in *principle*, and in such a country as ours, must tend to very unpleasant results. Will any man in this free and independent nation, venture in the face of open day, to affirm or prove the contrary? Such a man will be told at once, by a thousand *tongues*, and by a thousand *pens*, that *science* can only *advance*—that *civilization* can only *progress*—that *governments* can only be *improved*, and that *religion* itself, can only extend its *reign*, in proportion as discussion is allowed on a *liberal scale*. In speaking thus, I speak the language of a great and happy people, and I have no doubt, but that I speak the language of bishop Hedding too, in reference to all subjects except this one. O, how detestable is the maxim, that "the doings of the clergy are to be kept from the eyes of the world." I hope the day will speedily come, when this proverb shall no more be used to the disgrace of our Israel.

I will now answer to the charge of ascribing to Bishop Hedding "a thirst for power and desire of dominion which is only equalled by the papacy," p. 57. This is a charge of some magnitude, and must therefore receive a candid consideration. If I really have conveyed the idea, that Bishop Hedding's *"thirst* for *power* and *desire* of *dominion,"* was *equal* to that of the *popes* of *Rome*, I am not sensible of it. The prosecuting committee only adduced one passage from my address to Mr. Hedding, in proof of this charge, which is as follows:—"We should be more inexcusable than the members of the christian church in the rise of popery, if we were to suffer our spiritual rulers to enslave us; we have many advantages unknown to them, particularly the printing press. What a blessing this has been to the world, what a scourge to wild and law-

21

less ambition!!" ibid.—In order that it may be seen, that their charge is not supported by this quotation, the reader will indulge us, in submitting the following remarks. 1st. Bishop Hedding is no more concerned in this passage, than the travelling preachers generally, for they are the "spiritual rulers" intended. 2d. Let it be distinctly recollected, that these our "spiritual rulers," have all *legislative, judicial* and *executive power—all creed-making, property controlling, officer appointing power*, now in their own hands, and Bishop Hedding, who is presumed to speak the language of at least, a majority of our itinerant ministers, did strenuously oppose our preachers and members, publicly examining into this order of things. 3d. Although our "spiritual rulers" have hitherto been good men in general;—indeed it may be acknowledged, that their *goodness* so far, has been almost the only earthly *safe guard* of the church; there being *very few redeeming principles in the government;*—yet this *safe guard* is beginning to be *less worthy of trust*, than *formerly*. The *arbitrary* government of our church is a continual temptation to the itinerants to become *arbitrary*. We are certain that long possessed, unchecked, unbalanced, irresponsible power, is calculated to spoil the best men in the world, and as the principles of the government are unrighteous and enslaving in their character; how then was I to shut my eyes against the direct tendency of this order of things, to enslave our people, in its practical operations? Dr. Paley says, in his evidences of christianity, "that they who are in possession of power, do what they can to keep it," and that "christianity does not universally condemn this principle, because it is not universally wrong," p. 377. The power to do good, is also the power to do evil. Good men may desire to get, and keep power for good purposes; this "christianity does not universally condemn." And evil men may desire to get and keep power, for evil purposes; this christianity cannot *allow*—and since power, or something else, may spoil any of the frail sons of Adam now, as well as in former ages, and in other countries, it therefore, clearly follows, that for our preachers to have all this *unchecked, irresponsible* power, in their hands, is wrong; because human nature *now*, must be greatly altered from what it used to be, or it will end in *absolute ecclesiastical slavery*. 4th. In order for this quotation to have supported their charge, it should have made our "spiritual rulers," to be as bad men as the popes of Rome; as wickedly *athirst* for *power*, and perfectly given up to the "desire" of temporal and spiritual "dominion," as they. This I have not said, neither came it into my heart. Of course their charge is wholly unsustained by this quotation. 5th. I refer to popery in its *rise*, without saying one word about the goodness, or the badness of the ministry in those days. We may suppose the teachers of religion to have been good men. We may suppose people to have voluntarily given their share of church power, into the hands of their ministers, for the purpose of increasing their usefulness: but what was the result? Ask history, it can tell. All the *sighs, groans, tears* and *miseries*, of the *papal world*, from Constantine down to the present day, now call on us to learn *wisdom*, by the *folly* and *miseries* of others, and not to play the old game over again. 6th. As to the "printing press" being a "blessing to the world," do our prosecutors deny this? If so, let them speak out, that we may understand them. Let them tell whether, in their opinion, matters would not move on much better, if men of their *views* could control all the "printing presses" in this nation. Had the first christians been blessed with "printing presses," as we now are, perhaps they would have remained *free* from ecclesiastical slavery. 7th. As to the *"wild and lawless ambition"* spoken of, however applicable such a remark may be to some of the itinerant clergy, yet it never was intended for them as a body, as all candid men must allow. I think that *even* our prosecutors might have perceived, that as I represented the "press" as a "blessing to the world," in one part of the sentence: so in the other, I meant, that it had been a *scourge* to the "wild and lawless ambition" of the *world*, and I here add, that the press has been a very necessary *scourge*, on the "wild and lawless ambition" of men, *high in ecclesiastical power*. So may it still continue to be, and if "our spiritual rulers" need *scourging*, let them have it; and let all the people say amen.

Two of what the committee are pleased to call my "unwarrantable inferences," must receive some attention. I have inferred from the bishop's *opposition* to *reform*, and to *public discussion*, that he held the *doctrine*, that *"to obey was enough for the people,"* p. 58. And is this an unwarrantable inference? Will the bishop, the prosecutors, or any other thorough going old side man affirm this? I think they will not—and I declare it to be the very spirit of our ecclesiastical government. So far from calling it an "unwarrantable inference," these brethren ought to write on their *phylacteries*, and wear it to the house of their solemnities, in order to let all the zealous sons of the church know, that "TO OBEY IS ENOUGH FOR THE PEOPLE" CALLED METHODISTS.

The other inference from the same premises was, that the "bishops rule by a divine right, which ought not to be examined, or called in question," ibid. The former part of this inference, may possibly be incorrect, since without believing in the "divine right" of episcopacy, he might have manifested the same opposition to reform. But the latter part of the inference, namely, that the "right" by which our bishops do *"rule*, ought not be examined or called in question" stands good, and will, until the right of *free discussion*, is allowed to the whole church. The prosecutors speak of me as "holding up the bishop to the political execration of the people," p. 58. This charge deserves particular attention. To support it they make the following quotation from my address to Mr. Hedding. "I do sir think it my duty, to hold up your conduct to public *view*, (not execration) that all men may *know* what a genuine friend to the rights of man you are, and how entirely republicanism governs all your movements," ibid.——And are the prosecutors opposed to the bishop's principles being *known* by the community at large? To make them *known* was all I aimed at. Must we all get back to the hateful maxim, that "the doings of the clergy"—especially, the *principles* and *doings* of bishops, "are to be kept from the eyes of the world?" No, indeed, the *principles* and *conduct* of all *public men* should be *known*, in order that every man may pass for what he is worth, and no more. On the above quotation the committee remark: "Now would not any man *infer*, from all this vituperation and abuse, that the bishop had greatly infringed on this author's *rights*, or uttered some opinions on government subversive of our civil institutions? yet nothing of all this had happened," ibid.—Here we shall take occasion to observe: 1st. The *irony* of this piece might have been spared, as too *nettling* in its character; but to hold up the bishop's *principles* and *"conduct* to public *view"* for a valuable purpose, was not "vituperation and abuse"—the real truth, told for beneficial purposes in *church* or *state*, is not *abuse* on *public officers*. 2d. The liberty of public discussion, is the *indubitable right* of the *church*, as well as the *state*.——Bishop Hedding did oppose public discussion, any and every where, save on the floor of the General Conference, and I have not questioned his good intentions in doing so. He no doubt meant to preserve the church from "agitation." 3d. But the course adopted by the bishop in order to accomplish his wishes, in the preservation of *tranquillity*, was a little *unfortunate*, and can never be *reconciled* with the *rights of man*, or sound *republican principles*. God does not save us by destroying our freedom: so neither should bishops undertake to save the church from "agitation," by laying an *embargo* on the *liberty* of *public discussion*—this the bishop did, with all the force of *emphatic exhortation* and *advice*—aye, he threw all his *influence* against it, before the whole conference and many citizens who were present. 4th. The prosecutors may glory in declaring that my humble "rights were not infringed upon," if they will;—they very gravely tell us, that "nothing of all this had happened," but what is all this but to say, either that I was *already* a *slave*, and had no *rights at all;* or that the bishop never opposed public discussion, for which I contend, as a right of the church. 5th. Let some politician undertake to assuage the "agitations" of the American people, in the true style of Bishop Hedding, by opposing public discussion, any, and every where, save on the floor of Congress, and see if he is not immediately charged from all quarters of our happy country, with "uttering opinions on the subject of government, *subversive* of our civil institutions." Would not Mr. Hedding himself charge him?—would not our prosecutors come out *long* and *loud* against him? Aye, and the editors of the "Christian Advocate" too. Let all candid men reflect a little on this matter.

We have one item more to notice, and then we are done. The prosecutors say:—"As to the *stealing march of ecclesiastical power*, which is complained of, the writer knew that the march had been retrograde," p. 58. Is this so? Have I, with perfect knowledge of the *contrary*, stated *"the stealing* march of power," to be onward? No truly, what I stated, I knew to be the fact, and I shall now sustain myself, by an induction of particulars, and leave the community to judge, whether *"ecclesiastical power"* has been on the *"stealing march,"* *backward* or *forward*.

1st. In 1784, in the city of Baltimore, on Christmas day, at the organization of the government of the Methodist E. Church, the itinerant preachers did *then*, and *there*, boldly march up to a principle of ecclesiastical polity, *and take it into their safe keeping*, after which the Roman clergy struggled, by trick, stratagem, and pious fraud, for 1160 years before they laid their hands upon it, *and took it into their safe keeping;* and when they got it, the church was ruined. The principle is this, namely, *that to the itinerant clergy alone, does pertain of divine right, all legislative, judicial and executive power, over the whole church; leaving nothing to the local preachers and the lay members, but absolute submission to their will, or expatriation from the church.*—*Their will officially expressed, by a delegation of one for every seven itinerant ministers, in the General Conference, is now the law of the church, against which there is no balance of power, no check, or defence in any way.* A single pope never sat on St. Peter's chair at Rome, for 1160 years, without the elective voice of the people, as may be seen by an appeal to Mosheim's and Gregory's Church Historys; but when had our local preachers and members a voice in the election of a bishop of the Methodist Episcopal Church? Never!

2d. In changing the *title* of *superintendent*, in 1787, for that of *bishop*, without the consent of the American Conference. See Lee's "History of the Methodists," p. 128, and contrary to the express instructions of Mr. Wesley. See "Moore's life of Wesley," p. 285, and when becoming an independent Methodist Episcopal Church, doctor Coke, Mr. Asbury, and the itinerant preachers, did abundantly strengthen themselves in the possession of the power which they had *assumed* at the time of the organization of the government.

3d. According to Lee's "History of the Methodists," p. 183, the power to make presiding elders, which was first *assumed*, and "used for several years" *without law*, and was finally in 1792, established to the bishops by the General Conference, "gave them a power over the whole church," which indeed, "really looks alarming!" No man in his senses will pretend that the power of episcopacy is weaker by the presiding elder system. This system renders the whole government, in its practical operations, vastly more powerful in every way.

4th. In 1796, according to Lee's History, p. 234, a "deed of settlement" was got up, to be carried into execution throughout the whole connexion, as far as the civil authorities and laws would allow. This deed makes the property a kind of common stock, or at least, the use of it is made common to all the Methodists in every state and in every conference. It is placed under the *absolute legislative* control of the "General Conference, of ministers and preachers," for the people can only use it according to their *legislation.* It is placed also under the *absolute appointing power of the bishops*, who have power to put the occupants into the pulpits and parsonages, without consulting any *will* but their own. Thus, the itinerant clergy, by taking this *anti-christian hold* of the temporalities of the people, have immense power over them. By controlling the property, they control the people themselves: *"for power over a man's substance, really does in most instances, amount to a power over his will."* Is this march retrograde, or onward?

5th. In 1808, the restrictive instrument, improperly called a constitution, was formed, by which our bishops became *officers for life.* The General Conference became a delegated body, and the whole government was so *saddled upon the Methodist community, by the itinerant ministry alone,* that no *vital changes can be effected or hoped for, without the consent of all the Annual Conferences, and a vote of a majority of two-thirds of the subsequent General Conference.* This the bishops can easily hinder, as they hold all the *appointing power,* and consequently all the *church livings* in their hands. This is onward too.

6th. In 1820, if I mistake not, our bishops became pensioned upon the book concern, at New York, for all their table expenses. Henceforth, they are not to know want like other men. Their support is as certain as that concern can make it. Numbers have given them power. Wealth has given them power; for what would a King be, with all his arbitrary principles of government, without men and money?

In this induction of particulars, we think we have shown *"the stealing march of ecclesiastical power"* in the Methodist Episcopal Church, to be *onward, fearfully "tending towards accumulation,"* and yet we are told by the prosecuting committee, because Mr. Wesley's general assistant, and the itinerant preachers had done pretty much as they pleased, before the church had any thing like a settled government i. e. before the revolution, "that the march of ecclesiastical power is retrograde!" What candid man, who knows any thing of our history, can allow this? The fact is, the principles *assumed* by the itinerant clergy in the organization of the government are without parallel in our country, for this *tyrannical character;* and these principles the itinerant clergy have become amazingly strengthened in, by their various additions, and by nothing are they more strengthened, than by their firm grasp on *church property,* through the medium of the "deed of settlement," and the constitution, as they call it, of 1808—this girds the government fast upon the people, and leaves them no hope, but in ecclesiastical expatriation.　　　　　GEORGE BROWN.

STEUBENVILLE, May 1st, 1828.

CHAPTER XIX.

Miscellaneous remarks by Dissenter, published in January, 1827.

The extracts, from this paper, like the rest of Dr. Bond's selections for his Narrative and Defence, could not have had their intended effect, had they been so exhibited as to have conveyed the true and entire meaning of the writer. We have revised the paper and can find nothing, considering the occasion which produced it, to which we can raise any reasonable objection. It is only necessary to replace the extracts and read them in their proper connexions with the whole essay, to be convinced of their *truth.* We proceed therefore to submit the paper in its own justification. In order to assist the reader, the parts selected by Doctor Bond, will be printed in Italics; and a few notes will be appended. The reader is requested in the mean time, to keep it in his recollection, that the travelling preachers, by the aid of those under their influence, had begun to expel reformers, for partaking in the formation and exercises of union societies, before these remarks were admitted into the Mutual Rights.

MESSRS. EDITORS,

Under the date of October 20th, I sent you some thoughts on the subject of reform in the Methodist Episcopal Church. In that communication I briefly suggested, first, that there are multitudes in the bosom of our church, distributed over this continent, who are decidedly favourable to many changes in the government of the church, but who from motives of prudence, remain silent on the subject, and probably will continue to do so, until this controversy shall assume some conclusive aspect. Of the truth of this remark I have additional confirmation since the date of my last. I suggested, secondly, that there were many weighty reasons for the silence and neutrality of our preachers and members, on this momentous question, and a principal one is, that a system of oppressive treatment and persecution has been organized and acted upon, from New England to New Orleans. It is the policy and practice of those in rule, to place in as obscure and irresponsible relations and stations as possible, all our travelling preachers who are suspected of being friendly to the proposed reform in the government of the church, while local preachers, leaders, stewards and trustees are placed under the ban, and in the back ground of the administration, for the same reason. And to finish this ominous specimen of papal manœuvre, numbers have been expelled from the church, simply because they are reformers. This will doubtless deter and intimidate many, but not all. There are those who will speak and write; and there are those who will bear and read, maugre all this threatening array of distrust and persecution, held up to reformers *in terrorem:* A third remark was, that those who wish for reform, and act from conviction in trying to obtain it, should be firm and fearless in the assertion of their rights.

I confess it is a source of peculiar gratification to me to see the spirit of determined inquiry so extensively diffused among our people, notwithstanding conference lectures, pulpit hints, and class room lessons to prevent it. These warning voices so often lifted up in our hearing, are the evident misgivings of power, and so many proofs that our arguments in favour of reform, are felt even by those who affect to despise them. A fourth of my prefatory remarks was, that although much good feeling may be lost in this controversy, yet as the present and future interests of the church require it, reformers ought not to blench from their purpose, whatever social sacrifices they may be *called upon to make; but ought to continue in the church, and multiply and vary their efforts, until the existing anomaly of government in the Methodist Episcopal Church, shall revert to its primitive Wesleyan standard; in which state, if we can credit Mr. Wesley's declarations, it was never intended that the Methodists should become an ecclesiastical establishment, headed by an episcopal hierarchy, consisting of an indefinite number of incumbents, all possessing the same powers, and ruling the same diocese.** The model for such a state of things, is not to be met with in the whole range of church history, except when four individuals at the same time, claimed by divine right, the chair of popedom in the Roman see. If the reader is startled at this, let him recollect that things that are alike in their nature and progress will be compared by the human mind and classed accordingly.* A fifth remark, was on the right which every reformer has to remain in the church. Why leave it? They believe and speak the doctrines of the bible, as taught by Mr. Wesley and his venerable associates. They do not object to the moral discipline of the church. They are pleased with and determined to support the Wesleyan plan of itinerancy. They are attached to all the peculiarities of original Methodism, as taught by the Wesleys, such as class and band-meetings, love-feasts, and free-seated churches. A charge I am aware, has been published by our patent rulers, from Maine to Georgia, and from the Gulph of St. Lawrence to the mouth of the Mississippi, that reformers intend the destruction of all these, but we ask for the proof. Have reformers ever said it? Have they written it? Is it to be inferred from their known character and conduct? Have they not uniformly disavowed it? It is in this way, I regret to say, the motives of reformers have been gravely libelled, in order to maim and cripple their efforts in an attempt to improve the church, and promote its best interests; but I sincerely hope none of the friends of reform will be provoked to leave the church. If the work of extermination be commenced, they will find enough to do. Every such outrage will be avenged by an attitude of resistance and defence on the part of scores, who but for such measures would have gone to their graves without marshalling themselves among those with whom on this subject they had long thought and felt. I repeat, therefore, a former suggestion, that separation from the church is to be deprecated, until heaven by "obvious indication" shall point out the time. *We cannot expect to succeed immediately in the great objects we have in view. I have no hope that the next general conference will do any thing for us. We have too many men in power, bishops and would-be-bishops, that are hovering over the nucleus of eclesiastical aggrandizement; and already laying their plans to prevent the election of reformers to the general conference, to indulge the hope, even for a moment, that we shall be able to accomplish much in that short time. But the fact, that they are thus industrious to defeat the objects of reform, is the proof of our*

---

*Mr. Wesley's letter to Mr. Asbury as published in his life by Mr. Moore, puts this question for ever at rest. "How can you—how dare you suffer yourself to be called a *bishop?* I shudder, I startle at the very thought, &c! &c!" Moore's Life of Wesley, vol. 2, page 285.

success. *Let them manœuvre, let them caucus, let them buy men by the "sale of indulgencies," all will ultimately operate in our favour, and only multiply our friends.** Witness the re-action of their conduct at the Baltimore conference in 1824. Witness the unintended effect of bishop Hedding's famous address at the Pittsburg conference in August last. Also the effect that has followed the defection of three or four half-hearted reformers in different sections of our country; men who publickly and privately committed themselves to the interests of reform, and then for the sake of a place, as it would seem, cowered down most civilly at the feet of episcopal patronage. That this was their motive, I infer from the fact, that reformers only ask now, what they then prayed for, a representative government. Reform is now, what it was then. If their change has been the result of honest conviction, why not let us know the powerful reasons which produced that conviction? If we are in an error, and they have the proof of our folly, why not let it be known? Why not declare this part of God's counsel that has been so useful to their own souls? The result has been, that their former friends on both sides of this question think, that these men will, at least, bear watching.

Another method by which our views are furthered, is, the abuse of "Mutual Rights," by old side brethren indiscriminately. They denounce this publication as utterly treasonous:—Immediately the people start up, and wish to see the odious thing.†—They seek it, read, and become reformers. It is really surprising that so many hard names, so many ill-natured epithets, should be given to a little monthly paper, gotten up as its title imports, to evince by argument, that the rights of legislation in the Methodist Episcopal Church belong to the *many,* and not the privileged *few.* One says it is "inflammatory;" another, it is "too sour;" a third, it is a "wicked bitter thing;" a fourth, it is edited and supported by a group of "backsliders;" a fifth, that the writers withhold their names, and that nobody will notice it, not even to review it. These, Messrs. Editors, are grave episcopal objections, and have all been urged by our pious rulers. Now I would ask all who may happen to be my readers, whether there is any thing in "Mutual Rights," from its first to its last number, more inflammatory, sour, bitter, wicked;—that furnishes more stubborn signs of backsliding;—that has greater reason to be anonymous; that ought to excite less admiration, or that should sooner shrink from a review than this language of our overseers. Is the work good for nothing because no one has replied to it? What then will become of scores of publications that issue from our book room? Who reviews the Meth-

---

*The appeal which the writer makes to the facts which immediately follow, is sufficient explanation of the extent of his meaning and amply justifies his statements.

†We know there are few exceptions to this statement. Some read the work to find additional ways and means to sustain their power. And there are others, the slavish adherents to the powers that be, who read to find fault, that they may better please their masters.

22

odist Magazine? Bangs on Episcopacy, McKendree's Address, the famous circular of the Bishops in 1824, and so of other publications stamped with the magic authority of the Methodist book room. All these have received as little notice in the light of review, as Mutual Rights, and less, except from reformers themselves. But the work is anonymous, and therefore unworthy of confidence. And does the intrinsic value of a work, professing to state facts, and discuss principles which every one has the means of investigating, depend on the authority or credit of a name? If so, what will become of some of the most valuable productions of the literary world, even a portion of the Holy Scriptures? the books of Judges, Ruth, Kings, Chronicles, Job, many of the Psalms, and the Epistles to the Hebrews? These were all anonymous, and the writers only ascertained from the internal evidence of their productions, and some of them remain unknown to the present day. Were the papers of Hamilton, Jay, and Madison, now forming the political text book of this country, unworthy of confidence because they all withheld their names at the time of publication? Have the letters of Junius been of no service to the world, the author of which is still unknown? Should Belshazzar have been unmindful of the hand-writing on the wall, because he did not know the hand that traced it? Ought the blind man in the gospel, to have listened to the advice of the Pharisees, because the character and claims of his benefactor were only accredited by the convictions of his own understanding? But Messrs. Editors, I will not proceed. Every reader will perceive, that these are the arguments of children, although urged by men grown. The fact is, these men perceive that their idol is in danger; if light be diffused on this subject, principle will become triumphant. A church ruled and governed by men and laws, whose official creation does not emanate from the intelligence and will of the people, was the capital blunder of the primitive church, and gave birth to popery with all its train of debasing and damning evils. Are we better than the primitive church? if not, the warning voice of history tells us we are in danger. But say the advocates of the present monopoly of power in the church, the people do not *ask* for their rights; for even a bishop has admitted in my hearing, that if they did, they ought to have them. This is well enough, it is conceding, at least, that all is not right; and, that when the people have sense enough to find it out, and independence enough to induce complaint, then they must be attended to, on this subject. It would seem then, that we are not to "render to all their dues," unless we are *asked* to do so. We are not to do justice unless the injured implore mercy. * * * * Messrs. Editors, what we ask is, that Methodism may be in these United States what it was under the eye and management of Mr. Wesley, with this difference, that the government of the church shall correspond with the genius and policy of the political institutions of this country. This is plainly suggested, as I conceive, in Mr. Wesley's letter to Dr. Coke and Mr. Asbury, in relation to the civil rights of American Methodists. *But Mr. Wesley seems not to have contemplated an episcopacy in any shape. It* is, to be sure, asserted in the preface to our book of discipline; but the oldest preachers in the United States, with whom I have conversed and corresponded on the subject, never saw the warrant. It has been called for by friends and foes for thirty years, but is not yet forthcoming. If such warrant exists, why is it that we can learn nothing about it? I have a letter in my possession, saying that a venerable old preacher in the neighborhood of Baltimore, for whom I have the highest regard, is in possession of this document;—that is, written instructions from Mr. Wesley recommending a Methodist episcopacy in the United States. Now if this highly esteemed contemporary of Mr. Wesley, will give this document to the world, he will confer a singular favour on thousands in the Methodist church.* But until such a document or warrant from Mr. Wesley, be produced, I as an individual, must of necessity continue to doubt the historical probity of the preface to our book of discipline, in relation to this particular. I am the more confident that no such document exists, because Mr. Wesley has expressly, in a letter to bishop Asbury, now before the public, ridiculed his pretensions as a bishop, in a way that plainly says, Mr. Wesley never intended Mr. Asbury to be one of the type he was. But as this subject is soon to be discussed by an able hand, I forbear saying more than is necessary to my present purpose. Again, Mr. Wesley definitely disavows his belief in the validity of a third ordination differing from that of presbyter. Finally, as Mr. Wesley was only a presbyter himself, he could not, if disposed, have conferred a third and higher ordination on Dr. Coke, and directed him to confer the same ordination on Mr. Asbury; and if he even had done so, it is no reason why we should perpetuate the error: Mr. Wesleys' motto was, "follow me when I follow Christ."

The object of reformers, therefore, is, that Methodism in this country may be what it was under the personal inspection of Mr. Wesley, subject to such revision and changes in its external discipline, as shall best accord with the rapid increase of knowledge and the improving spirit of the times. As an individual reformer, I am convinced that I contend for nothing that Mr. Wesley would object to, under similar circumstances; and this I propose to shew clearly and unequivocally from Mr. Wesley's writings, in a future communication. When, therefore, our bishops, presiding elders, preachers and people, of the old school, sound the note of alarm, that Wesleyan Methodism is in danger, they either no not know what Wesleyan Methodism is, or they subject themselves to the charge of disingenousness. What had Wesleyan Methodism to do with our self-created and self-styled episcopacy? For I repeat it, Dr. Coke was only set apart as a superintendent of the American Methodists, and not ordained to a third office as a prelatical bishop. The ceremony of separation was only intended to confer Mr. Wesley's authority to oversee the American Methodists upon another, as Mr. Wesley could not attend to them in person. What did original Methodism know of

* We are assured, that the preacher alluded to has no such document in his possession.— Eds.

*our order of presiding elders? One man having power to appoint
seventy, to overrule and remove at pleasure fourteen hundred. Where
in the annals of original Methodism did the framers of our discipline meet with the ceremony of ordination for a bishop?* What
hand had Mr. Wesley in the selection? If original Methodism
was the object of the establishment in this country, why was Mr.
Wesley expelled from his own family, by the official decision of
his own children, in striking off his name from the American minutes? And why did Dr. Coke declare, when preaching the funeral
sermon of Mr. Wesley, that he deemed it the greatest sin of his
ministerial life, that he did not raise his voice against this act of
treacherous cruelty, from one side of the continent to the other?
The truth is, our brethren have widely departed from primitive
Methodism, and the principal object of reformers is to bring them
back.

Reformers are charged with "disaffection." But if their object
is simply to deprive Methodism of its adventitious incumbrances,
and adapt it, in its external organization, to the primitive mode of
operation in the New Testament, surely the charge of disaffection
lies at the door of anti-reformers who first corrupted the simple
plans of Methodism, and now wish to give immortality to their
folly in refusing to reform.

We are told, reproachfully, that reformers are "few." We need
only ask, were not the knees in Israel unbent to Baal few, in Elijah's
time? Were not the apostles few, when they went out to evangelize the world? How many were with the Saxon reformer when he
commenced his career of glory? How many with Wesley when
he began a reform in the church of England? If the majority are
most likely to be right, in any organized body of people, why withhold the privilege of election and representation from three hundred thousand ministers and members of the church, and place it
in the hands of a "few!"

But we are told the "missionary character" of our ministry will
be destroyed if we alter the present system. But as in other cases
of objection, the proof is omitted. Did not missionary enterprize
succeed in the first ages of the church, when all the bishops of the
church together, did not possess as much power as one of our's
does now? We might quote here, the Waldenses and Albigenses,
the Moravians and others, who have been as truly primitive and
missionary in their character as ever we were, and yet without an
episcopacy resembling ours. So far from this being true, the fact,
I apprehend, is beyond cavil, that multitudes of the most able and
worthy ministers we have ever had among us, have been driven
from missionary toil altogether, because of the arbitrary and capri-
cious notions of the episcopacy, in sending them whither they
could not go, without a violation of other and paramount duties.
But it would seem anti-reformers "know nothing" of these things.

*The improvements proposed in our present form of government, are
openly denounced as "innovations." This is somewhat singular when
every man of information knows, that our whole system of episcopacy
in the United States, is to all intents and purposes, an "innovation"*

upon the genius and plans of Wesleyan Methodism, and one expressly disapproved and disavowed by Mr. Wesley.

We are told by some, with an air of great confidence, that we enjoy all the "rights and privileges stipulated for or acquired," at the time of joining the church. This is not true of any minister or member of the church on the continent, who became members prior to 1808. Our restrictive bill of rights of this date, deprives ministers and members of rights with which they were introduced into the world, and born into the kingdom of God, and our book of discipline has undergone alterations and received additions quadrennially ever since. When a few travelling preachers, who meet in general conference, each representing his "sacred seven," and to the whole body of the church beside, utterly irresponsible, see proper, then our code of laws is incomplete; but when multitudes, here and there, throughout a community of nearly four hundred thousand human beings, complain of the unnatural and unscriptural distribution of power among us, then we are hushed by an argument, that it seems must be received without defence or proof, whether it is because it is too forcible to require proof, or too feeble to admit of it, I cannot pretend to say, but the argument is, reformers are "few—disaffected, and innovaters;" and what is worse than all, will say what they think; the prudence of the determination *not* to defend this position, must be obvious to every one.

It is said by our friends of the old side (not Mr. Wesley's side, however,) that our plans and efforts to obtain a representative government, and have the thousands of our Israel duly represented in the legislative councils of the church, are "visionary theories and uncertain speculations." This dexterous stroke, obviously an "appeal to the political feelings" of those concerned, betrays a fearful want of attention both to civil and church history, and is broadly contradicted by the records of ages and nations. The alleged incompatibility of representative government with successful missionary enterprize, is equally contradicted by the history of man and the bible, and a discerning public cannot fail to mark this item of Methodist policy, as worthy of being called up again.

One remark more, Messrs Editors. It is said reformers "inveigh against the discipline of the church." This charge we deny. We think the discipline of the church defective, and wish it improved; but where is the reformer that refuses peaceably to submit to the order of the church? While we remain in the church, and its present discipline is retained, it is our intention to submit to it. May not a man find fault with the government under which he lives, without treasonously inveighing against it? But if the discipline be really, as we conceive, in many respects inconsistent with the scriptures, and unprimitive in its character, where is the sin of opposing it, provided it be done in a proper manner? The framers of our discipline doubtless saw, that this clause on the subject of "inveighing" would be of great importance, in support of the unnatural and almost non-descript form of government, they were about to adopt. We beg leave to ask, however, whether those preachers "inveigh against our doctrines, who do not believe some of them, and publicly preach and openly write against them. That the doctrine of Christ's eternal Sonship, is a doctrine of Methodism, the merest novice knows full well, and yet this is denied and denounced, by scores of our preachers every Sabbath. The absolute omniscience of God, is another doctrine of Methodism, as it is of the bible; and yet, I have frequently listened to Methodist preachers, trying to demonstrate that the prescience of Deity is only contingent,—that he could, but does not know every thing. In a sermon, recently published under the sanction of the Methodist Book-Room, it is expressly asserted, that Jesus Christ possessed "two distinct persons," contrary to the express language of one of our articles. If this is not inveighing against the "doctrines" of the church, surely *we* have not inveighed against its discipline. Our friends, therefore, need not talk so piteously about the "impunity" extended to reformers, for some of them stand in more need of this grace than we do. I suppose it was by a constructive torture of this part of the discipline, that the wary trustees of the Methodist churches in Baltimore, recently refused their houses to a man, whose genius and piety for thirty years past, as a Methodist preacher, have thrown nine-tenths of the pulpits of this country into shade. These men may account to their own consciences for their conduct; but, the question arises, will their contemporaries and posterity receive their plea?

I close by simply remarking, that it is my sincere wish that this controversy may be conducted with the temper and dignity becoming the importance of the subject. The discussion, if properly managed, can do no ultimate harm to the church; truth and facts will be elicited and brought to light; our people will be able to prove all things on this subject, and hold fast, in their form of government, that which is good. That much feeling will be excited, is to be expected: this will occur on both sides, and, if duly managed, is not to be deprecated.

One thing is certain, reformers, so far as I know them, have not manifested the uncharitable disposition that has appeared in most of our active anti-reformers. The former admit the piety and integrity of the great mass of the travelling preachers; they only doubt their policy, or rather are convinced it is both unsafe and unscriptural: while on the other hand, it is, I am sorry to say, the *staid* effort of those who oppose us, to represent us as fallen from virtue and destitute of piety. This conduct may have the credit of zeal— it may be glossed by the casuist, so as to appear plausible to many, but still it is invidious in the judgment of the judicious, and immoral in the sight of God. Let reformers, while engaged in the laudable work of reformering the abuse of church power, not forget or neglect the moral discipline and practical purity of Wesleyan Methodism. Let them remain in the church till they be cast out or compelled to leave it; an event, at present, not to be strongly looked for; but, should it occur, we shall then, in the order of providence, be under the necessity of resting our cause and appeal, with men and churches, better informed, and God, the judge of all.

December 29th, 1826.   DISSENTER.

The remarks which we have in view respecting this paper are. reserved, with intention to present them together with something additional, at the conclusion of the paper by Neale. The propriety of this, will be seen when the intended remarks shall be submitted.

CHAPTER XX.

Presbyter to the Editors of the Mutual Rights.

THIS paper was published in the April number of the Mutual Rights for 1827:—the month in which the Baltimore Annual Conference suspended Rev'd. Dennis .B. Dorsey. Considering the previous expulsions of reformers and the accompanying circumstances indicative of the arrogant purposes of the power party, men of good sense will say, that we, as the editors of the periodical, ought not to have rejected any such papers . as those bearing the signatures of Dissenter, Presbyter or Neale.

Presbyter to the Editors of the Mutual Rights.

MESSRS. EDITORS.
· Permit an individual unknown, and unnumbered in the ranks of reform, to say one word to you, and through the medium of your increasing popular paper, to the world, on a subject in which he feels a deep and an abiding interest. It affords me no ordinary pleasure, to witness from time to time, in various ways, and through different channels, the enlarged borders, and abounding prosperity of the American Methodists, and I should deeply regret the occurrence of any event that might tend in any way, or to any extent, to prevent the unrivalled success, so invariably attendant upon the evangelizing labours of our ministry. It has been suggested to me, by many in different departments of the church, that the influence of the present controversy, on the subject of reform, is directly and extensively hurtful to the interests of practical piety among us, and likely to render us less zealous and primitive than we have heretofore been. This opinion, I conceive, is plainly an error; so far as I can judge, it has no foundation, either in fact or moral probability; as it respects the best means, and the grand elements of ministerial success, in labouring for the world's conversion, we are all agreed, and all united. · The only question of difference among us, is purely a question of government, and hitherto has been, with few exceptions, and I think will continue to be discussed and canvassed apart, from the more immediate concerns of the pulpit, the altar, and the closet. That this has been the aim and course of the principle reformers, admits of no doubt, unless we refuse to believe men who are as fully and fairly entitled to credit as any men living; that there are men among us, professedly in favour of reform, who are as rich in character, talent and usefulness, as any among the thousands our church embodies, not even

excepting the "episcopal board," is a truth, that must be felt by all, unless grossly ignorant. Now to withhold confidence from such men dictating their sentiments without disguise or equivocation, is to insult the human understanding, and outrage christian charity; for it is obviously a departure from all those maxims, that govern men in their intercourse with one another. Our controversy therefore, is one respecting discipline, and I sincerely trust, if our brethren of the old school, are determined to remain unyielding, that they will not attempt to impress the uniformed with an idea that the friends of reform of the discipline of the church, are the enemies of real and vital piety; that this has been extensively attempted, by our non-reforming brethren, is, I think, in proof before the public; and this single circumstance, in my opinion, (although others of a bolder character are not wanting) would justify "Dissenter" in all he has said in his "Miscellaneous Remarks" upon this subject. It seems to have been agreed upon as an "argumentum ad hominem" and this "Dissenter" calls a "system," and that it is "oppressive" will be questioned, I apprehend, by no impartial examiner. What reformers ask for is, that we may have (if any) a presbyterial episcopacy, and a representative government, while our brethren of the majority publish to the world, in no ambiguous language, that such a form of government would prove "ruinous" to the best interests of the church, and that *prelatical diocesan* episcopacy and non-representative government are necessary to the being and perpetuity of Wesleyan Methodism; and this is the actual state of things among us, although Mr. Wesley declares his belief in presbyterial episcopacy and no other.* If the reader be startled, I refer him to our old minutes, where Dr. Coke and Mr. Asbury styled themselves bishops, "by order and succession!" It appears, however, they reformed in a short time and dropped this pitiful figment, as carrying its own refutation with it. In 1789, an attempt was made to conciliate Mr. Wesley, by calling him "bishop of the Methodist church in Europe in the American minutes; and what is indeed remarkable, this was done after Mr. Wesley had written to Mr. Asbury, definitely declaring he would never be called "bishop with his consent." *Now the object of these remarks, Messrs. Editors, is to show that our episcopacy has nothing to do*

---

*After a careful attention to this subject, our deliberate judgment is, that a presbyterial superintendent, was the official character, with which Mr. Wesley, assisted by two other presbyters of the church of England, considered himself to have invested Dr. Coke. That he in like manner, ordained Richard Whatcoat and Thomas Vasey, and sent them with Dr. Coke to America, that they might ordain Mr. Asbury a joint presbyterial superintendent, to co-operate with Dr. Coke in supervising the societies. And that in this manner, he expected to continue his authority and exercise it, by making any other similar appointments, or by recalling any one or all of those who might be appointed from time to time, to act as superintendents. In course that he did not intend, that any one of them, should be an incumbent for life. It has been noticed in a preceding part of this work, that Mr. Asbury got himself elected to prevent his being subject to the recal of Mr. Wesley. And Mr. Freeborn Garretson in his last letter, certainly gives confirmation to this view of the subject.

with original Wesleyan Methodism, and is disowned by it. It cannot therefore, be in any way essential to our prosperity, for the history of the British Methodists, and that of the American Methodists for eighteen years, proves clearly and indubitably that its alleged importance, in order to the success of christianity among us, is a perfectly gratuitous assumption, unsupported by reason, history or common sense. On the other hand, if our bishops, and their pertinacious supporters as high-toned episcopalians, ill as it may look, (for such they really are,) would yield and distribute throughout the different departments of the church that part of their power, that has come into their hands "surreptitiously,"* it would abate the honest inquietude of thousands; it would remove the just apprehensions of the discerning, and bring worthy multitudes into the bosom of the Methodist church, whose names, as things now are, will never adorn our calendar. Of the truth of these remarks, I have no doubt, and surely one who has travelled as a Methodist itinerant preacher, at least fifty thousand miles, may be permitted to speak on a subject that lies so near his heart, and is vitally connected with the individual and social interests of living and unborn millions! With these remarks, Messrs. Editors, I close; but as I have passed the Rubicon, you may hear from me again about the ides of March.

February 28th, 1827. PRESBYTER.

P. S. In the number of Mutual Rights for the month current, I observe some remarks fixing a difference between the terms "discipline" and "government," as used by some writers on the subject of reform. I had observed this distinction in the singular publication of twenty-four "trustees, local preachers, stewards, and leaders," of your city, in December last; but, like many other things in

---

*In addition to what is adduced in justification of Mr. Walker, Luther, &c. in proof of *"assumption,"* and in explanation of the manner how, the influence of the British preachers and Mr. Asbury, prepared and enlisted the American preachers, to go with them and lay hold on all power, legislative, executive and judicial. We here insert an extract from Mr. Freeborn Garretson's letter, alluded to above, and as published in the Wesleyan Methodist Magazine, for the year 1828.

In the year 1787, May 10th, perhaps, he says, "Dr. Coke had just arrived from England, with directions of considerable importance from Mr. Wesley, which caused much agitation in our conference. The business was Mr. Wesley had appointed Messrs. Whatcoat and Garretson, to be consecrated for the superintendency. The former (Mr. Whatcoat) as joint superintendent with Mr. Asbury in the United States;—the latter (Mr. Garretson) to have charge of the societies of the British dominions in America." It is known, that the conference rejected Mr. Whatcoat. After this occurrence took place, Mr. Garretson, speaking of himself and Dr. Coke, says, "We were grieved for the rejection of Wesley's appointments, and for the loss of his name from our yearly minutes. After Dr. Coke returned to England, I received a letter from Mr. Wesley, in which he spoke his mind freely. He was dissatisfied with three things:—the rejection of his appointments;—the substitution of the word bishop for superintendent—and the discontinuance of his name from our minutes."

23

that production, I thought it more the effect of negligence and
inattention, than the result of discriminating reflection. I find,
however, that the Rev. A. Shinn, in his masterly and triumphant
appeal to the public, in reply to this imposing, but every way vul-
nerable document, has admitted and carried out the distinction.
Now, Messrs. Editors, however I may admit the abstract propriety
of this distinction, and I really think it ought to exist and be uniformly recognized, as one of obvious practical utility; and although
I am aware this distinction exists in its full force in the Methodist
Societies in Great Britain, yet I am compelled to think the sagacious masters of our present form of government, did not intend to
make or *allow* the distinction under notice. I refer you to our
Book of Discipline, title page, "The doctrines and discipline,"—
by *doctrines* the authors of this book undoubtedly mean articles of
faith, and, in some editions, a few essays illustrative of them : by
discipline, every thing else in the book. Thus, you will perceive,
that the just and important distinction noticed by your able and
judicious correspondent, Mr. Shinn, is not in reality admitted, in
the authorized nomenclature of episcopal Methodism. If any man
among the thousands who belong to our establishment, should
venture to find fault, or suggest improvements in the government
of the church, be it done never so temperately or calmly, it is not
material, he is liable to arrest; the displeasure of that establishment is sure to reach him, and the chances are ten to one if its
foot of oppressive memory be not placed upon his neck. In confirmation of an opinion of so serious a character, I offer the conduct of the late Virginia conference, in *sanctioning* the expulsion
of several members of the Methodist Episcopal Church, for no
other reason than that they were reformers. It may not be amiss
to remind our readers, that *three* of our bishops were present at
this conference, and no doubt, felt their hands much strengthened
by the primitive zeal of "Benton Field," and the *approving* majority who gave the salutary vote ! Mr. Wesley, in his "Appeal to
Men of Reason and Religion," declares *opinions* in matters of
church government are *no part* of Methodism: but, our more sagacious bishops, and others, seem to think *opinions* vitally essential,
at least to *episcopal* Methodism. Mr. Wesley was right, and so
are our bishops; and the remark is perfectly consistent, when we
recollect that episcopal Methodism is plainly and incorrigibly
anti-Wesleyan. The preceding remarks, will, perhaps, satisfy
many readers that I am correct in using the term discipline in its
ordinary acceptation with our men in rule : but, I beg leave to
state distinctly, that I mean by it precisely what Mr. Shinn means
by *government*, as in strict propriety distinguished from *discipline*.
I used the term in accommodation to established usage in our
church. If discipline mean only our "general rules," as given us
by the Wesleys, I am satisfied ours is the best discipline of human
construction, on earth: but, if I am to understand the term, as
used by Coke and Asbury, to cover all the flimsy and fallacious
pretensions of Methodist Episcopacy, then, and only in this event,
I am opposed to *some* parts and features of what is called our

discipline; and I claim the privilege of stating freely and fairly, the nature and extent of my opposition: and, in doing this, I cannot conceive that I *inveigh against the discipline* any more than our reverend bishops themselves, who have consented to the *repeal* of many things contained in the discipline, at the time this politic precautionary clause, on the subject of inveighing, was introduced.

If the time has arrived, when a man cannot express his opinions as to the scriptural character, and relative legitimacy of our mode of church government, without subjecting himself to ecclesiastical censure and anathema, as exemplified in the proceedings of the late Virginia conference, then in this case, I think, the sooner we arrive at a crisis, the better. The world ought to know, and heaven and earth record, that the Methodist Episcopal Church of the United States, is to be governed by human authority, and not by moral evidence, as found in the Bible, and other kindred sources of accredited information. The intelligent reader may startle at the sentence he has just read; but let him recollect, remarks of this kind, are not without foundation in truth, and support from facts. Why are our friends, of the reigning administration, so vigilant in their endeavours to ascertain who are the real authors of various productions on the subject of reform? Obviously, that they may reach them by a process, other than that of argument and fair discussion. If the friends of the present state of things in our government, were disposed to confine themselves to the merits of the controversy on the subject of reform, it would be entirely immaterial to them, who "Spectator" and "Dissenter" are; and so of others: they would reply to them, and attempt to refute them, as individuals who have a right, from God and men, to say what they honestly think: we should not see so many engaged in a furious hunt, or epistolary crusade, after writers, who are too well acquainted with the PRESENT TEMPER OF METHODISM, to disclose their names; but whose productions, at the same time, must convince good sense, wherever it is found, that they are entitled to be heard, and will be read with interest, by all who love and appreciate freedom of inquiry: even *bishops* can guess at authors, to whose arguments they do not choose to reply; and the conjecture is received as *oracular* and published by pious *minions* accordingly. Allow me, Messrs. Editors, to ask, what does all this prove? To me, it demonstrates most irrefutably that one of your correspondents, the influence of whose pen will be felt by posterity, is correct in saying, we are to be silenced by *authoritative* and not by *rational* arguments. As an individual, it is very possible, I may feel in no very pleasant way, the force of this reasoning; that I shall never be convinced by it, I am entirely certain. I respect the sayings and the authority of the Son of God too much, to call any man "master" in things affecting my eternal interests, and those of my fellow creatures. John Wesley, the enlightened and beloved founder of Methodism, was only a presbyter in the church of England; Doctor Coke was nothing more: from these the Methodist ministers in America, have derived their ordination. Confident that the latter could not derive from the former, what

they did not possess themselves, I renounce, as perfectly gratuitous and trifling, the episcopal pretensions of those among us, with whom the abused epithet of *bishop* means any thing more than a primitive New Testament.   PRESBYTER.
March 27*th*, 1827.

CHAPTER XXI.

Reasons in plea for reform in the government of the Methodist Episcopal Church, by Neale. This paper was published in the number for July, 1827.

THE same departure from candor and propriety was practised in this, as in the two preceding instances; and, as in those, so in this, an exhibition of the paper entire will justify its publication. The part extracted will be recognized by being printed in italics.

It should be remembered, that this paper was published subsequently to the suspension of Rev'd D. B. Dorsey.

GENTLEMEN,—I propose sending you a few brief essays on the subject of Episcopal Methodism, the *distinctive* character of which will be understood from the caption above. I shall avoid all elaborate discussion, because I know your list of correspondents is rapidly increasing; and I am deeply solicitous that my brethren, who may think with me on this subject, should severally speak for themselves. I wish to be distinctly understood, I have no controversy with original Methodism, I have no dispute with the doctrines and duties of Methodism, considered as a *systematic* exposition, or practical *illustration* of the word of God; and in the remarks I have to offer, I have no concern (unless it be allusively) with Methodism as it exists in Europe; my only concern is with *episcopacy* as an appendage of Methodism in the United States. The distinguishing system of religious doctrines and duties styled Methodism has existed in Europe near a century, without the unnatural appendage of which I am now speaking, and it existed in this country without any such burdensome adjunct for eighteen years. It is plain, therefore, that episcopacy is no part of Methodism in its primitive character and operations; it is not, in any way, essential either to its being or success, as the creed and manual of one of the reformed churches, and it remains to be inquired into, whether it be a *good* or an *evil*, in its rather mysterious connection with American Methodism. Hitherto it has been the policy of Methodism, at least in most cases, to be bold and unshrinking, she has not declined the light nor shrunk from inquiry, but has fearlessly challenged the most acute investigation; and if the *supernumerary* badge, under which she now appears, in the United States, I mean episcopacy, suggests the propriety of adopting any other policy, it is obviously a suspicious circumstance, and calls for examination.

Impressed with the correctness and importance of this view of the subject, we proceed to inquire into the *origin* and *establishment* of episcopacy among the Methodists in the United States; on this subject I submit to the reader a concise *syllabus* of facts, the greater part of which, admit of *positive* proofs, and the truth of the rest is fairly inferable from an *induction* of authentic particulars. 1st. The Rev. John Wesley, the father and founder of Methodism, expressly avows his belief, founded *especially* upon the reasoning of Lord King, that there are but two orders of ministers by divine appointment in the church of Christ;—deacons and presbyters, and that a *third* order differing from and superior to presbyters, is an unscriptural and gratuitous assumption. He also affirms in so many words, that a presbyter has the same right to ordain, that a bishop has; hence Mr. Wesley, in language that nothing but ignorance or want of candour can misconstrue, definitely renounces episcopal ordination, when we understand by it a *third* order of ministers, in the church of Christ. 2d. Assuming that Mr. Wesley acted consistently (and a charge of inconsistency here would argue want of principle) we are only allowed to suppose, that Mr. Wesley's ordination of doctor Coke, Mr. Hanby, Mr. Taylor, Mr. Pawson, also Messrs. Mather, Rankin and Moore, was simply an appointment to labour and govern, in given sections of the vast field of missionary effort and pastoral care, to which the personal inspection of Mr. Wesley could not extend, and *not* the creation of a *third* order, as asserted and contended for, by the bishops and their apologists of the Methodist Episcopal Church.

In the ordination of these men, Mr. Wesley conferred equal powers upon all, at least we can find nothing to the contrary; one was as much a bishop as another; and the power conferred by Mr. Wesley, as the great father and leader of all the Methodists, was simply to create them *superintendents* under himself, with the express understanding that they were to continue united to the established church, or at least were not to seek a separation from it. If, however, Mr. Wesley had intended his ordinations to create a third order of ministers in the character of bishops, this would have been *publicly to disown* the discipline of the church of England, and must have been considered by all, as a *bona fide* separation from it. It is, therefore, clear as the light of heaven, that all these were ordinations of appointment and not of office, they created no new relations or powers, but simply gave the pre-existing relations and powers of these men a new direction, in reference to the *specific* divisions of labour for which they were set apart. 3d. We have positive proof from the pens of the living and the dead, that in the case of Dr. Coke, Mr. Wesley instructed him in the most explicit and "solemn manner," not to take upon him the name of bishop, nor allow himself to be so called; and we have it from the pen of Mr. Wesley himself, that three years after this had been done, by Dr. Coke and Mr. Asbury, in the United States, he *conjured them in the name of God*, to redeem themselves from the disgrace, by putting an end to their episcopal pretensions at once. Now it must occur to the reader, that few men ever made a better use of language than Mr. Wesley, he was in the habit, proverbially so, of calling things by their proper names; and had he considered doctor Coke and Mr. Asbury as possessing episcopal powers, in any other than a *presbyterial* sense, he would have joined with the world, and christened them by their *favourite* self-selected title, bishop. But Mr. Wesley tells them, that in his judgment, it would be more to their credit to be called *by men*, "a fool, a rascal, a scoundrel," than to be called "bishop," when they had nothing to entitle them to the distinction, in the sense in which they used it, except their own *affectation* of episcopal dignity. *4th. From the preceding facts, it appears, that the introduction of episcopacy among the Methodists in the United States, so far from being "recommended" by Mr. Wesley, was expressly disapproved and forbidden, and the proceedings of the General Conference of 1784, in establishing diocesan episcopacy among us, was in open violation of the instructions of Mr. Wesley; and, I now take the liberty of saying, to the Rev. Wm. M'Kendree, Enoch George, Robert R. Roberts, Joshua Soule, and Elijah Hedding, that a statement on this subject, to which I find their names subscribed, in the preface to our Book of Discipline, is believed by many to be a perversion of historical fact, and they are hereby publicly called upon, to furnish some evidence of the truth of the aforesaid statement; or leave us to infer, that such evidence cannot be produced. In justice, however, to these distinguished individuals in the Methodist Episcopal Church, I would say distinctly, I believe they are all innocent of having made this statement originally, but they have made it their own, by giving it the sanction of their names, as I have not been able to learn, that this preface has ever been sanctioned by any General Conference, if it has, upon learning it, I shall make (should God preserve my life) a similar on the next general conference, as the proper organ of information. At present the bishops appear to be the only responsible persons, and on them I call. Should the policy of the cabinet induce them to remain silent, as heretofore on similar occasions, I shall take the liberty of thinking they cannot answer me, without damage to their own cause, which it would seem must be supported by silence. 5th. As it is in proof before the reader, that Methodist episcopacy can derive no support from the name or sanction of Mr. Wesley, both having been definitely withheld, so also, does it admit of proof, that the great body of the Methodist ministers and members in the United States were not consulted at all, in the adoption of this enormously misshapen system of aristocratic government. It was the undivulged project, the favourite scheme of a few master spirits, who meeting in secret conclave, and excluding the junior members, even of their own body, (as living witnesses declare) acknowledging no constitutional rights, and comprehending no legislative privileges, as belonging to any except themselves, proceeded to the hasty formation of the present plan of government among us, and unblushingly palmed it upon posterity, as the offspring of Mr. Wes-*

*ley's wisdom and experience.** 6th. *The spurious origin of Methodist episcopacy, is to be inferred from the fact, that those very individuals who made these pretensions, were unsettled and felt misgivings on the subject.*

Dr. Coke, in a letter to Bishop White, of Philadelphia, doubts the power of Mr. Wesley to confer legitimate episcopal authority; he does the same in a letter to the bishop of London, written subsequently, in both of which he modestly asks for re-ordination. Whenever doctor Coke was absent from this country, he was by common consent *unbishoped*, both in Europe and America;—even the *mitre* could not preserve those who wore it from *doubts*, and *fears*, and *change.* Coke admits the whole system to be an "aristocracy."

At *one* time they attempted to establish their episcopal pretensions in one way, at *another* on very and widely different grounds. In 1785, the bishops say, in their Book of Discipline, 3d section and 6th page: "The uninterrupted succession of bishops from the apostles, can be proved neither from the scriptures nor from antiquity." In 1789, while this statement was fresh in the recollection, and lying on the shelves of the Methodists throughout the United States, these *same* bishops, publish in the minutes as follows:—"Ques. Who are the persons that exercise the episcopal office in the Methodist Church in Europe and America? Ans. John Wesley, Thomas Coke, and Francis Asbury, *by regular order and succession.*" All this is passing strange! I will not dwell on the *fact*, that the Methodists have *never* assumed the style of a church in Europe, much less at the time that this was written. I will not pause to animadvert upon the *groundless* assertion, that Mr. Wesley exercised the "episcopal" office in Europe, although every man of reading knows he *did not.* He himself affirms it was the office of a "presbyter" he exercised; but, I come at once, to notice the *change* of sentiment in these men, in the short space of four years. In 1784, scripture and antiquity demonstrated the doctrine of "uninterrupted succession" to be a *fable.* In 1789, they have ascertained that they are bishops "by regular order and succession." Now scripture and antiquity have become a little more pliant, and speak a different language. Now that these self-created bishops have a little more power, and are likely to become established in the exercise of it, the *want* of countenance from "scripture," and the misty lore of "antiquity," are *ingeniously* kept out of sight, and the hasty admission in the discipline, that bishops are *not* the regular successors of the apostles, is *struck out for ever.* Reader! as a man of sense and candour, I ask you to stop and look at this, re-read the above, and ponder well its bearing. The documents are all before me.

In the present preface to our Book of Discipline, the adoption of our present form of government is attributed to the express instructions of Mr. Wesley; but the venerable Wesley has, unequivocally, disavowed the honour, and no one has ever shown or quoted the doc-

* Witness the transactions of 1773, 1779—1784.

ument, paper, or verbal instructions of *Mr. Wesley.* It is now nearly a year, since all our bishops were respectfully invited to furnish information on this subject, if they had any to furnish;—they have not even deigned a reply of any kind. Passing by the uncourteousness of such an act, and the insult it offers to the wishes of inquiring thousands, who it is known to the bishops, feel a deep interest in the subject, I shall plead their apology, by taking it for granted, that they would have replied, if they had been able to do so, without defacing the beauty of those "institutions received from their fathers," many of whom are still living; or, perhaps, like the Chinese historians, they are unacquainted with their own origin, because their living fathers conceal it.

But finally, *Mr. Asbury* pleads his authority, as a *Methodist* bishop, on the following grounds: '1st. *Divine authority.* 2d. *Seniority in America.* 3d. *Election of the general conference,* 1784, 4th. *Ordination of Coke, Otterbine, Whatcoat and Vasey.* 5th. *Because the signs of an apostle were found in him."* See *Asbury's Journal for May,* 1805, third volume, page 168. *No "succession"* directly hinted at here, no allusion to *Mr. Wesley.* On this expose of the *arcana of Methodist* Episcopacy, I would only say it is plain, *Mr. Asbury* is here speaking of himself as a bishop of the third order, and superior to presbyters. Of his *"Divine authority"* we can say nothing, only we know it was not received from the Scriptures. As to *"seniority"* we have yet to learn that it ever creates any new civil or religious rights. With regard to the vote of the *"general conference"* electing *Mr. Asbury,* it is only necessary to observe, they might have acted unadvisedly in this vote of the conference of 1784, as well as in others, and we know that many of the acts of that very conference, have been since repealed, as improper and disadvantageous. On the subject of *"ordination"* as it was only an ordination by presbyters, we cannot admit its *"episcopal validity,"* if more be meant than a presbyter. As it respects the last item, the signs of an apostle can only be seen in an apostle, and of course have not been seen since the apostolic age. Thus the reader will perceive that our *"fathers"* acted a palpably inconsistent part, in the introduction of episcopacy among us, and have been under the necessity (created by their own indiscretion) of acting an equally awkward, and I fear posterity will think, ridiculous part, in defending themselves against the charge, of a reckless usurpation of unwarranted power. For the present, Messrs. Editors, I must let this subject rest; but by divine permission, its examination shall be resumed in a subsequent number, of the series of essays; I propose to send you.

To *reformers* I would respectfully suggest, "the signs of the times" are becoming rather squally and ominous. We have at present a troubled atmosphere, the clouds lower and the tempest impends, but we need an "Euroclydon" of the moral kind, to purify the air. The only way to get rid of legalized error, and pernicious practices consecrated by long usages, is fearlessly to attack by argument, and urge by expostulation, until you reach the point of proper excitement, when those concerned will begin to *think* and *act* for themselves. I am more astonished that we have done as *much* as we have, *than* that we have not done *more*. When my attention was first called to this subject, I stood alone in one of the largest conferences in the United States. Now I have a score of travelling preachers within the same limits, beside a large number of local preachers, and hundreds, if not thousands of private members who think as I do. These changes are working every where, and their influence *must* be felt. A few here and there, like my unknown friend D. B. Dorsey, may be *put down*, by some of our testy "lords over God's heritage," but they are destined to *rise.* Sage deliberative bodies, like the Baltimore conference, may *pass* and *enforce* and *defy the contravention* of such "resolutions" as those offered by Mr. Roszel and Mr. Guest; these may be *rubricked* on the journals and minutes of the conferences, as important precedents and mere *specimens* of what *can* and probably *will* be done hereafter, "but the end is not yet," these delectable *morceaux* in ecclesiastical legislation, have to pass the ordeal of *public opinion.* The above named gentlemen will be honoured with *readers* as well as *hearers*, and their singular efforts to *loyalize* the Methodists, so as to preclude even the freedom of social inquiry, and epistolary correspondence, may not only affect the *character*, but may induce their contemporaries to write their epitaphs before they are dead! This "Bellum Episcopale," as bishop Pierce calls it, this "war in support of episcopacy," is not ended, they may yet need all the *recruits* their present superiority, in point of numbers, will be able to furnish them. *We* have the Bible on our side; the practice of the primitive church sustains us; public opinion is our friend and ally; the civil institutions of our country lend us aid, and the *genius* of American freedom, throws her protecting shadow over every friend of equal representation and mutual rights. If we should not live ourselves to witness the achievement of the objects we have in view, the "clods of the valley" will be sweetened by the reflection that our children *may.* Let us, therefore, labour and faint not; if "cast down we are not destroyed."

In this contest, my brethren, the similitude of our trials, may be the "smoking flax and the bruised reed," but the one shall *smoke on*, and the other *unbroken*, shall continue to *bend* before the blast. Let your rulers *insidiously* expel you (as ministers) from their pulpits, *by not inviting you there*, it will only *lessen* the number of their own hearers, while the good sense and discernment of the public, will take you up, and you will find yourselves cherished in the high places of their affection and esteem, where your oppressors will seek in vain to intrude.* To conclude, our attitude

---

*We had been excluded from the pulpits in Baltimore, because we had the impudence to espouse the cause of Rev. D. B. Dorsey in defiance of the Baltimore Annual Conference.

24

is one of petition and address for our rights; rights which we claim as Christ's freemen, in the bosom of a branch of his church and people; rights founded on the testimony of God's word, and the practice of the primitive church; we *resist* only when we are *oppressed ;* as members of the great family of our common father, we *ask* to be treated as his children, and we shall continue to ask. If *tauntingly* requested by "the powers that be," to *leave* the church, we reply, if you *wish* a division, separate *yourselves;* if required to lay down our arms, (they are those of reason and scripture) we say to our rulers, "*Come and take them.*"

June 1, 1827.   NEALE.

Doctor Bond, having selected those fragments which are printed in italics, proceeds to make his remarks; and instead of touching the merits of the papers, he flies away from the arguments and attempts to hide behind the cloud of ill founded prejudice, which his party had raised against a certain pamphlet entitled "The History and Mystery of Methodist Episcopacy." * * * "The co-partnership" says he, "is obvious."

Previous to the publication of the Narrative and Defence, unbounded pains had been taken, to raise the prejudices of the Methodist people against Mr. M'Caine's pamphlet. Mr. Emory had attempted to answer it, and in the opinion of Doctor Bond and his friends, had produced a "masterly refutation of *all* the allegations in the History and Mystery, &c."   Relying upon *this "masterly refutation"* and the existing prejudices of his party, he seems to have thought it all sufficient to secure our condemnation, if he could shew, that Dissenter's, Presbyter's and Neale's papers contained "assertions" which had an "*obvious coincidence*" with those published by Mr. M'Caine—This, by the way, was an argument for the good people who were prepared "*unanimously*" to condemn the Mutual Rights "without having read the work at all." Dissenter's paper is dated December 29th, 1826; Presbyter's March 27th, 1827. And on the 30th of March, 1827, Mr. M'Caine obtained from the clerk of the District of Maryland, his certificate of copy right. The writer of Dissenter and Presbyter was also the author of Neale; and his residence too remote from Mr. M'Caine to justify the conclusion, that there was any co-partnership or collusion practised between them. The Doctor and his friends must not be surprised if they learn before they die, that many men of sound judgment are not quite satisfied with the "masterly refutation." Any man of good understanding who shall chance to read these papers of Dissenter, Presbyter and Neale, will perceive, that the writer is not a man of ordinary attainments. The papers speak in a language irresistible. And neither Doctor Emory nor Doctor Bond has succeeded in shewing that they ought not to have been published in the Mutual Rights. Besides it should not be overlooked, that, outrageous as they have represented the History and Mystery to be, and wicked as they would have their people to believe the writer of that pamphlet is, they found it necessary to prepare the "*masterly refutation*" with the hope of preventing its effect. If the refutation was so complete, why did they not trust to the corrective power of this masterly work, instead of having recourse to expulsion? Doctor Bond says there is no doubt that we generally encouraged Mr. M'Caine to publish his work. On the supposition that we were acquainted with Mr. McCaine's intended publication, in reply to which the "masterly refutation" had not then been published, was it at all inconsistent with our duty, as editors of the periodical which was open for essays upon the government of the Methodist Episcopal Church, to admit papers written in the best style, because they possessed point, more especially when we knew they would be sustained by a pamphlet which would require a "masterly refutation?" and which, after all this boasting about its "refutation," in respect to the great question at issue, still remains unanswered? Every sensible man in these United States must see, upon an investigation of the subject, that our expulsion for admitting these papers into our periodical was altogether out of character. The perpetrators of this outrage may keep one another in countenance, but the day will come, when those who may wish to revere their memories, will not find it an easy task.

From the two succeeding papers, the one by the Rev'd. N. Snethen, the other by the Rev'd. Asa Shinn, extracts were taken which are represented by doctor Bond to be very objectionable. They are therefore printed at large. Considering the occasions which produced them, nothing more is necessary. The parts extracted, and commented on by doctor Bond, are in italics.

It is proper to state as a prelude to Mr. Snethen's address, that it was written and published, immediately after the Baltimore Annual Conference had suspended Mr. D. B. Dorsey.

CHAPTER XXII.

An Address to the friends of reform, by N. Snethen.

DEAR BRETHREN,

You have heard of what was done in the bounds of the Virginia Conference; and will hear of the proceedings of the Baltimore Annual Conference, in the case of Dennis B. Dorsey. I notice this last case as proof of the fact, that the itinerant preachers have taken a stand against reform, or representation, which must change our relation to reform. We are no longer to consider ourselves as standing upon the open and equal ground of argument with those brethren in behalf of a principle; but as the supporters of what we conceive to be truth and right, opposed by power. From the beginning, I have considered the avoiding of written discussion by almost all the itinerant preachers on the old side, as ominous of this issue, and have not ceased to anticipate the time when a display of the plenary powers in their hands would in effect place us as lambs among wolves, and call upon us to be "wise as serpents and harmless as doves."

I understand the text in its original application, "I send you forth as lambs among wolves," that is, with truth and right, among those who have both the power and disposition to resist your principles and to destroy you, but I give you no means of self-defence, but the wisdom of the serpent, tempered with the harmlessness of the dove. We have all along asserted, that there is power enough in the rulers of the Methodist Episcopal Church, to excommunicate us all, and we are still of the same opinion; but if any one should doubt it, let him remember, that the body of men of whom we mean to ask for a fish, may give us a scorpion; that the very general conference of 1828, may make rules, if they conceive they are not already made, to reach every reformer.

Our relation I say was changed in point of fact, from the day the power of the itinerant preachers waked into action. The most distinguished preacher who should advocate the principle of representation would find himself obnoxious to power, as well as the least member in the church. No man among us has power to oppose to power; and truth or right in the mouth of a minister would not lose its lamb-like helplessness, when assailed by the power of a majority of itinerant preachers. This majority have all the claws and all the teeth, and therefore, every man may be made to fear.

This fact, brethren, we ought not by any excitement of zeal, to lose sight of for a moment. I therefore repeat it, truth or right in the grasp of power, is like lambs among wolves. Hitherto reformers have spoken and written freely and openly, they have had no secrets, the wisdom of the serpent was not necessary. The charge of imprudence and the general cast of all the objections brought against them, goes to shew, that power was not roused, that the prey though within reaching distance, was not seized. Henceforth the character and conduct of Methodists must rapidly change. On the side of power there will be fierceness, and on the side of right concealment. Threatenings and suspicions will mightily prevail. A name has already been demanded, not I suppose to satisfy curiosity, or to confute arguments, but for punishment, or at least impeachment.

Heretofore it is doubtful if a single travelling preacher has written for the Wesleyan Repository or the Mutual Rights, who was not known to his superiors. The writers themselves often confided their proper names to their brethren, and so they felt not like lambs among wolves; but a few examples in the Annual Conferences will put an end to this kind of generous rivalship. Travelling preachers themselves will be thus painfully taught the wisdom of the serpent—taught to elude power by policy. What a temptation will this prove to trespass upon the innocence of the dove? Brother Dorsey, it seems, was advised by his friends (in this advice I did not participate,) not to answer any question which might criminate himself. This refusal to answer questions, this putting the conference upon the proof of his guilt, made a part of his offence. Who then did he thus offend? No one but the members of the Annual Conference. Now mark brethren, the importance of this whole transaction: not to brother Dorsey merely, but to us all. Let this procedure be established as a precedent, and of what avail will the maxim of our Master be to us? How can we maintain the harmlessness of the dove? How escape the jaws of power without dissimulation? Surely if we have no right to keep our own secrets among *those who make a man an offender for a word, we have no means of self preservation, but in the unqualified wisdom of the serpent.*— Brother Dorsey by a vote of the Annual Conference, is deprived of a station for one year. Will either of these voters feel any twitches or qualms of conscience in treating either of us relatively in the same way, if we refuse to answer and to promise as they may please, and to punish us for contumacy, or contempt of court?— And that too, while in our courts of law no man is required to answer any question which goes to criminate himself. If brother Dorsey were imprisoned or banished for one year, by an Annual Conference for contumacy, all the state of Maryland would be up in arms. The sound of the outcry of the deed would reach the ends of the earth. Persecution! would be re-echoed in all directions; and yet, in case either of imprisonment or banishment, he might preach as much in the capacity of a travelling preacher as these brethren intend he shall in this case. The truth is, brethren, that there is the very essence of persecution in this act of the Baltimore Annual Conference. As a precedent, it deprives us of our last, our only resort to defend ourselves against power, which we can employ consistently with our christian character. Is not punishment for telling the truth and a reward for dissimulation, in effect, the same? I know brethren, that we shall be accused of party spirit and party purposes, in espousing the cause of this brother, but it is not so; by this dispensation we are sent forth as lambs among wolves. Power has usurped authority over truth; *we are not to be reasoned with, but punished.* In this new condition, what are we to do? We must go to the New Testament for direction and instruction; and there we learn, that we must be wise as serpents and harmless as doves. Must we not then espouse the principle, and can we do this, without espousing the cause of the first martyr of it in the Baltimore Annual Conference? Your turn, my turn, may come next. It is an awful thing to be driven by the power of a majority from the last asylum of harmlessness—to be reduced to the dreadful alternative of dissimulation or bearing witness against one's self.

On the critical situation of brother Dorsey's health, passing from his bed to the conference for several days, in which he was kept in painful suspense, I shall not enlarge; for though these circumstances may have produced a crisis in his disease, though his death may be thus accelerated, even this would be a small matter compared with the consequences of this principle as it relates to the souls of men, this sin against the brethren! It is not to your sympathies that I am addressing myself; but to the sacred regard which I hope and trust, you feel for the vital principle of all human society. Let the wolf of authority, the unrelenting majority, either in church or state, leave us to a harmless silence, let them not compel us to bear witness against ourselves, and the wisdom of the serpent may shield us, may yet enable us, in the enjoyment of a good conscience, to elude their death-grasp.

I deem it proper, brethren, that in this portentous change, in this

*state of our affairs, that you should hear my voice, should see my
name. It will, I know it will, it must be asked, now the time is
come to try men's souls, where is Philopisticus? Where is Ady-
nasius? Where is Senex? Where is the man who was among the
foremost to challenge us to the cause of representation? Where is
Snethen? I trust that while he is among the living, but one answer
will be given to this question—he is at his post, he is in the front of
the contest, he is shouting, on, brethren, on! and if he fall, it will
be with a wound in his breast, and with his head direct towards the
opponent.*

It is the command of the great Captain of our salvation, that we
may not hurt even a hair on the head of those who hold the power
to hurt us, even by the wisdom of the serpent. We may not lie,
even for the glory of God; but we may be silent, we may leave
those in ignorance whom we know will not only not see, but punish those who offer to give them light. The old side men have
done a strange thing in the earth: they have placed themselves
hors du combat; they have done more, they have tempted us to smite
them in the back, to aim invisible strokes at them—to conspire for
their overthrow. Let us not avail ourselves of the advantages
which their folly or want of foresight has given us! But I call
upon you by every sacred name, to resist this inquisitorial power,
this attempt to renew in America, the old, the exploded principle
of torture, this monstrous outrage upon the principles of civil and
religious liberty;—the punishing of men for not submitting to criminate themselves. O defend to the last extremity, this final sanctuary of oppressed innocence. What may not the traitor to this
cause expect? Where can he find shelter from the frowns of
Heaven and earth, and the self torture of his own reflections?

Of the labour of seven years, I make no account. I was not a
lamb among wolves. My courage, my resolution was not put to
the test. I have never been questioned, never called to account,
not even threatened. The fiery trial has come upon one who is as
the shadow of a man, a walking skeleton, and I yet go free!—
Mysterious providence! Thank God, the afflicted man's soul is in
health, his fortitude is unimpaired by disease, he has the courage
and the constancy of a martyr: Lord, let the young man live and
not die! Let not the wife of his youth be a premature widow.
I cannot now desert the cause and be innocent before God or
man. I cannot now be silent and be harmless. I therefore ad-
vertise you of the change, and earnestly entreat you to conform
to it by conforming to the directions of the Master, "Be ye,
therefore, wise as serpents, and harmless as doves." Your affectionate fellow labourer in the great cause of church representation.   N. SNETHEN.

Every reader must see that the occasion called for this paper;—
and that the paper speaks for itself.

CHAPTER XXIII.

The sovereignty of Methodism in the South.

PETERSBURG, Va. Feb. 22, 1827.

"THE Virginia Annual Conference, which sat in this place, has just risen. The Granville Union Society of North Carolina, presented to it a petition, praying that seven members, lately expelled from the Methodist Episcopal Church for joining the Granville Union Society, be restored to their former standing. The petitioners alleged, that although the charge exhibited against them was that of inveighing against the discipline, yet nothing was proved against them on the trial, but their having joined the Granville Union Society. That when the preacher in charge*, found he could not substantiate his charge, he put the following question to the society, "You that believe their being members of the Union Society will have a bad effect, will rise up." That a majority of those present were of that opinion and rose up, upon which the preacher read them out as expelled. With the petition, the Granville Union Society presented a charge against the preacher for mal-administration; but the conference decided that it was not mal-administration. Thus the door is closed on our unfortunate brethren, and opened for all the reformers to be pushed out of the church.

WILLIS HARRIS."

The first thing here demanding attention is, the charge presented against those brethen of "inveighing against the discipline." If the true notion of "an inveigher" is, "a vehement railer," as our learned men have told the world it is, then surely it is possible for a man to *object* to a principle or rule of government, without "inveighing" against it. But let us have divine authority: "Michael the archangel, when contending with the devil, durst not bring against him a *railing accusation*, but said, the Lord *rebuke* thee." Jude 7. Hence it appears, from the authority of God, that if we should so remonstrate against a law of discipline, as to say to the author of it, "The Lord rebuke thee," this would not be "a railing accusation," and consequently would not constitute us guilty of the charge of "inveighing."

But the members of our ecclesiastical courts, doubtless claim the right of explaining the law, as well as executing it. If they refuse to receive the explanation above given, they must believe that all objecting, reasoning and petitioning against a rule of discipline, is to "inveigh" against it. If they mean this, let them say so in plain language; and let the free-born sons of America open their eyes, and see what is claimed by these men: first, they claim the right to *make* laws at pleasure, without having a single *representative of the people* among them; secondly, they claim the right to be the judges and explainers of their own laws; thirdly, they claim the right to enjoin *silence* on all their subjects, so that they shall

---

* Mr. Benton Field.

not *speak*, or *reason*, or *petition* for amendment, on pain of excommunication! If all this can pass in the United States of America, and pass without the indignation of the community, I have mistaken the sense and spirit of my countrymen.

These august law-makers are free from all restraint.—First, they are free from the restraints of *representation:* no delegate of the people can open his mouth in their legislative assemblies. Secondly, they are free from *constitutional* restraint: for though they have a little instrument of their own making, which they *call* a constitution, yet it is evident to common sense, that it is no constitution of the people; and the makers of it can alter it when they please, without the people having a single voice in the matter. Thirdly, they are free from any restraint of *scripture:* for in their law-book we read, that when members have broken their rules of discipline, "If they do not amend, let him who has the charge of the circuit, exclude them, [the church] shewing that they are laid aside for a breach of our rules of discipline, and not for immoral conduct." Book of Discipline, page 82. Thus it stands glaring in the open face of heaven, that the "Methodist Episcopal Church" claims authority to expel members from the church of the Lord Jesus Christ, who are guilty of no breach of his laws ("not for immoral conduct") but merely because they have violated such "rules of our discipline" as, according to her own confession, involve no immorality! It is evident, if the church has authority to make *one* such law, she has authority to make a *thousand:* of course she can make laws, and expel members, independent of Divine revelation.

But, our Virginia brethren, in expelling those members in such a lordly manner, practically assumed the principle, that in their administration they need no law at all, save the *will* of the executive officer. He put the question, "You who believe that their being members of the Union Society, will have a bad effect, will rise," &c. What law can this brother find, even in "our discipline," which says a committee or society have authority to expel members for any thing which they "believe will have a bad effect?" This would put supreme power in a court of judicature, and would supersede the necessity of every other law: let the legislature pass a law, that the court may condemn men for any thing, which they "believe will have a bad effect," and this law alone will be sufficient to regulate all judicial proceeding. Such was the conduct of "the preacher in charge!" Who might as well have said, "You who *wish* the brethren to be expelled, will rise up!" And, more astonishing still! This pitiful and contemptible course of conduct, we are informed, was brought before the Virginia Conference, and they "decided that it was not mal-administration!" This loyal and orthodox conference, appears to claim the right of exercising the authority of Eastern despotism: "All people, nations, and languages, trembled and feared before him: whom he *would* he slew: and whom he *would* he kept alive; and whom he *would* he set up; and whom he *would* he put down." Dan. v. 19. So "the preacher in charge," whose "administration" is before us: "he *would* that

those "radical" members should be expelled; and as he had no law
of God nor man to support him, he had them expelled by a law of
his *own will:* "You *that* believe that their being members of the
Union Society will have a bad effect, will rise up!" And because
"a majority happened to be of this opinion," he "read them out
of society."

If a single preacher can exercise such power, and be patronized
by an annual conference, what may we expect to hear, when the
time shall come, for people to go up to the general conference?
If the bishop should be there, and have the weight of the conference made up with his presiding elders, will it be said, "All people, nations, and languages, trembled and feared before him : whom
he *would* he slew; and whom he *would* he kept alive; and whom
he *would* he set up; and whom he *would* he put down?" Suppose
the next general conference should pass a law, that every man
who has written any thing for the Mutual Rights shall be forthwith
expelled; and that every member who has a single number of this
"extraordinary publication," shall commit it to the flames, on pain
of excommunication: will any man question their right to pass
such a law? They evidently have as good a right to do this, as
to pass any law whatever to dismember the disciples of Jesus
Christ, who are at the same time acknowledged to be free from
"immoral conduct." It appears they not only claim the right to
enact such laws, and expel members for breaking them, but also
to expel them for making any *objection* to the law! Do these men
really think they can keep the people of the United States hood-
winked in this manner? If they are unwilling the people should
enjoy the liberty of speech and of the press, do they not give a
demonstration in the presence of heaven and earth, that ecclesiastical power has far greater eagerness to destroy the just freedom
and rights of mankind, than civil power has? Here, our civil rulers
let us quietly enjoy those privileges, without manifesting any signs
of reluctance; nay, they appear to take pleasure in protecting us
in the enjoyment of this liberty: while professed ministers of the
meek and benevolent Saviour of mankind, who call themselves the
followers of the great and amiable Wesley, wish to deprive us of it,
under pretence that we are inveighing against their laws! Tell it
not it Gath; publish it not in the streets of Askelon; lest the Ma-
hometans and Pagans rejoice and triumph, to see us equal or sur-
pass them in priestly insolence and dominion.

By the late act of the Virginia annual conference, in sanctioning
the administration of Benton Field and others, it is practically
avowed, that the Methodist people are not under a government of
laws at all. There must first be a law in existence, by which members can be expelled for doing what the court may believe "will
have a bad effect," before "the preacher in charge" can *execute*
such a law; there must first be an act of the legislature, saying,
members shall be expelled for joining the Granville Union Society,
or signing its constitution, before an executive officer can arrest
members under such a law, and before a jury can have authority to

25

judge of their innocence or guilt in the breach of it.   This conduct is still worse than passing an *ex post facto* law, which according to our American constitution, is destructive of civil liberty, and inconsistent with all good government.   Let "our people" duly consider what will be the consequences, if they tamely look on, and see such precedents sanctioned by the high authority of "the Methodist clergy."   They will not stop at the Granville Union Society; they will not stop at the reformers, for after all these "restless spirits" shall be put out of the way, such "true friends of old Methodism": as Benton Field and his coadjutors, will soon be on the look-out for new offenders: and any persons among the "laity" or "locality" will be liable to arrest and expulsion, whenever "the preacher in charge" shall be displeased with any part of their conduct, and shall be able to persuade his jury, "it will have a bad effect."

If the Virginia brethren should urge, that the Granville members were expelled under the law which forbids "inveighing against our discipline," it would be well for the Methodist people to reflect seriously upon this plea.

The Bible, being clothed with the grandeur, of Divine Authority, demands our implicit submission; so that we have no right to *object* to any of its laws, to *petition* for amendment, or to use any *efforts* whatever, to bring about any alteration.   Now if the above rule of discipline is intended to lay on us the same restriction, and to enforce the Methodist episcopal government, as absolutely as the government of the Almighty is enforced; does not this look like *the man of sin seating himself in the temple of God, and shewing himself that he is God?*   But the Methodist Episcopal Church, it would seem, claims even higher authority than the Bible does; for she not only prohibits all objecting and petitioning against her *present* laws, as the Almighty does, but also demands the same implicit submission to all the laws she may see proper to enact in future!   We know not what her future laws may be, but we are bound before hand, not to "inveigh" against them: that is, not to *object*, or *petition*, or use any *efforts* towards any alteration or amendment!   If this be the "system" which is "approved" by the "best judgment" of our official brethren of "Baltimore city station," let this fact stand as the eighth wonder of the world; and if this explication of the "inveighing" rule be not contended for, then let the Virginia annual conference confess, that the administration of Benton Field was perfectly *lawless*.

But, it seems, we must argue upon *principle*, as well as upon *law*: William Compton says, in his reply to Ivey Harris, "You inquire under question 2d, 'Was our aged brother convicted, or even charged with any thing that, in your estimation, would exclude him from the kingdom of heaven?   If not, why give your vote to exclude him from the church militant?'   The plain English of this is, that no person ought to be excluded from the Methodist (which you are pleased to call militant) church, unless he be guilty of something that would exclude him the kingdom of heaven.   This plea, I think, was sufficiently met by brother Howard.   But, as most of us are forgetful hearers of those things which confute our strongest arguments in favour of a beloved theory, it may not be amiss to repeat the substance of, at least, a part of what he said. And to make this more forcible, permit me to preface it with one or two questions. Will you say, that the Presbyterians because they are Calvinists, or the Baptists because they deny infant baptism and free communion, or the Protestant Episcopalians because they contend for a regular succession in the ministry, are heretics, and ought, therefore to be excluded the kingdom of heaven? Let your conscience answer. Now, if the opinions of neither the one nor the other of these denominations are sufficient to exclude a man the kingdom of heaven, then neither are the opinions of the whole, provided they were concentrated in one man. Let us then suppose Lewellyn Jones, to be this man. In sentiment he is a Calvinist—he denies infant baptism and free communion—and contends that none ought to preach the gospel but those who can prove their ministerial authority in a direct line from Christ;—through the apostolical church—through the church of Rome—and through the Protestant Episcopal Church. You, I suppose, would say, that he is not to be excluded the Methodist (that is to say, the militant) Church; because of the peculiarity of his sentiments. Is this the way you argue? Or, is this the "freedom" of which you so often speak, and which, from your course of reasoning, one would think is one of the constituent parts of your contemplated change in the government of the Methodist Church? If so, what I did in the case of your "venerable father in Israel," I conceive to have been one of the best acts of my life. L. Jones may, or may not be a good man, and so of I. Harris, it is not for me to say." Answer;

1st. Supposing it were true, that L. Jones, in being "in sentiment a Calvinist," in "denying infant baptism and free communion," and "contending that none ought to preach the gospel but those who can prove their ministerial authority in a direct line from Christ," would thereby be guilty of a sin against "Methodism," while it is acknowledged he would be guilty of no sin against God; —still he could not be legally expelled, even upon "Methodist" authority, until a law shall be found in the discipline, saying members shall be expelled for being "Calvinists in sentiment," for "denying infant baptism," &c. Is there any such law in the discipline?

The act of "inveighing against our doctrines" may be plead, but there is no "inveighing" in the case: Mr. Compton supposes L. Jones ought to be expelled for being "in *sentiment* a Calvinist," and for "*denying* infant baptism." But perhaps after a while the word "inveighing" will be made to signify *denying, objecting, petitioning, doubting* or *presuming!* Nor can he plead the act of "holding and disseminating doctrines contrary to our articles of religion;" for, though he supposes L. Jones to "*contend* that none ought to preach the gospel but those who can prove their ministerial authority in a direct line from Christ," yet said Jones could not be condemned on this ground, by any law in being; because brother Compton cannot put his finger on one "article of our religion" in the discipline, which this sentiment contradicts. And how could L. Jones be expelled, for "holding and disseminating" a sentiment which is not mentioned or alluded to in any one of our articles? This same brother Compton appears to have been so long in the habit of acting "without law," in his administration, that he probably begins to imagine he has a right to do so; and that "true friends of old Methodism" ought not to be restrained and hampered with legal rules and provisions.

2d. It is matter of public record, that Mr. Wesley received Calvinists into his societies in England, and openly disavowed the practice and the principles, of expelling any "merely for their opinions." I appeal to the case of Mr. Cennick and other members at Kingswood. After Mr. Wesley had read several of them out of society, for various crimes which he alleged against them, that they had "belied and slandered Mr. John and Charles Wesley," that "they had been guilty of tale-bearing, back-biting, and evil speaking, dissembing, lying and slandering." T—B—replied, "it is our holding election, is the true cause of your separating from us." "I answered," says Mr. Wesley, "you know in your conscience it is not. There are several predestinarians in our societies both at London and Bristol: nor did I ever yet put any one out of either, because he held that opinion." See "the works of the Rev. John Wesley," volume 1, page 339, 340. Now as Mr. Compton and "all" his "fraternity" take pleasure in announcing it "from New England to New Orleans," that they are all good old "Wesleyan Methodists," why should poor "Calvinists" meet with so much worse treatment in their "*Episcopal Church*," than they did in Mr. Wesley's "*United Societies?*"

3d. Brother Compton appears to be a great advocate for "free communion." Suppose on one day, he should solemnly invite our Baptist brethren to the Lord's table, who "*deny*" this sentiment; and on the next day expel several Methodists for holding the Baptist sentiment on the subject; ought he not on the third day, upon his own principles, to admit those expelled Methodists back to the communion table, who are owned to be no more disqualified for it, than the Baptist brethren whom he invited? Ought he not to receive those brethren back to the "communion" whose expulsion he "conceives to have been one of the best acts of his life?" Suppose he should say, you Presbyterians, who are Calvinists, we invite to our "free communion," you Baptists, who "deny infant baptism," we also invite; you Episcopalians, who contend for an uninterrupted succession in the ministry, we likewise invite: but if after the service is over, we find any of "our people," who agree with any of you in sentiment, we will immediately expel them from the church; and they shall have no more communion with us "without confession, contrition, and proper trial."

4th. "The plain English of this is, that no person ought to be excluded from the Methodist (which you are pleased to call the militant) church, unless he be guilty of something that would exclude him the kingdom of heaven." The plain English of the matter is this, brother Compton:—the church is *under law to Christ*, or she is not—her members are to be governed by his law, or they are not; if they *are*,. then, as the subjects of his government, they, in their christian character, and church membership, must stand or fall by his law, and by that alone; if they are *not* under law to Christ, then please to tell me, how Christ lost his authority, and by what means an usurper has got into the seat of Majesty? If Christ's government cannot protect his own faithful subjects, while they *obey* his laws, this must result from one of two causes,—either that his government was originally defective, or that its salutary influence is supplanted by an usurped administration. You may adopt which alternative you please; and if you reject both, you will be so good as to point out a third. Do not the citizens of the United States consider themselves protected from condemnation and banishment, so long as they continue obedient to the laws of our government? And have not the subjects of our Saviour's government a right to expect equal protection, while they continue obedient to *his* laws? Or will you say, that the act of expulsion did not expel the Granville brethren from the church of Christ at all, but only from the "Methodist Episcopal Church?" This seems to be twice intimated in your reply to I. Harris; for you seem quite unwilling that the Methodist should be called "the militant church." Do you mean, then, that she is the church triumphant, or that she is not the church of Christ at all? Your only evasion must be, that she is a *part* of the church of Christ; and that the intention was not to expel those brethren from "the church militant," but only to expel them from a *part* of the church of Christ, that they might go to *another part* of it: if so, you own they stand in the same relation to Jesus Christ, and to his church, in which they stood before. I entirely concur in this sentiment; because I believe they were expelled in *defiance* of the Saviour's laws, and therefore, in reality they stand related to him and to his government, as they did before.

But Mr. Compton meant expulsion from the church of Christ, in the full sense; and he believes all reformers ought to share the same fate: for thus he speaks: "I think it very advantageous to Methodism, that those who are dividing our Zion against herself, should be traced out and exposed in all their ramifications, both as it relates to themselves, and to those with whom they are connected in the great work of *revolutionizing* the government of the church. I will suppose a case, C. is found carrying off the body of a murdered man, upon examination, it is ascertained that A. caught the deceased and held him fast, that B. threw him down, and that C. stabbed him through the heart. They are all tried, and being found accessary to the man's death, are all brought in guilty, and must all die. In vain A. pleads that he only caught and held the deceased, and B. that he only threw him down; the law says that they shall die. But Ivey Harris asks, "whether it is just to name what B. and C. did on the trial of A. and so try to tranfer their guilt to him," who perhaps may say that he had no idea that matters would have been carried so far. "But the law says that he must die."

From this illustration, it is plain that Mr. Compton meant expulsion from the church of Christ, as fully as banishment would be expulsion from the United States, or even as a public execution would be expulsion from the protection and privileges of our government. For "the law says that they shall *die.*"—"The law says that he must *die.*" Strangel that his mouth should be so full of legality—"the law says"—"the law says"—after his perfectly *lawless* career, and that of his "fraternity," in condemning our Granville reformers, in committee, in quarterly conference, and in the annual conference, through "all their ramifications." How he intends his illustration to apply to the reformers, we may be able to ascertain. He seems to consider them, some how, as moral murderers. By the "murdered man," he may probably mean *episcopacy;* for this is sometimes represented as the nerves and vitals of the church; and when our opponents speak of the *church* being in danger, their real meaning is, that the absolute power of the *hierarchy* is in danger. It is supposed then, that at some time or other, this formidable power will be slain, and that "C." will be "found carrying off the body" of the "murdered man." "Upon examination" it will be "ascertained that A. caught the deceased and held him fast, that B. threw him down, and that C. stabbed him through the heart. The law says that they shall die." Mr. Compton will be pleased, however, to wait till the law is enacted, before he attempts to put it in execution. *Suppose some President of the United States should succeed to establish himself in the presidential chair for life, and should have a law enacted forbidding the citizens on pain of imprisonment, banishment or death, to "inveigh" against the government, either by objecting to any of its laws, by petitioning for their repeal, or using any argument, through the medium of speech or of the press, to evince their impropriety; would not the American people find this to be a "gag law," a hundred degrees worse than any they have ever yet had to complain of? And in what would such a law differ from our present "gag law" in the discipline, on supposition that it is to be so explained as to sanction the administration of Benton Field? It will require all the clerical talents of old Virginia to point out any difference, excepting that the latter only involves the church penalty of expulsion: in principle, they would be precisely the same; and this principle, with a sufficient enlargement of power in the hierarchy, would soon bring the christian community again under the penalties of corporeal punishment. Yet this tyranny is sanctioned by the Virginia annual conference!*

An orthodox brother took an early opportunity to give the public the following information: "We have had a fine conference, and the appointments of the preachers you will receive in a few days. Three bishops attended—bishop M'Kendree, whose health and spirits are better than usual, and bishops Roberts and Soule, who are in good health." Why, herein is a marvellous thing, that the preacher in charge had several members expelled from the church, in defiance of all laws, both human and divine, and yet "a fine conference," with "three bishops" at its head, and could not discover this to be "mal-administration." The next number of the Christian Advocate (the 27th) contains a more full account, in which we are informed "the venerable bishop M'Kendree addressed them in a very affectionate and feeling manner.——He then concluded with an exhortation to holiness," upon which the conference afterwards "adopted the following resolution."—"That the doctrine of holiness recommended by our discipline, and forcibly impressed in the address of the bishop, be duly weighed and enforced by the members of this conference."

It is hoped, "the members of this conference," in "duly weighing" the subject of christian holiness, will try to acquire just views of its nature and extent; and that while they justly expostulate with those who oppose the doctrine, as being advocates for sin, they will not forget to raise a warning voice against those who make professions of holiness and sanctification as a cloak for their sins. By what tests is it to be ascertained that a man is not sanctified? They are such as the following: "He that saith he is in the light, and hateth his brother, is in darkness even until now." (1. John ii. 9.) "If a man say, I love God, and hateth his brother, he is a liar." (1. John iv. 20.) "But, why dost thou judge thy brother? or why dost thou set at nought thy brother? For we shall all stand before the judgment seat of Christ." (Rom. xiv. 10.) "But Diotrephes who loveth to have the pre-eminence among them, receiveth us not—prating against us with malicious words: and not content therewith, neither doth he himself receive the brethren, and forbiddeth them that would, and casteth them out of the church." (3. John, ix. 10.) For a man who is in the habit of such conduct, as is thus condemned by the divine laws, to get up in love-feasts and say, "at the last prayer meeting, or at the last camp meeting, I was sanctified," is an insult to God, and to all christian morality. Alas! how many thousands are zealous advocates for the doctrine of sanctification, and are ready to fly into a passion in defence of christian perfection, who are merely fond of the sentiment, not because they have a true hungering and thirst after righteousness, but because the doctrine is a distinguishing peculiarity of Methodism? The doctrine of holiness is valuable beyond expression, and may be justly regarded as the great consummation of christianity; but sectarian partiality appears to corrupt every thing it touches; and such are the mysteries of human nature, that it would be no matter of surprise if the time should come, when a man would be ready to cut his brother's throat, in defence of the doctrine of christian perfection. In what way our Virginia brethren intend to "enforce" the "doctrine of holiness," they have not explained: perhaps their conduct will hereafter explain it.

By what tests are we to ascertain that a man is sanctified? They are such as the following: "Take my yoke upon you, (that is, the law of Christ, and not the yoke of "episcopacy") and *learn* of *me;* for I am *meek* and *lowly* in heart: and ye shall find rest to your souls." Matt. xi. 29. "Therefore all things whatsoever ye would that men should do to you, do ye even so to them: *for this is the law and the prophets.*" (And of course, is christian perfection.) Matt. vii. 12. "But the wisdom that is from above is first *pure,* then *peaceable, gentle,* and *easy to be entreated,* full of *mercy* and *good fruits, without partiality,* and *without hypocrisy.*" (James iii. 17.) Let our brethren measure their sanctification by these rules, and not suppose it sufficient merely to be said in familiar conversation, at the last camp-meeting brother —— was sanctified, or at the last prayer-meeting, sister —— was sanctified. And let them not forget to pray that the general conference may be *sanctified;* that is, that the members of it, in their official deliberations, may be *entirely set a part for God,* and not "reject the commandments of God, that they may keep their own traditions."

As to the objection so repeatedly and confidently urged against reformers (and which has been urged in the same way through all past ages) that they intend to injure and destroy the church, we reply: it is our design to guard and benefit the church, by opposing the progress of that clerical dominion which has been injurious and ruinous to her, for more than a thousand years. When we make a stand against the high career of ecclesiastical episcopacy, it is fondly pretended we oppose the progress of the christian religion, and are secret friends to infidelity; whereas the truth is, that the sovereign power of the priest-hood, which we oppose, has greatly promoted infidelity in all ages, and has furnished deists with a more plausible and influential argument against christianity, than they otherwise could have ever got hold of: for they appeal to the conduct of "the clergy," in proof that Jesus Christ has authorized a succession of men to establish and perpetuate a tyrannical hierarchy over the human understanding, and the human conscience. But any set of men, who practically and officially say, the Lord Jesus has authorized them to be tyrants, slander and blaspheme his gracious character; and the only way to repel the infidel argument, is to demonstrate that in all ages, tyrannical hierarchists have been usurpers, who have assumed and maintained their unholy power, in *defiance* of the Saviour's laws.

A keen-eyed opponent will be likely to perceive, with terrible indignation, that we are waging war against "the episcopacy!" Yes: this absolute sovereignty is the centre point of our opposition; while it stands, in its present mighty energy, all reformation is hopeless, and an increase of moral darkness and corruption will be inevitable. We have no quarrel with our present bishops: we believe them to be good men; and that none of them have become by many degrees, so corrupted by this same great "Episcopacy," as many of their tame underlings and dependents have become.

If our brethren suppose any thing in this communication is too sharp, the author, confident that nothing here expressed needs an apology, requests of them to recollect what has been the *occasion* of this paper; and then to read Tit. i. 13, 14. "This witness is

true. Wherefore rebuke them *sharply*, that they may be sound in the faith: (and the faith is to be found in the Bible, not in ecclesiastical canons) not giving heed to Jewish (or Gentile) fables, and *commandments of men*, that TURN FROM THE TRUTH." "For the time will come when they will not endure sound doctrine; and they shall *turn away their ears from the truth*, and shall be turned unto fables." 2 Tim. iv. 3, 4. A VIRGINIA METHODIST.
APRIL, 1827.

CHAPTER XXIV.

Rev'd. Dennis B. Dorsey's case, &c. before the Baltimore Annual Conference.

LETTER FROM REV. DENNIS B. DORSEY TO VINDEX.

Rev. and Dear Sir,

I have had the pleasure of reading your affectionate communication, addressed to me through the medium of the Mutual Rights, and now enjoy the equal pleasure of returning you, through the same medium, my grateful acknowledgments for the solicitude you evince in my behalf. In the mean time I am not unmindful of the great principles, on which this matter is predicated, of which I presume you are an advocate. And as you put several interrogatories relative to the case, for your personal information, I will give you a glance at the whole affair. I am the more inclined to this than to entire silence, under existing circumstances, for two reasons. The first regards the reputation of our conference, which is as liable to be tarnished as my own; and the second is grounded on the special regard which I must necessarily feel for my own character, as a christian, and a minister of the gospel. This brief history shall be given from my best recollections, and the least exceptionable means of information. If there should be any apparent mis-statement, I hope no brother will attribute it to design; and that if any one be prepared to correct it, he will do so through this *public* medium, before he undertake to contradict or criminate in a *private manner.*

Some time last February, I wrote a few lines to a friend, Mr. Hugh M. Sharp, in which I gave him information "of a work on church government, publishing in Baltimore, by a committee of Methodist preachers and members, exposing to open view, some of the errors in our government and administration." I also informed him that the work "was a very satisfactory one, well worth his attention;" that I had "taken it more than eighteen months, and was well pleased with it;" that it contained so many pages, and came at so much per year; that several in that part took it, and were well pleased with it; and, finally, requested him to let me know immediately, if he desired to have the work, and to inquire

26

of a brother, whom I named, whether *he* would take it also. In conclusion, I remarked to him, "You need not mention this to any other person, if you please." But when Mr. Robert Minshall, the preacher in charge of Huntingdon circuit, came round, my friend Sharp betrayed me, by giving him my letter to read. Mr. Minshall then, according to his own telling in conference, asked him for a copy of the letter, to which he replied, that he might have the *original*, as it was of no use to him.

About this time there was a letter written by Mr. Minshall, to Mr. David Steele, giving him information, that I was actively engaged in circulating the Mutual Rights, and probably censuring me for such conduct. This information was communicated to Mr. John Davis, who, in his turn reported it again, until, finally, it was brought before the late Annual Conference, first in the form of an *objection*, and then as a *charge*.

After the commencement of the conference, I had an interview with Mr. Davis, who gave me an assurance, that as I would give him no satisfaction in his interrogatives, he could not *pass over* it on the examination of my character. Accordingly, when my name was called, in the examination of characters, Mr. S. G. Roszel arose and made some *objections*, stating, as I was informed by members of conference, (for I was too unwell to be present,) that I had been away from my circuit during the last year, under the pretence of being *afflicted*, but had been travelling extensively, circulating a work derogatory to the interests of the church. My case was then postponed until I could be present.

The following, or second day after, I was present, when my name was called, and the inquiry instituted, whether there was any thing against my character: certain members of the conference replied that there *was*, but the brother who had made the objection was absent. Mr. Roszel being sent for, came in and stated his objection, on the ground above mentioned. This led to reference for information, and Messrs. Steele and Minshall were referred to as informants. My letter was now produced by Mr. Minshall, who stated how he obtained it, and intimated that it had now accidentally come in place, as he thought when he obtained it, might sometime be the case. The letter was then read, and the president, Mr. Soule, remarked, that if I had any thing to say in reply, I was now at liberty to speak for myself. As I saw no formal *charge*, I had nothing to say, only to acknowledge the letter read to be my own production. I then retired, and after considerable deliberation on the subject, the case was decided. Some brother, in passing out of the conference, remarked to me that I could now go in, which left me under the impression that my character had passed. I then went in and remained until conference adjourned; but heard no official announcement of the decision, until the next day. I learned however, in the mean time, the nature of the decision, in part, but could find no one to give it me in full.

The next morning when the journal of the preceding day was read, there was a formal charge recorded, which was "*for having been actively engaged in the circulation of an improper periodical work.* The president then announced to me from the chair, that the decision of the conference in my case was, *"that my character should pass, upon my being admonished by the president; and promising the conference that I would desist from taking any agency in spreading or supporting any publications in opposition to our discipline or government."* The admonition was then given from the chair; after I had signified my disposition to submit to it, for the sake of brethren's consciences. I was then required to give a pledge that I would comply with the latter part of the resolution; which I *refused* to do, while the resolution remained in its unqualified form. I then replied to all the important items of the admonition, and gave my reasons for not complying with the latter part of the resolution. The following is the substance:

MR. PRESIDENT,

With you I admit the importance of clearly ascertaining that we have *found* the truth, before we undertake to *communicate* it; and that when we do communicate it, we ought to be careful to cultivate the spirit of christianity, lest it be attended with greater injury than good, to our fellow men. These considerations have governed me throughout: and God forbid that I should *ever* depart from them!

As it regards the allusion to my promises before I received ordination, to be obedient to my superiors, and not to "mend our rules but to keep them,"* I reply, that I regret exceedingly, that when I made such promises, I was not better qualified to *judge* of our discipline and government. I was young, inexperienced and uninformed. I perceived no errors in either of these. But, Sir, if I *now* had to pass that examination, I should certainly be strict in *qualifying* my promises; as I do believe there are *rules* of *Discipline*, as well as *practices* in our *administration*, which ought to be modified.

I do, Sir, as firmly and fully believe in our *doctrines*, generally, as any brother; and have endeavoured since I became a member of our church, to obey them: nor do I now feel any abatement of my purpose, to persevere in this path of duty to the end, by the Grace of God assisting me. I have uniformly recommended our *discipline* to others, as well as laboured to conform to its mandates myself: and in this course too, I feel inclined to persevere, until some better modification of them shall be introduced by the proper authority of the church, or until they be repealed. And as to the grand *fundamentals* of our *government*, (meaning the itinerant operations,) no member of this conference feels more disposed to support them than I do. But, Sir, believing as I do, that there are some of the minutiæ of our discipline and government, which could be modified to advantage, I wish to enjoy the privilege of examining the subject, by reading ecclesiastical history, the Mutual Rights, or any thing else which will afford me the necessary information. And when I am fully convinced that I have obtained a knowledge

*Mr. Dorsey neither broke the "rules" nor mended them.—*Eds.*

of the truth, I desire the privilege of *communicating* it in the best possible manner to the church and the world, either verbally or otherwise. And, although I should rejoice to have the sanction of this conference, in so doing, yet if it *cannot* be obtained, I must beg the privilege of pursuing the course which my judgment and conscience dictate.

You admit that the *preachers* have a right to *read* and *examine* the Mutual Rights, or any thing they please. And is it not admitted, that they have the same right to communicate to *others*, what they learn? Are we to retain our information, and neither speak nor write about it? No, Sir, I cannot suffer any man, or body of men, to trammel my rational faculties, in their search for truth; nor to restrain them from promulgating it when obtained: and I now reserve to myself the entire privilege of doing so, either verbally, or in any other manner I judge most expedient.

I have read the Mutual Rights, Sir, for myself, and think highly of the work, and recommend it to every member of this conference.

The *bishops themselves* read it,—the *preachers* read it,—the *book agents* read it, and exchange the Methodist Magazine for it;—and will any one say, that the *people* have no right to read it? Without an act of reason, my intelligence itself on the first blush of the subject, forces this language upon me:—If *bishops*, *preachers*, and *book agents* read this work with impunity, then all the *members* of our church, ought to enjoy the same privilege. But I must come to the conclusion and application of this argument.—If the members have as good a right to read the Mutual Rights, as the ministry, (which all must admit, or else deny that they are free,) and if the ministers *undoubtedly have* this right, as has been admitted on this floor, by bishops and others, then there is no argument to set aside the consequence, that it is the right of any preacher to *recommend* the work to the people, if he judge it would be profitable to them. [And every attempt to inflict punishment on a preacher for recommending it to the people, is an absolute, though indirect, declaration, that they are *not* at liberty to read and examine for themselves.] And if it be a preacher's *right*, how can you punish me for so doing? Yet I have been punished with an *admonition*, for *recommending* the Mutual Rights to one or two members; for this is all the proof you had against me.

After this I retired, and the sense of the conference was taken, whether my reply was satisfactory, and the vote was given in the negative. I was again called in and interrogated on the subject; but replied as before, in *my own* language, qualifying my promises, and yielding *so far* as I could, without sacrificing the clearest dictates of my judgment and conscience. I *again* retired, and as I was informed, the question, "whether my character pass," was again put to the conference, and answered by a vote in the negative. It was then "moved, that the case be postponed till to-morrow."

The next day the case was again resumed, and I was once more interrogated. I replied in substance as follows:

MR. PRESIDENT,

Upon a candid re-examination of the subject, I am prepared to reiterate the remarks which I offered yesterday, relative to my disposition to render a respectful obedience to our discipline and government. But I request the conference, if they please, to favour me with the *rule of discipline* on which I have been *charged, tried* and *punished*, that I may be better prepared to conclude how to shape my course. (No law was given.) If there *be* any rule, and you have proceeded according to it, then I am subject to no *further* penalty, unless I can be punished twice for the same offence.

It has just now been suggested to me, by a brother at my left hand, that there is a law of the general conference, passed at their last session, *requiring* our preachers not to become agents for other booksellers, &c. Now, supposing this law to apply to the case in hand, (which we believe it will not,) *I* knew nothing about its existence until half an hour ago; and how then could I *keep* or *break* it? *It is not in our discipline.* A law must be promulgated before it can be in force: for, "where there is no *law*, there" can be "no *transgression.*" How then can I be punished for the transgression of *that* law? I feel myself as much bound as any member of this conference, to keep the laws of the general conference, until they shall be amended or repealed. When I violate any one of those laws, I am amenable at this tribunal; and, if found guilty, subject to punishment and am willing to submit to it. But I cannot be punished *now* for an offence which I *may* or *may not* commit hereafter, without a violation of justice.

Moreover, it has been suggested, (by the president,) that an "annual conference has authority to make rules and regulations for its own members." Admitted. *Rules* and *regulations* are not *laws* to regulate *moral conduct*, I presume. This conference is now sitting in an *executive*, or *legislative capacity*. If the former, then not the latter; and if the latter, not the former. If you are sitting in an *executive* capacity, how can you *enact* laws for yourselves to execute? If in a *legislative* capacity, how can you *execute* your own laws? Unless you prove that these two powers should be united in one body; which would *astonish* my understanding, and form a monstrous anomaly in ecclesiastical government, in *this* country.

But if this conference *had* the power both to *enact* laws for the regulation of the moral characters of its members, and to *execute* such laws, when enacted, surely none would argue that you had authority to punish one of your members for a breach of a law *before* it is *broken*, or even *enacted!* And when was the law enacted, which prohibits any of your body from *recommending* the Mutual Rights?—the supposed offence for which I have suffered the punishment of an admonition.

I might easily say much more on the subject: for it is one of the deepest moment to me: but suffer me to close my remarks, by referring brethren to the many hard things which some of them have said on this floor: and also, to what some of them have written and published, in opposition to certain parts of our discipline and government; and let me request them to refer to those things, when they shall give their vote in this case.

I now retired again; and Mr. Roszel offered the following motion: "*moved that the character of brother Dorsey pass, upon his being reproved by the president, for his contumacy in resisting the authority of the conference.*" This motion did not prevail. The following motion was then offered by Mr. Job Guest, but written as the secretary says, by Mr. F. S. Evans: '*Moved and seconded, that the bishops be, and hereby are requested not to give Dennis B. Dorsey an appointment for the present year, and that his name be so returned on the minutes, with the reasons assigned why he has not an appointment; viz. his contumacy in regard to the authority of the conference.*" This motion was divided, and the first and second parts adopted separately. The resolution being read to me, when called in, I requested a transcript from the journal, of all the proceedings in the case; and signified a probability of my appealing to the general conference against their decisions. My request was laid over, however, till the next day.

When the case was called up on the following day, on motion of Mr. Joshua Wells, it was resolved, that the last resolution passed on yesterday, relative to the return of the name on the minutes, be amended,' and "that the words, '*with the reasons assigned why he has not an appointment; viz. his contumacy in regard to the authority of the conference,*' be retained on the journal, but not published on the minutes." This motion was adopted.—The same day, as I could not be present on account of bodily indisposition, I wrote to the conference, informing them of my determination to appeal to the general conference, and requested them to pass a resolution, that this appeal be inserted in the minutes along with their former resolution. In that letter I renewed my request for a transcript from the journals. Mr. Robert Cadden then moved, that my "*request be not granted;*" The secretary, Mr. Waugh, and others, made some remarks on the impropriety of my obtaining such a document, without some restraint not to publish it until the general conference. This motion was lost. After this, it was, on motion of Mr. Roszel, "*resolved that*" my "*request be granted.*"

Thus, dear sir, you have an outline of this afflictive and protracted trial; and you are now left to form your own opinion concerning the nature and grounds of the charge—the manner in which it was introduced—the proofs by which it was sustained—the decisions of conference on the case—and my merit or demerit of the penalties inflicted.

Soliciting an interest in your petitions to the God of all grace, that I may have that love which "endureth all things," and "thinketh no evil," I subscribe myself, dear brother, your fellow labourer in the cause of religious liberty, and in the ministry of reconciliation. DENNIS B. DORSEY.

To Vindex.

Baltimore, May 15th, 1827.

CHAPTER XXV.

A short address to the Members of the Baltimore Annual Conference by Bartimeus.

FATHERS AND BRETHREN,

Permit an old friend, and an old member of your conference, to address you in the language of mildness and expostulation. One who was brought out of the kingdom of darkness, by the instrumentality of the Methodist ministry, and who has been raised up among you, as an advocate for the pure doctrines of original Methodism. One who, in the twenty-second year of his age, being ordered by the bishop far hence into the wilderness, was noticed by a distinguished member of your conference, who, casting a benevolent glance at the timid young man, silently retired from the busy scenes of the day, and went from house to house, to procure a little money from the generous friends in Baltimore, to aid him through the dangers and hazards of his western tour. A member this, who then stood so high in your ranks, and in the public estimation, that when he had an appointment to preach, his name was previously announced from the pulpit, that the citizens might know when they could have an opportunity to hear him. What distinguished member of your conference was this? It was no other than that same Nicholas Snethen, who is now regarded as the great troubler of Israel. That mild, inoffensive man of God, who, for more than thirty years, through a variety of trying circumstances, has held fast his righteousness, and maintained his integrity. Shall I forget thee, Snethen! Now the shafts of reproach fly thick around; shall I hide myself, and leave thee to the pelting of the storm? I have arisen, thou knowest, to aid thee in the mighty contest, and to share in thy reproach. I will be thy fellow-labourer through the cloudy and dark day, until summer suns shall break the dense vapours of the storm, and clear up the troubled atmosphere. Then like weather-beaten and war-worn soldiers, lifting our eyes to the tranquil stillness of the heavens, and looking abroad through the surrounding beauties of spiritual vegetation, we will sing together:—"For lo! the winter is past, the rain is over and gone; the flowers appear on the earth; the time of singing of birds is come, and the voice of the turtle is heard in our land; the fig-tree putteth forth her green figs, and the vines with the tender grape give a good smell."

You, my brethren, who are yet members of the Baltimore annual conference, will forgive this involuntary digression, this grateful recollection of past events, and pleasant anticipation of the future, while I solicit your attention to the intended suggestions of the present address.

I am not insensible of my obligations to you, and have long admired that dignity and intelligence, which have caused you to hold a distinguished rank among the annual conferences of the United

States. You possess advantages which other conferences do not. Occupying a central situation, and having easy access to the first sources of information, you have it in your power to sustain a valuable weight of influence, and to stand among the most useful bodies of men in our nation. The principles of reform have long been in operation among you; and you have had ample means to know and appreciate the evidence on which they rest. I retain a lively recollection of the times and seasons, when an Emory, a Ryland, and a Griffith, made a noble stand on your floor; and when other intelligent brethren with them, plead the cause of liberty, against the dangerous accumulations of ecclesiastical power. Whence is it, then, that in your late session, you have laid an embargo upon the Mutual Rights? Is Emory gone from among you? Is the voice of Ryland no more heard? Has Griffith retired to the mournful solitudes of discouraged silence? Does modest Hanson still refuse to open his mouth? And have Waugh and Davis found out, that truth reaches too deep, to be safely followed in all its connections? Does the thunder of S. G. R. still terrify the rising ministry? And have your young men "stipulated" to enjoy the consolations of passive obedience and non-resistance? Whence is it, that these dismal tidings have come out from Baltimore? Refusing to notice our arguments, and unable to obstruct their influence on society, by manoeuvre, are you now resolved that absolute authority shall take our citadel by storm? An embargo is not unfrequently a harbinger for an open declaration of war; and we may so regard it, perhaps in the present case.

You have resolved, have you, that the members of your conference shall not recommend or circulate the Mutual Rights? Why is this? Have you given any reason for such an extraordinary resolution? Or have you avowed your determination, not to enter into any "discussion or controversy" upon the subject? If you will not give a reason for your conduct, let your expostulating brethren do it for you. We think the plain English reason why you will not read the Mutual Rights, is, that the work contains more truth than you are willing to endure. Ecclesiastical power will not come to the light, lest its deeds should be reproved.

You have laid the heavy arm of authority on a young man, it is said, because he has recommended and circulated our periodical publication. Have you any law for this? Where is it? In the discipline? In the scriptures? In the codes of the United States, or of the state of Maryland? If in none of these, must you not own that it was a perfectly *lawless act?* And is the Baltimore annual conference *without law* to God? or is she *under the law to Christ?*

Brethren, what do you intend to do? To prohibit the freedom of inquiry, and of reading, is a greater outrage upon civil liberty, than to take away the freedom of speech, or of the press. It is rumoured that some great man among you, intends publicly to vindicate the conduct of the Baltimore annual conference, in this case. If I cannot fairly shew his arguments to be inconclusive, I promise I will yield to them, and give up the cause of reform.

If you forbid travelling preachers to circulate the Mutual Rights, why not lay the same prohibition upon the local preachers, and the private members? You profess to have equal authority over them in your law-making power; and why not in your sovereign prerogative to act without law?

If you resolve still to be inattentive to our arguments, and to our rights, have some regard, I beseech you, to your own standing in society. Will your daring efforts to abridge the freedom of thought and discussion, pass unnoticed in this land of justice and independence, which reflects the light of civil and religious liberty over both hemispheres? Will the free born sons of America, whose fathers had such struggles to cast off the yoke of European despotism, be silent and respectful spectators of your ecclesiastical march after absolute dominion? Will not Methodists every where open their eyes, and see that the efforts of reformers have not been made without a cause? Think you, that, with trembling steps, they will begin to gather up their scattered numbers of the Mutual Rights, and commit them to the flames, lest the second edition of the Baltimore act, should involve *them* also in its penalties? Will they break up the Union Societies, and implore your royal clemency, pledging themselves no more to peruse the forbidden pages? Will the reformers belonging to the Baltimore annual conference tamely surrender to your high-toned injunction, and with an abject meanness, go and ask you what books they may be permitted to read and circulate? As well might you expect them to bow down, and kiss the great toe of his holiness at Rome.

If you are men of reason, why spurn from you the many appeals made to this noble faculty in the Mutual Rights? If you are men of one book, the Bible, why forbid the reading of those pages, where so many sacred quotations are to be found? If you are Wesleyan Methodists, why interdict a book, which contains so many respectful appeals to Mr. Wesley's authority, and so many quotations from his works?

A respectable number of you were zealous reformers four or five years ago. Have you taken a retrograde motion, or become lukewarm in the cause? If so, how is this fact to be accounted for? Has it arisen from a dread of novelties, and a sanguine confidence that nothing is true but "the old gospel which we had from the beginning?" That nothing is true which contradicts the gospel of our Lord Jesus Christ is very readily admitted, and it would be well for the christian world, if it were more generally admitted than it is. But I beseech you to reflect, that many of the warm advocates for *old* things, with all their fondness for antiquity, do not look so far back as to the days of our blessed Saviour and his apostles. Many things have been invented since that time, which have now become old; and these are the things which excite the greatest outcry against novelty, and for which the most zealous efforts are made, to magnify the argument of antiquity; because it is well known, if this should be torn from them, they would have no other argument to rest upon. Because the gospel is old, must we therefore support
27

all the old absurdities of popery? The mere argument of antiquity proves this, or it proves *nothing*. We believe the gospel, not because it is old, for it was as true eighteen hundred years ago, as it is now; and will not be any *more* true, after the lapse of ten thousand years to come. And as to church government, if you insist on antiquity, we join in with you immediately, and invite you back to the apostolic age. Is not this old enough for you? Or will you make your official conduct demonstrate, that you think it quite too old?

You are ready to say, perhaps, that one thing will open the way for another, that for another, and if these reformers can have their will, we know not where they will find a stopping place. If you see them going beyond the oracles of God, and beyond the apostolic age, then I will join you with all my heart, in endeavouring to stop them. The church of Rome, in her church government, went beyond the oracles of God, to borrow pagan rites, and beyond the apostolic age, to borrow many of the pompous and obsolete ceremonies of the Jews: had she regarded, and been governed by divine authority, in all her discipline, what superstition and bloodshed would have been prevented through the following ages! You have no fears, have you, that Methodist reformers will wander as far out of the way as she did? Allow us the stopping place just mentioned, and we will never ask you to go beyond it. Nor do we wish to urge a rapid motion, in our return to primitive usage and simplicity. We only request you to take a step at a time; but in the mean time, we wish to be looking forward, and clearing the way for future movements, when the proper season shall arrive.

Remember, brethren, the interest you felt in the cause of reform, in 1823—4. Where was then, *your* stopping place? Was it the election of presiding elders? The election of a stationing committee? or both? Now, both these points of reform evidently contemplated an enlargement of general liberty, and an abridgment of episcopal power: and if we now request that the representative principle should properly run through the whole connexion, what is this but maintaining that *consistency* and *impartiality* in our claims, which truth and righteousness require? Will our old reforming brethren in the travelling ministry, forsake us on this account? Or, if we plead for such abridgement and responsibility of episcopal power, as shall make it correspond with the executive power of the United States, will the free born sons of America find fault with us for this? Will they go back, and support episcopal sovereignty in all its extent, giving up the presiding elder question, and every other question of reform, merely because we want Methodist bishops put upon a level with the dignified ruler who presides at the head of the nation? Is it possible, that this will frighten away any of the reformers belonging to the Baltimore annual conference? Will they now give up their own rights and privileges, rather than see local preachers and lay members have the enjoyment of theirs? To keep down the laity and locality, are they now willing to surrender their own claims, yield a passive obedience to their masters, and do all that in them lies, to perpetuate an absolute hierarchy, to the end of the world? We hope better things of Baltimore reformers. Too many in that conference, we know, are not reformers; too many are violently opposed to reform; from them we hope but little.

But brethren, who are in any degree favourable to reform, would do well to consider, that, however desirous they may be, to take a neutral stand, or to pursue a middle course, the time appears approaching when our rulers will not suffer them to do either.—— They may pass along for a year or two; but an inquiry will probably be commenced before long, on the conference floor, to ascertain who has been guilty of reading the Mutual Rights; or, who has been guilty of conversing with others in favour of reform.—— Every thing of the kind will be considered "inveighing against our discipline." Our bishops, presiding elders, and their admirers, will be likely to insist, that every man must come out, and let the conference know where he stands.* It appears to be high time, therefore, for every man to examine church history, search his Bible, read the Mutual Rights, consult his conscience, exercise his understanding, and deliberately make up his mind, concerning the course he is to take, through the portentous and eventful scenes which are before us.

Some of the brethren will probably reply, the eventful scenes referred to, are the very things which stagger us. We were reformers, until we saw there was danger that the church would be torn to pieces; and now we are afraid to persevere. Well, brethren, you are perfectly right in resolving not to do any thing that would injure the church. This resolution, it is to be hoped, will be abundantly confirmed, in the mind of every one of you. And what, think you, will injure the church? Will reason or revelation do it? Will the church be injured, by her members searching for the truth, or by assisting each other in the diligent communication of it, through every lawful medium? Pause and think. Will the church be injured by an increase of light on the principles of government? Will *truth, justice, equal rights*, and *equal liberty*, ever do her any harm? Will it tear the church in pieces, to ask a Methodist bishop to yield the least tittle of his power?. Or to ask "the Itinerancy" to do unto others, as they would have others do unto them? And who intends to divide the church? Will reformers do it, by voluntarily separating? Or will it be done by the episcopacy, through the sovereign power of expulsion? Time will answer these questions. Can the Baltimore Annual Conference find no other way to avoid injuring and destroying the church, but the old way of absolute power maintaining *silence*—forbidding to *read, think, judge,* or *converse* on the subject of church government? And pray, then, where did this conference receive her education? Where did she learn such a lesson? You will have to look across the great water, to the Southern regions of Europe, for an answer to this question.

But why do I write this address, to be published in the Mutual Rights, after that publication has been proscribed by the very per-

*This prediction was soon fulfilled.

sons to whom the appeal is made? Some of them may feel indignant at it, and may be disposed to ask: "What emboldeneth thee, that thou answerest?" I answer, because if you will not read in order to inform your minds of what is going on in the earth, it is probable some of your children will. If you are too wise, either to yield to our arguments, or to answer them; your posterity will be able to judge, whether our arguments were too weak to *need* an answer, or too strong to *admit* of one. They will discover, whether your declining cause had no *occasion* to defend itself, or that you had no *ability* to give an answer which would bear the public scrutiny.

Information has been received more than once, that some of our old side men, among other schemes of low-cunning, have fondly whispered that Bartimeus is *crazy*. A clerical friend, within the United States, lately expressed himself as being apprehensive that brother S——, from the appearance of his late writings, had fallen into a state of insanity; and seriously inquired of a Western acquaintance, if this were not the case. Bartimeus thinks it best to meet, this friendly and sympathising suggestion, with a smile, and to wait patiently until the *sane admirers* of episcopacy, will condescend to answer his crazy arguments. On this subject he deems it sufficient to reply, "I am not mad, most noble Festus, but speak forth the words of truth and soberness."

May, 1827. BARTIMEUS.

CHAPTER XXVI.

Proceedings of the Baltimore Union Society, in relation to the Rev. Dennis B. Dorsey's case.

AT a meeting of the Baltimore Union Society of the Methodist Episcopal Church, held on the 15th day of May, 1827, it was deemed proper to lay before the public, the following brief narrative of facts relative to the case of the Rev. Dennis B. Dorsey.

On Wednesday, the 18th of April, the Rev. Dennis B. Dorsey, "was charged before the Baltimore annual conference, with having been actively engaged in the circulation of an improper periodical work." A confidential letter from Mr. Dorsey to a friend, recommending to his attention the Mutual Rights, as an important work on church government, was produced in evidence, and read in the conference. Mr. Dorsey acknowledged the letter to be his; but did not consider that he had violated any law by recommending the above work. After Mr. Dorsey had retired, the following resolution was offered by the Rev. Stephen G. Roszel, and adopted by the conference; "Resolved, that Dennis B. Dorsey's character pass, upon his being admonished by the president; and promising the conference that he will desist from taking any agency in spreading or supporting any publication in opposition to our discipline or government."

On the following day the admonition was given in due form, from the chair; but Mr. Dorsey could not be induced to make the promise required by the resolution. He objected to it as unreasonable and unjust—there being no law in the discipline, prohibiting any preacher from recommending or circulating such works as the Mutual Rights. He stated that he was willing to promise the conference to be submissive to the discipline and government of the church; and to recommend like obedience to others, until by the legislative authority of the church, some modification of the government could be effected. A promise embracing more than this, he informed them he *could not* make.

On Friday the case was again resumed, and Mr. Dorsey was pressed to make the promise required by the resolution, which he still declined, urging as before, the injustice of the requirement. Upon which, the Rev. Stephen G. Roszel made the following motion: "Moved, that the character of brother Dorsey pass, upon his being reproved by the president for his contumacy in resisting the authority of the conference." This motion; however, did not prevail. After considerable desultory conversation on the case, the following resolution was offered by the Rev. Job Guest, and adopted by the conference: "Moved and seconded, that the bishops be and hereby are requested not to give Dennis B. Dorsey an appointment for the present year; and that his name be so returned on the minutes, with the reasons assigned why he has not an appointment, viz: his contumacy in regard to the authority of the conference." On Saturday, the *latter* part of this motion was so far rescinded as to omit the publication of it on the printed minutes of the conference, but to retain it on the journal.

Thus was brother Dorsey, a presbyter in the Methodist Episcopal Church, without any charge against his moral or religious character, left, by the order of the conference, without a prospect of support for himself and family; and that too, with a constitution seriously injured in the service of the church.

Now as it is the undoubted right of every man, to express his opinion of the *official conduct* of his ecclesiastical as well as his civil rulers; and whereas we deem the proceedings, against Mr. Dorsey as intended to prevent the diffusion of light on a subject of vital importance to the Methodist Episcopal Church, and the community at large.

Therefore, *Resolved*, 1st. That the conduct of the late Baltimore annual conference, in the case of the Rev. Dennis B. Dorsey, was oppressive in its character, and not warranted by the scriptures, nor the discipline of the church.

Resolved, 2dly. That in the opinion of this society, the conference in thus oppressing Mr. Dorsey, has evinced a determination, not only to withhold representation from the membership and local ministry, but also to keep them in ignorance of the true principles of church government.

Resolved, 3dly. That this society duly appreciate the firm and dignified stand taken by Mr. Dorsey in the conference, in favour of the principles of religious freedom, and tender to him their most affectionate regards.

Resolved, 4thly. That this society deem it but just to say, that several members of the conference, together with bishop Roberts, manifested a liberal spirit on the occasion.

Resolved, 5thly. That the above narrative and resolutions be published.

JOHN CHAPPELL, SEN. *President.*

CHAPTER XXVII.

Letter addressed to the Rev. Dennis B. Dorsey, by a travelling preacher.

MY DEAR SIR,

Not knowing you *personally,* nor the *place* of your residence, I ask the privilege of addressing you through the medium of the "Mutual Rights," for *approving* and *recommending* of which, you now stand *suspended* as a Methodist travelling preacher! The Baltimore annual conference of the Methodist Episcopal Church—with three or more bishops present to direct and shape its measures, have, by a solemn resolution, after several days' deliberation, *officially* decided that a presbyter in the church of God, deserves *punishment* and *disgrace,* because he adopts opinions and sentiments on the subject of church government, which are received and acted upon by a large majority of protestant christians, throughout the various divisions of the religious world! I cannot pause my brother, to write the many denunciations that common sense, throughout an outraged community, will pronounce upon this overbearing act of abandoned tyranny! But I hasten to inquire why were *you* selected as the *victim,* the *sole* victim, when it was in proof before them that others were in the same condemnation! Why did not my lord of Canterbury, who "rides in the whirlwind and directs the storm" among you, and by whom *even* bishops are tithed at will, together with the active and zealous Doctor, the principal officer in his "star chamber," select a goodly number of victims, and offer an *appalling* hecatomb at once! Was it because heaven had deprived you of health? Was it because you were remote from home and friends? Was it because like your Master you were poor, and with the humble sharer of your fortunes, "had scarcely where to lay your head!" Did they wish by increasing your *mental* inquietude, to strengthen the desolation *without,* and so send you to a premature grave? Or was it intended by the *horror* of the example made of you, to say to other reformers "if *you* have the *word, we* have the sword!!" I cannot refrain from asking where *three* or *four* members of the Baltimore conference were during this *laboured* deed of *hard-earned* infamy? Did they sit by, in inglorious silence? But my brother, be not discouraged, recollect that the great father of us all, as Methodists, was by a similar body, and in the *same* city, forty years ago, declared unworthy of a name or place, in that communion, in the bosom of which, you now find yourself honourably degraded. When Mr. Wesley was informed of this, he declared in a letter, now in my possession, that the American bishop had "no more connection with him——" But I trust you will not so decide in relation to your blinded and prejudiced brethren—"yet a little while," and this stupid, *laudean* zeal, will be cooled in the humiliation and disgrace of your prosecutors; public indignation will chastise their pitiful pretensions, to *lordly* inquisition over the rights and consciences of those, who have too much intelligence and too much candour to think and act by their prescription! To conclude, my dear sir, I beg you to accept the best wishes of a stranger. "Faint not in the day of evil." The honorary overthrow you have sustained, for the rights of conscience, will make strangers your friends. On hearing of the treatment you and others received at the Baltimore conference, ten or twelve persons within my charge have declared for *reform*, and are ready to aid you with their *influence* and *purses*. Wishing the speedy restoration of your health, and that you may live to see the curse of religious oppression banished from the church and the world—I remain yours in the kingdom and patience of *Jesus Christ*.

Rev. D. B. Dorsey.   VINDEX.
     April 27th, 1827.

Upon the receipt of information from Baltimore, that the foregoing letter had given great offence and that it would have a place among the papers "indicated" for the purpose of sustaining the prosecutions which were then pending, Vindex forwarded the following note of explanation, to be inserted in the Mutual Rights.

Note of Explanation from Vindex.

GENTLEMEN,
    I regret that you are about to be *troubled* on *my* account. My letter to Mr. Dorsey, was written immediately on the receipt of a letter from an *old side* brother in Baltimore, *detailing* the facts in Mr. Dorsey's case, not one of which has been contradicted by the famous manifesto of Mr. Wilkins & Co., but rather *confirmed*; with the exception of a little *varnish* and misrepresentation. I admit that I have expressed myself in *strong* and *severe* terms, and have all along been willing to have it in my power, to *correct* and *recall*, by learning that my information was more or less incorrect. But after hearing all that can be said on the subject, I am perfectly satisfied that my error, if any, has not been a very serious one. That the *act* of the conference, was an *"overbearing"* one; tending to *repress* freedom of inquiry, and punishing an individual for holding opinions which we have published to the world in our *standard* works, are not *essential*, is an assertion I shall prove by indubitable evidence, when it becomes necessary. That the act was an *"abandonment"* in *executive* practice of *law*, *brotherly love*, and that *liberality* every where characteristic of the more enlightened Methodists, is a *proposition* I am equally competent to prove, when it is

called for by any thing, but *abuse* and personal vituperation. That the act was *'tyrannical,'* that is, that it resembled the *policy* of tyrants punishing *without* law, and *beyond* its provisions, acting an inclement, imperious part, in relation to one whose conduct did not deserve punishment, and who had not the means of successful resistance and defence, at the time, is a position, the assumption of which I again renew. I have said that the deed, by which Mr. Dorsey was degraded, was an *infamous* one, that is, a notoriously improper and unjustifiable one. This is what is always understood by the term, I believe, when applied to acts of administration: at all events, it is what I meant by it. I intended to convey the idea, that the conduct of the conference would become the subject of open censure, of public reproach, and that the affair of punishing Mr. Dorsey, in the anomalous way in which it was effected, would be a matter of deep and burning shame, to those men, who in the character of heaven's *best* messengers to the present generation, are continually praying "forgive us our sins *as* we forgive those who sin against us?" And are daily haranguing thousands on the *duty* and *importance* of forgiveness, forbearance and brotherly kindness. Upon the whole, I consider my letter to Mr. Dorsey, substantially correct, in its general meaning and bearing. Had I written under different circumstances, I should probably have expressed myself with less severity; but the conduct of the reigning party in Baltimore has shown, that I anticipated their real temper and disposition, and developed pretty correctly their *collective* character. I must atone therefore for the *style* of that letter, by an expression of regret, that *facts* and *principles* subsequently disclosed, have fully authorized my impressions and fears at the time of writing. Mr. Wilkins and Co. in their declamatory address, assert, with as little regard to *truth* as "decency," that I have employed the "*most* abusive epithets to which malignity itself could resort." In reply, it will be sufficient to say, no *honest* man will believe the assertion, who has seen my letter; and those who do, are at liberty to *bundle* with my detractors. I am also said, to be among the "enemies of Methodism;" public opinion, however, will set this down also, where it ought to be, on the score of malice and misrepresentation. To conclude, if in my strictures upon the conduct of the Baltimore conference, in the case of Mr. Dorsey, there is to be found any thing *vicious*, on account of its *severity*, it is a *vice*, so nearly allied to *virtue*, that my defence will not be difficult, and so for the present I let it rest. VINDEX.

Sept. 21st, 1827.

A copy of the Narrative and Defence having reached Vindex, he wrote and forwarded the following address to the Editors, which the reader will find to be such as the occasion called for, and the prosecutors and the agent justly merited.

Vindex to the Editors.

MESSRS. EDITORS,

I perceive I am so unfortunate as to have fallen under the displeasure of Messrs. Earnest, Rogers, Toy, Harden, Yearley, and

Israel—(or rather, as some think, the spleen of their pugnacious secretary,) on account of the letter I addressed to the Rev. D. B. Dorsey, in May 1827.—In the remarks upon my letter to which these gentlemen have *appended their names*, found on pages 16 and 74 of their late "Narrative," I see nothing worthy of particular notice, except the want of *truth* and *candour*, manifested in every line, they have so flippantly conjured into a phillipic, upon the writer of "Vindex." Every single statement they have made in relation to my letter, betrays the facility and "recklessness" with which they are capable of misrepresenting facts, connected with the subject of reform. As it respects the relative "decency" of my letter, it is not destined, I apprehend, to lose much in comparison with the productions of my critics in reply, whether of "star chamber" or "Pitt street" memory.—The conduct upon which I found it necessary to offer a few strictures, had but slender claims to Christian "decency," or religious propriety, and *hence* it was the less necessary for me to be particularly *select* in the choice of language. But after all that has been said upon the subject, the charge of *indecorum* in the use of terms, can only be fixed upon VINDEX by showing that he had no *occasion* to use severe language;— and until this is done the writer of the "Narrative" (if I conjecture right) or those who have kindly consented to stand *godfathers* to "the precious bantling"—will receive no apology from the object of their abuse. The allusion to the "star chamber" in my letter to Mr. Dorsey, was intended to call the attention of those concerned, to a few individuals, some of them members, and some of them *not* members of the Baltimore Conference; who were trying, as I conceived, by very unfair and high handed measures to injure and degrade reformers—that the conference was not intended, is plain from the connexion of the letter.—Vindex is of opinion, further, that a legislative body, or executive tribunal, may enact a law, or make up a decision, oppressive and tyrannical in its nature and tendency, without deserving the denomination of "tyrants" applied to the individuals composing the body, or tribunal in question—such a law may be the effects of haste, surprise, or passion, it may result from want of information, or a few artful leaders may impose on the rest, even when there is the appearance of serious and solemn deliberation. The influence, therefore, of the sagacious committee of "inquiry" that I have charged the members of the Baltimore conference as "infamous tyrants," is far from being either logical or just; it was not my intention to do so, and I take pleasure in avowing it. But should that body, by a repetition of similar acts, approve and perpetuate the *policy* of the single measure alluded to, then I should be disposed to apply to them the language I have applied to a solitary isolated action of their lives. Permit me to ask, was it the intention of the evangelists, to characterize the apostle Peter, as a profane swearer and common liar, when they narrate, that when under severe temptation; "he cursed, and swore that he knew not the man" whom he had been following for years? Or did St. Paul intend to denounce him as a dis-

sembler, when he affirms that on one occasion at least, he was
guilty of "dissimulation?" or again, we ask, did our Lord intend
to be understood, that the apostle was a devil, when he said "get
behind me Satan?"—If these questions are negatived, as they must
be by every man of common sense, then surely it does not follow
from the facts involved, that Vindex has said what the Baltimore prosecuting committee and council make him say.   Have not deliberative assemblies as well as individual rulers in all ages, been oc-
casionally guilty of cruel and oppressive enactments, without for-
feiting their claims, to general and enlightened benevolence?   No
inference, therefore, can be drawn from the remarks of Vindex,
that will justify the language of his accusers—he indignantly ani-
madverted upon conduct, but except an allusion to one or two individuals, left general character alone.

Thus far I had proceeded when I received the intelligence, that
the Baltimore conference had expelled the Rev. D. B. Dorsey for
circulating the "Mutual Rights," and the "History and Mystery of
Methodist Episcopacy"—and also the Rev. Wm. C. Pool, for aiding in the formation of a Union Society, and subsequently deliver-
ing an address before said society, in furtherance of its objects.   Such
conduct, I confess, I consider, as inexcusably oppressive and
tyrannical, and I moreover believe it to be the natural offspring of
ignorance, bigotry, and misguided zeal.   The committee who have
honoured me with their notice, can think on this subject as they
please, I want no higher praise than the censure of men who are capable of approving such unmanly and unholy persecution.   Before I
close, I must beg leave to correct an error on the part of the committee, which must have resulted from ignorance, or a disposition
to garble the truth in imitation of one who had preceded them in
the business of studied defamation, they say, Vindex was a new
or "late recruit."—*This happens not to be true.*   Vindex was one
among the reformers who drafted a memorial to the general conference in 1816, 12 years ago, praying for important alterations in
the government of the church—and as early as 1822, published
his thoughts at length on this subject, in the "Wesleyan Repository."   It is therefore, in conclusion, respectfully recommended
to the "committee" having the supervision of *morals* in Baltimore,
that *hereafter* they should pay a little more attention to their *own!*

With all due respect,

April, 1828. VINDEX.

We never yet have thought Vindex too severe.   The Baltimore
Annual Conference had determined to sacrifice Mr. D. B. Dorsey,
at the shrine of clerical power, in expectation, that such a decisive
step would deter our friends, and put a stop to the further progress
of reform.   Their proceedings, therefore, merited a severe rebuke;
and no man was better prepared to do them justice, than Vindex.
Our readers have learned from the accompanying documents, that
the proceedings in the case were without law or established precedent;—in course they were *arbitrary* and *tyrannical.*   It put in requisition all the talent and consumed much of the time of the con-

ference, to accomplish their purpose. Vindex, therefore, said of it, *truly*, that it was "*a laboured deed.*"—In pursuing their victim, they were obliged to overcome all their personal regards for an afflicted brother!—They had to resist the relentings, which are universally felt by men of merit, on seeing such firmness as Mr. Dorsey evinced in asserting his rights before his oppressors;—and which he did in a manner that will long be remembered to his honour, as a man and christian minister!—They had to suppress the disposition to forgiveness, which was excited by an affectionate assurance of his desire and purpose, as far as he could, with a good conscience, to submit to the will of his brethren!—They had to overrule all the sympathies which pleaded in behalf of a fellow servant of Jesus Christ, standing on the verge of the grave, out of sight and out of the reach of any sinister interest!—Every tender emotion, which the oppression of a brother in circumstances so loudly calling for compassion was calculated to excite, they were obliged to smother!—Surely then it was a "*hardly earned*" triumph. And in despite of their hopes to escape merited reproach, the disinterested part of the community and posterity will brand the proceedings with "*infamy.*"

CHAPTER XXVIII.

IT appears from the letter of Vindex to Mr. D. B. Dorsey, that by some means, he has learned that doctor Bond, was a chief officer in the Star Chamber. This notice of the Doctor, led him to retort upon Vindex, in his epistle dedicatory, addressed to Mr. Snethen, and introductory to his appeal to the Methodists, in opposition to the changes proposed in their church government, p. 6. "The subaltern alluded to," says the Doctor, has already distinguished me as the chief officer of the star chamber, to my lord of Canterbury. Notwithstanding, I have the misfortune to be out of favour with you, I will do you the service to rebuke the indiscreet ardour of this recruit, lest he should do you more harm than good, by his temerity. Let him know then, that his fictitious signature has not concealed him as well as he intended; we have had a peep under his mask, and would advise him to be careful in future not to expose his ignorance, in print. The star chamber was a civil not an ecclesiastical tribunal, and therefore neither my lord of Canterbury nor his chief officer, could have had any thing to do with its decisions. Let him keep his LEARNING for the pulpit—a rhetorical flourish ad captandum vulgus, may pass as well as crude *geological* arguments, when mixed up with the desultory matter of a very LONG sermon, but it may not be safe to place either before the public, through the medium of the press."

The Doctor ought to have been sure he was right, before he ventured so bold a challenge. Now to let our readers see what kind of a guide was followed by the Pitt street meeting, and again by the quarterly meeting conference, when they voted *unanimously* agreeably to the agent's wishes, the condemnation of the Mutual Rights, without having read the work for themselves, we here insert the reply of Vindex to doctor Bond's rebuke and accusation of ignorance.

Vindex, in Controversy with Dr. Bond.

Messrs. Editors,—I send you a few *proofs* and *authorities*, demonstrating the correctness of an *allusion* to the "star chamber," in my letter to the Rev. Dennis B. Dorsey, published in your May number for the year current. The *testimonies* I send you, will satisfy the *judicious* and *discerning*, that my allusion was historically *correct*, and strictly *in place*. As it respects the *application* of it in the case of Mr. Dorsey, I would simply remark, I thought it just and proper at the *time* of writing, and taking into consideration all the circumstances of the case, I think so *still*. So far as *individuals* are concerned, my communication left them to be "distinguished" by the *notoriety* of their conduct, or not at all; and in this attitude, I consider it fair and honourable still to recognize them. My only concern, therefore, with doctor Bond, at present, is, to let our readers know, that but for *his* "ignorance," I should not have been charged with want of information, in relation to the "star chamber." The following authorities, will perhaps satisfy the public that the star chamber *had cognizance of ecclesiastical matters.* This is *expressly denied* by doctor Bond, and we are fairly at *issue.* The doctor says, "the star chamber was a *civil*, not an *ecclesiastical* tribunal, and therefore, neither my lord of Canterbury, nor his chief officer, could have *any* thing to do with its decisions." To this assertion, I oppose the following authorities.

"The star chamber was a court, composed of twenty or thirty noblemen, *bishops*, judges, and counsellors, nominated by the crown, with the king or queen at the head, who was sole judge when present, (which was seldom,) but in the absence of the king or queen they decided by a vote of the *majority*, the lord chancellor having the *casting* vote." Neal's History of the Puritans, vol. 1. page 455. "The star chamber, camera stellata, was a court of very ancient original, consisting of *divines*, lords, *spiritual* and temporal, being *privy* counsellors, together with two judges of the court of common law, without the intervention of any jury." Blackstone's Commentary, iv. vol. book 4, chap. 19, page 265—6. "The star chamber consisted of the lords *spiritual* and temporal," with others, "they stretched their power beyond the utmost bounds of legality, punishing small offences, or no offences at all, but of their own creating." Nicholson's Encyclopædia, art. star chamber. *Bishops*, therefore, as lords over God's heritage, *had* something to do with the "decisions," of the star chamber, and so had "my lord of Canterbury," as we shall see by and by.

"The star chamber was the most intollerant of all tribunals, and encroached on the jurisdiction of *other* courts, its punishments were enormous—Prynne, a barrister of Lincoln's Inn, for reviling plays, hunting and public festivals, and for *blaming the hierarchy and the new superstitions of Laud*, in a book which he published, was condemned to be put from the bar, to be pilloried in two places, to lose both his ears, pay five thousand pounds to the king, and be imprisoned for life." New Encyclopedia, art. Britain. "The star chamber was a court which exercised high discretionary powers, and had no precise *rule* or *limit* either with regard to the *causes*, which came under its jurisdiction, or the *decisions* which it formed." Hume's England, vol. 5, page 44. The *statute* of 1641 *abolishing* the high commission and *star chamber*, is said by Charles in his speech to the long parliament, to alter *fundamental* laws, civil and *ecclesiastical.* Ib.—In the reign of Elizabeth, 1584, bishop *Grindal* at the instigation of the queen, was by an order of the star chamber, *sequestered* from his *arch-episcopal function*, and confined to his own house. Hume vol. 4, page 25. Hume says, Laud's vengeance was the principal cause of the degradation of bishop Williams, in the star chamber, and that the *severity* of Prynne's sentence in the star chamber, is to be attributed to his *religious opinions* as a Puritan. vol. 4, page 246—Bishop Williams, of Lincoln, was cited to trial before the star chamber, by the instigations of *Laud*, upon a charge of *Puritanic* principles. Neal, vol. 2, pages 172, 282. Prynne, Bostwick, and Burton, were all cited before, and condemned by the star chamber, because they pleaded for *reform* in the government of the church. Neal, vol. 2, pages 250—1—2. see also contents of chap. 5, page 23.—Mr. Neal says, If they will call a relation of the *illegal severities* of the star chamber a *satire* against the present *establishment*, they must use their liberty as I shall mine! vol. 2, page 15.—In 1627, Prynne, Bostwick and Burton, were again cited before the star chamber, "my lord of Canterbury" being present, and *passing sentence!* vol. 2 pages 278—9, also 280, note; see also notice of a speech of archbishop Laud, in the star chamber. Page 285. "Laud who was sitting in the star chamber, at the time of Prynne's harangue, moved that he might be gagged." M'Cauley's England, vol. 2, page 243.

The court of the star chamber, punished individuals for *publishing* books and pamphlets, and in some instances, for "recommending" them *against* the hierarchy, page 286.—In 1632, Mr. Sherfield was tried and convicted in the star chamber for being *evil-affected* to the *discipline* of the church, and Laud *in person* moved his punishment! page 224. On one occasion, twelve laymen were fined in the star chamber for *employing ministers* in their families, without consulting "my lord of Canterbury!" vol. 2, pages 222-3. "The prosecution of Mr. Prynne *originated* with archbishop Laud." page 251. And yet Laud *pronounced* his sentence. "The report flew into Scotland, and the discourse was *there*, that they must also expect a star chamber to *strengthen* the hands of their bishops!" page 287. The celebrated Mr. Rushworth, says, the acts of this court were without *law!* Lord Clarendon states, that no man could any longer hope to be free from the *inquisition* of that court, than he resolved to *submit* to its extraordinary courses. The well known Mr. Cartwright, the father of the Puritans, and *fifteen* other dissenting ministers, were brought *twice* before the star chamber,

and were all shamefully degraded and punished by its decisions.
Neal, vol. 1, pages 445-6-7. "The archbishop sent the *most* of
his prisoners to the star chamber." page 460.

"My pains or weakness must excuse me herein, when I was
younger, and had my health, I so diligently attended the star
chamber, that for full seven years, I was not one day wanting."
Archbishop Laud's letter, see Rushworth's Collections 1628,
page 453.

Dr. Alexander Leighton, was ordered by the star chamber, to be
degraded from the *ministry*, pilloried, whipt, fined and imprisoned
during life, for *writing* against the *corruptions* of the hierarchy;
Neal, vol. 2, pages 209, 10—that he was degraded by the star
chamber *solely* on account of his principles, as a *reformer*, opposed
to the *lordly* pretensions, of an overbearing episcopacy, is the testimony of *Pierce*. See Vindication, page 177, and of Rushworth,
vol. 1, page 55, also Neal, pages 2, 9, 10. At one time, the king
himself, appeared in the star chamber and *preached* against reform,
his text was, Psalm 72, 1. The last sentence in this not "very
long sermon" would have been an excellent *motto* for doctor Bond's
book. "Plead not upon *Puritanic* principles, which make all
things *popular*, but keep within the *ancient limits!* " Rapin. vol.
2, pages 192, 3, and note 9, also Neal, vol. 2, page 101. I conclude these notices of the star chamber, as an *ecclesiastical*, as
well as civil tribunal, by citing another instance in Mr. Neal—
when the *infamous* sentence of the court of star chamber, was pronounced upon the venerable doctor Leighton, "my lord of Canterbury," Laud, was present, and evinced his *satisfaction*, on witness-
ing this *fiendish* deed, of religious cruelty, *by pulling off his hat
and giving God thanks!* vol. 3, page 210.

The preceding *proofs* will place the correctness of my allusion
to the "star chamber" beyond doubt. The remaining charges in
the notice the doctor has taken of "Vindex," are too paltry to
merit replication—their want of *fitness*, will furnish sufficient refutation, and I *return* them to the doctor, in company with the charge
of "ignorance," *non constat*. With these remarks, I take leave of
doctor Bond, until he shall feel it his "duty" to write again, when,
should he honour me with a second notice, I shall, if preserved,
attend to him as the nature of the case may require.

July, 1827. VINDEX.

After such a specimen of doctor Bond's information and accuracy, our readers will judge how formidable we considered his promise or his threat, to "*write down*" reform.

CHAPTER XXIX.

*An account of the Rev. Wm. C. Pool's trial before the Baltimore
Annual Conference.*

WE think it due to Rev. William C. Pool to insert in this place,
the following brief account of his trial before the Baltimore Annual
Conference.   We introduce it here because it will serve to give a
further illustration of the spirit and temper of the travelling preachers in respect to the friends of reform.   The account is copied
from the Mutual Rights and Christian Intelligencer, bearing the
date November 20, 1828.

MR. EDITOR:—To me it appears strictly necessary, that some one
should give an account of the trial of Wm. C. Pool, before the last
Baltimore Annual Conference; not only for the defence of his character, but also for the support of that cause with which it is connected, only to oppose which cause was it at all assailed.

As no one has, to my knowledge, attempted this act of justice
and kindness to his suffering character, I venture it, although I
may in consequence thereof, be made to follow him.

In poceeding to give some account of brother P's trial, it may
be proper for me to observe that he knew nothing of his accusation
until the conference had been in session five days; nor did he know
who was to be his accuser.   It is true, the presiding Elder did state
to him, some time prior to the conference, that it was likely there
would be something said about the pieces which he had written.
But surely no one would suppose this to be making him acquainted
with the charge against which he would have to prepare a defence.

When brother P's name was called and it was asked by the President, is there any thing against brother P.?   Mr. Shepherd and
others made some objections to him; but in consequence of the
absence of his presiding Elder the case was postponed until his return.   When he appeared in his place it was again asked, is there
any thing against brother Pool?   The presiding elder answered, he
had *nothing against brother P's moral character*, and stated he believed it stood fair: but referred at the same time, to some accusation which he believed others intended to produce against him.
Several members then stated the grounds of their objections to
brother P:, which were, his agency in the formation of a Union
Society in Harford, his address to that Society, and some other
pieces which he had written.   Brother P. then stated that, as he
was accused, and as what he had said before the Union Society,
together with the part he had taken in the formation of that society, were the grounds of the accusation, and as he could not know
the crime with which he was charged, nor consider himself in possession of the requisite means even to commence a preparation for
his defence, until he could have a list of charges, he wished to be
furnished with a copy of the charges before the conference proceeded any farther in his case.   Mr. Roszel, with others, argued

against the right of brother P. to have a written copy of charges, or else against the propriety of granting it, I know not which. Brother P. contended that his demand was just, and that a copy of the charges was his right in this case; urging that it was impossible for him to know against what he was to defend himself without it. At this time the president, bishop Soule, gave it as his opinion, that, when a brother comes up to the conference with any thing against his moral character, it is no more than just and right that he should be furnished with the charges, that he may prepare to defend himself at the conference. But, said he, in a case of mere improprieties, I say in a case of mere improprieties in a brother's conduct, I know of no instance in the usages of Methodism, in which an accused member was furnished with a copy of charges: such a practice is wholly new among us. These are as nearly the words of the president as I can recollect.

After this opinion was given the case was referred to a committee. The persons composing the committee were Edward Smith, James Riley, and John Thomas. This committee reported the following day, that brother P. was accused of immorality, as base as that of slander. He now asked for a copy of the charges contained in the report, referring to the opinion of the President, given the day before, for a support of the justness of his demand. Mr. Roszel again opposed his having that copy, as warmly as he had done the day before, and no copy was obtained.

The report, however, was recommitted, with the understanding that the committee was to make out a list of charges, and furnish brother P. with a copy. The committee then asked and obtained an addition of two: when Job Guest and Christopher Frye were added; and obtained leave to sit during the afternoon session, and retired. After sitting during the afternoon, and finishing their report, on the following morning, they came into conference and sat during the morning session; but made no attempt to report, until the afternoon. The chairman of the committee then expressed his readiness to report, and stated as a reason why he had not reported in the morning, that he had not time to prepare a copy of the charges for brother P. before, holding the copy in his hand at the same time. Brother P. discovering that the conference appeared disposed to act upon the report before he received the copy of charges, asked a third time, and on the third day after his case was taken up, for that copy. Mr. Roszel opposed his having it, as he had done for two days before, but with increased violence. Others joined him in this unreasonable course; and the Rev. John Baer, went even so far as to propose taking up the different items of charge in the report, and examine the documents, to see whether they could sustain the charges before that copy was given to brother P. Brother P. exclaimed against such sports with his character, and begged that the conference would not permit it. At this juncture, Mr. Emory rose, and expressed his disapproval of the course which the conference seemed disposed to pursue, remarking that he thought it appeared to be a distinct understanding with the whole conference the day before, that brother P. was to be furnished with a copy of the charges. After this, the chairman of the committee handed brother P. the copy of charges which he had held in his hand during the time that Mr. R. was endeavouring to prevent brother P. from obtaining it. I will place that copy before the reader.

CARLISLE, April 16th, 1828.

Dear Brother:—The committee appointed to examine and report in your case, have sustained the following items, and embodied them in their report:

1st. That you did take an active part in the formation of a Union Society, on Harford circuit, the acts of which go far to defame the government and administration of our church.

2d. That you have neglected meeting class on the Sabbath day, and instead thereof gave lectures on the subject of reform.

3d. That you have been actively engaged in circulating the Mutual Rights, and defending the Union Society of Baltimore in their defamation of this conference in the case of ————

4th. That you delivered an address to the Union Society of Harford, in which a highly inflammatory attack was made, both upon the preacher in charge and the constituted authorities of our church in the city of Baltimore.

5th. That you made in said address an unjustifiable attack on the episcopacy.

6th. That you represented the authorities of the church in Baltimore as conspiring against the rights and characters of the citizens of that place.

7th. That much of your conduct has been in direct opposition to the resolution of last conference, and contrary to the spirit of the gospel. You should have had notice sooner, but the committee did not find it until this morning.

Your brother, EDWARD SMITH.

Brother W. C. Pool.

After brother P. received this copy, the secretary handed him a copy of the report, which is nearly the same as the above, and it contains letters as marks referring to documents to sustain the charges, I suppose in the room of specifications. The report was now laid on the table, and brother P. asked permission to make some remarks respecting the time of taking up his case, but was informed *he could do that when the report was called up.* On Thursday in the afternoon, the report was taken up, at which time brother P. asked if he was to understand that in taking up that report, the conference had thereby determined to try him on the charges contained in it. Being answered by the conference in the affirmative, he took exception to their decision, and observed, were it possible, he would appeal from that decision, on the ground of its being a violation of one of their own rules recorded on the journal. He claimed a reading of that resolution, hoping it might procure him further time to make his defence. The secretary with others, admitted there was such a resolution, but as it was passed some years back, it would take some time to find it. From this cause, or from

29

some other, which I think it unnecessary to mention, it was not found, and consequently it was not read. The resolution referred to, was intended originally to prevent any advantage being taken of any member of the conference, by prefering charges against him without first giving him sufficient notice of such charges, in time to make his defence. When the effort of brother P. had failed to obtain a reading of the resolution above referred to, and the conference appeared inclined to proceed, he stated something like the following:—"I, am entirely unprepared to meet the charges. The conference have now been eight days in session, and I knew not until yesterday in the afternoon, against what I was to defend myself; and to-day, it is determined that I shall be tried on those charges, without any further time to prepare for a defence. There are items in the list of charges which are absolutely false, and which I can prove to be so, had I time to return to Harford. Besides, those items which embrace things that I acknowledge I have done and said, make it necessary that some further time to explain and defend, should be allowed me.

The president observed, addressing the conference, if brother P. says he is unprepared to meet the charges, and that there are charges in the report which he can prove to be false, if he had time to procure testimony, it would be unjust in this conference to try him on those charges;—I say it would be unjust to try him on those charges. But, said he, turning to brother P. Brother P. can point out those particular charges which he says are false, and which he says he is unprepared to meet, and the conference can omit them, and proceed to trial on the rest. Whether this was designed by the president as an ingenious turn to ensnare the accused, or not, I will not pretend positively to assert. But to me, it appeared to resemble nothing else. It did not, however, ensnare brother P. He rose and referred the president to the statements which he had before made with respect to the whole of the charges, and again declared he was unprepared to meet any of them; stating that he did not feel disposed to pursue the course proposed by the president, in pointing out any one charge, or in submitting to be tried on any, without further time to defend himself; because the time allowed him, being only one day, he could not think was sufficient to prepare for a defence against any one of the charges.

After much had been said against granting him any further time, he observed he wished it to be distinctly understood, that he did not design to treat the conference with contempt. But if the conference persisted in the determination to force him to trial on charges which he had again and again, said he was unprepared to meet, he would feel himself compelled as a last resort, to withdraw and let the conference try him in his absence. On receiving an intimation from the conference of their determination to proceed, he withdrew, and the conference entered upon the examination of documents to sustain the charges. The case, however, was not finished until the next day, Friday, when the following resolution was adopted, viz:

Resolved, That Wm. C. Pool, be, and he hereby is, expelled the Methodist Episcopal Church.

Having received official notice of the decision, and being informed that the conference would meet again in the evening, he appeared in the conference, signified his intention to appeal, and asked for a transcript of the proceedings in his case. Mr. Roszel, who had so violently for three days opposed his having a written copy of the charges, now argued against granting him that transcript. But some appeared to be disposed to allow brother Pool a chance of seeing the proof by which they had sustained the charges. Mr. Slicer moved the grant of his request. Considerable opposition was made to the motion. Perhaps some saw that if such a paper were put into the hands of brother P. the public would possibly see the whole amount of testimony, on which the conference had acted, and thereby have something more from which to form an opinion, than simply partial statements of those men who were concerned in transacting this business with their doors closed. Mr. Emory rose and instructed the conference to be cautious how they acted in their business, observing that it was not certain the General Conference would admit the appeal. This caution was well understood; for on motion of Mr. Roszel, it was resoved indefinitely to postpone the motion made by Mr. Slicer.

Thus brethren, I have given a brief sketch of brother P's trial, and know not how soon I may be made to follow him; but take leave to assure you, that I am yet in the Methodist Episcopal Church.   A Minister.

This account of Rev'd. William C. Pool's excommunication, will serve to shew, that he was expelled for being an active friend to the cause of reform; so that he and Rev'd. Dennis B. Dorsey are to be considered martyrs for the principle of a lay-representation in the legislative department of the Methodist Episcopal Church government. The many worthies, who have voluntarily withdrawn themselves from the communion of that church, for the sake of the same testimony, would have been noticed in this place, with suitable expressions of the high estimation in which we hold them, if it had been practicable to obtain all their names. But their numbers have increased exceedingly, amounting to hundreds. We therefore, can only say, they have individually acted a praise-worthy part; and having in a manner so commendably distinguished themselves, they will receive from their brethren that just respect, which is never withheld by men of true worth, from those who are ready to forego interest or convenience for the support of principle.

Those truly excellent men, who have devoted themselves to the itinerant work; and especially, the heroic individuals who have left the ranks of the itinerants where all power is in their hands, with intention to unite themselves with the friends of Mutual Rights, are entitled to very high consideration.

CHAPTER XXX.

A difference of opinion no just cause of discord.

The following essay, we wrote for the September number of Mutual Rights, 1826. It is reprinted and inserted in this place, to shew what was our disposition of mind and feeling towards our old side brethren, at the time when our expulsion was first talked of by them. We believe it to be a transcript of the temper of reformers generally. Our friends of after times ought to know this. Those who have read the essay, will indulge us in giving to all our friends this point of information.

A diversity of opinion is no just cause of discord.

The woman of Samaria, was greatly surprised, that a Jew should have asked, at her hand, a drink of water. To a liberal and enlightened mind, this might seem to be a strange thing. It would have been the mutual interests of the Jews and Samaritans to have maintained a commercial intercourse. It was a common duty of both, to have performed for each other, those acts of humanity and kindness, which constitute the bands of social life. And yet, it appears, that in all these respects, they looked upon each other as Barbarians. "How is it," said the woman, "that thou, being a Jew, askest drink of me, who am a woman of Samaria?—for the Jews have no dealings with the Samaritans." This statement carries on its face, an insinuation that the fault lay chiefly on the Jews; and in addition to the evidence afforded by the manner of the woman's reply, there are considerations which seem to favour that sentiment. The Jews thought themselves superior in point of privilege. Possibly they claimed precedence, because they were of the old establishment. Be this as it may, there is a general propensity in mankind, to disagree after the same manner, when there is no cause for it, except only, that they have different sentiments of religion, or are associated with a people of a different denomination, or think differently on the subject of church government. Those who once seemed to be unanimous in their religious opinions, and of one accord as to the system of church polity, by which they had been united; have, nevertheless, indulged in this propensity toward their brethren, because questions have arisen among them, about which they differ. And this is the unhappy state of things, however conscientious the party may be, with whom the questions originated. This evil, therefore, is not confined to Jews and Samaritans. It prevails among christians, and with strong symptoms of hatred, although the first principles of reason and the clearest precepts of revelation, discountenance and condemn it. Those who are chargeable with this unjustifiable conduct, seem to expect, that all others should think as they do, and subscribe to their principles and persuasions. And when this expectation fails, their affection cools, and their good will abates in proportion to the supposed difference. If any man presume to judge for himself and choose his own way of thinking, he is looked upon, by them, with a suspicious eye, and he forfeits some portion, at least, of their esteem. It may happen that he will become an object of their high displeasure, and be treated as an enemy. Why? What evil has he done? He has followed his own judgment and not that of others. And is this a reason which can justify such conduct? If not, why do men claiming respect, act in such a manner? Will any one say it is their love of truth, and their zealous concern for the support of truth, which impels them? A sincere and genuine love of truth, would produce very different effects. If it were even admitted, that the opinions of old-side brethren were in all respects, good and true, and of course that it would be right that they should be maintained and propagated, how would this be best accomplished? By ill will, hatred, injurious reproaches, or by love, good-will, kind usage and gentle treatment? If either party would recommend their opinions, ought they not to endeavour to procure them a fair hearing? Ought not each, at the least, to appear to be well affected towards those whom they are desirous to convince? Whosoever has a real regard for truth, and is honestly desirous to promote its interests, will correspond with men of different opinions, fairly and friendly. He will evince a spirit of humanity, equity and candour. He will not exasperate their minds by any expression of hatred or contempt, but will endeavour to conciliate their good will, and cultivate their esteem, by a willing discharge of all such good offices, as may reasonably be expected from him. He cannot believe that animosity will succeed, when argument proves ineffectual, or that reproaches will have a better effect than fair reasoning. "The wrath of man worketh not the righteousness of God." In fact, it is the most improper instrument in the world, for the maintenance of truth.

To publish for the benefit of others what either party conscientiously believes to be the truth, if it be done in a fair and amicable way, is undoubtedly a real service to the public. But strife and calumny, and uncharitable proceedings, are the bane of human society. It is right and proper that the one should be done; the other cannot be done without great wickedness.

These views appear to be so clear and conclusive, that it cannot be saying too much, to affirm, that every man of good sense, and good religion, must admit that diversity of opinion, is in no case a just cause of discord. And therefore, whenever a feeling of hostility is produced by such difference of opinion, it never can be ascribed to any cause or principle that is praiseworthy, no not even that is innocent. The plain truth is, that it springs from pride and immoderate self-love. Men become so swollen with a high conceit of their own opinions, that every opposition gives them pain, and their opponents become objects of their displeasure. And this spirit has produced all those rigorous judgements and rugged dealings, which have so often dishonoured our holy religion, and brought reproach upon human nature.

Reflections such as these, presented themselves after having read brother A. Shinn's Address to the readers of the Mutual Rights, vol. iii. page 12: where he says, "Therefore we *do* expect *punishment*, in some form or other," &c. "whether we are to be punished by neglect, or contempt, or ridicule, or suspension, or expulsion, remains to be explained hereafter; but every man among us may prepare himself, either to give up the cause of reform, or to *suffer*," &c. And will this prediction be verified? Is it possible that a body of men, distinguished for apparent zeal for God, can do this? They will have their difficulties to encounter, if they make the attempt. We know there are some, who have shown themselves willing to begin. But fearing consequences, have made their dispositions known, as yet, chiefly by the expression of wishes, that we would go out of the church. This, of course, would save necessity of turning us out. But these are hasty and inconsiderate men. Those who understand human nature better, and are better prepared to judge of the probable effect of measures on the public mind, will consider well before they begin to punish us openly. And every good christian among them, will refuse to punish us in any manner. A good citizen, much less, a true follower of the meek and lowly Saviour of the world, could not partake in such a work of barbarity? By the law of nature, as well as by all the rules which reason and religion have established, every man has a right to good will, whatever may be his character or conduct;—he is ever entitled to esteem, till he forfeits it by misbehaviour and demerit. —Therefore, whosoever entertains a hard thought, or an unfavourable opinion of any man, without good and sufficient cause, is manifestly "unjust and injurious." And we would ask the favour of every good man of sound understanding, to consider the following question, and answer it according to the dictates of his own conscience. Can any disagreement or difference of opinion on the subject of church government, be a just ground for dislike, or a real forfeiture of esteem? This question cannot admit of an affirmative answer. For no honest man's opinion on this or any other subject, which admits of a difference of opinion, is in his own power or subject to his own will. He must believe and conclude as he can. If he judge at all, he is under the necessity of judging according to the evidence of things, as they appear to his own apprehension. He may err in his judgment. So may all men. It pertains to human frailty. If it be said, he may be dishonest. That can be known only to God and his own conscience;—and, charity, that is, christianity, thinketh no evil. The law which requires every man "to do to others as he would have others to do unto him," makes it obligatory on him to admit, that other men use their faculties, and exercise their judgments, as fairly and uprightly as he does himself, and still that they may differ widely from him in opinion. Nothing else is to be expected among men. We differ from our old side brethren, and what is the offence which we have committed? What is the cause of blame? If we have carefully sought after the truth, and then sincerely followed the best light we could get, we are innocent in the sight of God, and are secure of his acceptance; even if our conclusions were greatly erroneous. And shall men, shall our brethren, be less easily satisfied? Will they take offence, when none is given nor intended? Our thoughts are not as their thoughts—our judgment in regard to church government is not conformable to theirs. And is it true, that we have therefore incurred their ill-opinions, their indignation, their censures? Do they, therefore, condemn us without mercy, and are they, therefore, ready to punish us? They might with as much propriety, quarrel with us, because we have different looks, different features, as because we have different opinions. Our features are the work of our Maker's hand, and our opinions are the result of the evidence and the reasonings on the subject, as they have been presented to our consideration. It may be said, perhaps, that we might have been satisfied; we might have refused to investigate; we might have shunned the evidence, by refusing to read or hear those reasonings. And will our good brethren say, it would have been more compatible with all the principles and considerations, which are implied in a proper sense of character and true worth, to have closed our eyes against the light? We think not. Many of them are unwilling to hear us, and refuse to read our papers. We are bound to believe they honestly think it right, and their best way. We think it right and our best way, to read, inquire, and inform ourselves on church government, as well as on any other subject in which we are interested. And we are very confident that candid and enlightened men, will say, our choice and conduct is more noble, in as much as it is more like that of the Bereans. Perhaps they think it their privilege to dictate to us, in this particular. Have we not as good a right to dictate to them? If not, then their opinions are entitled to the proud distinction of being the standard for all the world. But we say they are wrong, and we are willing, nay, we labour to shew them a reason. They say we are wrong, and neither answer our arguments, nor offer any in support of their own pretensions. And when this is known, and known it will be, is it possible that even the most bigotted will undertake to punish us? Brother Shinn, perhaps, may know more about men in power, than we do, and he thinks we must give up the work of reform or prepare to suffer for it. There are none more ready to meet the fate of faithful reforms, than we are. At the same time, however, we are determined to make it as difficult as possible to the lovers of punishment, to indulge in their wishes. In the most perfect accordance with Mr. Shinn's determination to appeal to the public, we also feel assured, that the people of these United States will approve our struggle; and therefore, if those who have the power, should undertake to punish us, the good sense of the people will avenge our wrong, and the intended punishment will recoil upon themselves with more than double effect.

CHAPTER XXXI.

Concluding Remarks.

THE reader has now an opportunity to make a proper estimate of the extracts from the Mutual Rights which were read before the Quarterly Meeting Conference of the Methodist Episcopal Church in Baltimore, as the testimony of the prosecutors, in support of their charges against us. The Agent in his Narrative and Defence, says, "from the extracts which we shall give from the Mutual Rights, it will be shown" that they have "impugned the motives of our venerable bishops and our itinerant ministers, with unrelenting severity—and accused them *without the shadow of truth.*" Can any of our impartial readers believe this? The writers were careful to avoid being personal? In fact, they could not have been less personal, and have done justice to their respective subjects. He says also, that from the extracts, &c. it will be shown that the bishops are represented to the world, as usurpers;—as tyrants and despots, lording it over God's heritage—as exercising an arbitrary authority, which was at first *surreptitiously* obtained, and which has been perpetuated by printing and publishing a falsehood in the preface to our book of discipline, and by forbidding the people to inquire into the truth of the affair." All such imputations are made without avoidable personality;—explanations are given of the intended extent of their applications; and, exceptions are furnished in favour of the men, at the same time that their government is impugned. And particularly, our complaints respecting the original assumptions of power, are carefully qualified and softened, with intention to save the feelings of present incumbents.

The extracts, when read in their proper places, so as to maintain their connexions, and when examined in view of the circumstances and occasions which led to their production, must forever stand justified in the estimation of disinterested good sense. And yet such was the effect of the Agent's garbling, or so great was the prejudice of the members of the Quarterly Meeting Conference, that although a majority of them had never read the Mutual Rights; upon the bare reading of the extracts, they unanimously voted our expulsion!!

These extracts together with the explanations and comments of doctor Bond and Mr. Hanson, in justification of the prosecutions, constitute the Narrative and Defence. Upon this Narrative and Defence, the Baltimore Annual Conference, and the General Conference must have relied in passing all those unfeeling and unjustifiable resolutions, which they adopted in respect to our expulsions. And as the members of the Quarterly Meeting Conference unanimously voted our expulsion, although a majority of them had not read the Mutual Rights, at all, in course without a proper acquaintance with the subject; may we not conclude, that the Annual and General Conferences, in like manner, without further investigation, acted upon the decision of the Quarterly Conference? Or what amounts to the same thing, the two superior Conferences acted upon the authority of the Narrative and Defence. Their organ, Mr. Emory, in his publications on the subject gives indubitable evidence, that the Narrative and Defence is considered by him, to be an infallible record of the transactions of which it treats. But we have demonstrated, that this work is disingenuous;—that it presents irresistible evidence of chicanery, in three important particulars.

1st. The extracts are garbled so that they convey a meaning, very different from that intended by the writers of them.

2d. They are distorted by comments in direct opposition to the true intent and meaning of the writers, whose papers they affect to explain.

3d. The garbled extracts accompanied by the distortions of the Agent, are all jumbled together, without regard to dates or circumstances, with intention to induce an opinion in the minds of his readers, that all those publications had appeared offensive as he represents them, before the patience and christian meekness of the constituted authorities of the church were worn out, so as to permit the angry passions of our prosecutors to expel us.

Our readers will now understand how greatly deficient in truth, in brotherly love, and in fair dealing the Narrative and Defence is: and will not believe that we were expelled for being the personal calumniators of the bishops and travelling preachers. They will know that a fear of our ultimate success in the work of reform, and a determination to rid the church of a work so offensive to clerical ambition, was the true cause of the shameful policy which, we think, we have now fully developed and satisfactorily exposed.

APPENDIX.

Bishop Asbury's Life.

We were much surprised in looking over an article, entitled "Bishop Asbury's Life," in the Methodist Magazine and Quarterly Review of January, 1831.

In a quarterly critique, we had been accustomed to expect enlightened observations upon important circumstances, connected with the general welfare, or entertaining and useful reviews of the different new publications, calculated to affect the taste, morals or intelligence of a community. Hence arose our surprise, that, instead of attending to these grave matters, the "Methodist Magazine" should lay itself open to the charge, of being an invidious review of private character. The manifest object of the article alluded to, (which takes up a large portion of the number,) is to degrade in public estimation, the character of a private individual. It will probably be alleged that, it was written in self-justification: but, besides that a Quarterly Review is not a fit arena for such self-advocacy, the discriminative reader will perceive that, we speak not unadvisedly, when we impute other and discreditable motives to the Editors of that Periodical. They profess to give a correct statement of the circumstances, connected with a projected biography of Mr. Asbury; but, they so cunningly interlard it with selfish impressions and suitable inferences that, while themselves are represented pure and faultless, the whole character, moral and intellectual, of the Biographer is involved in degradation. From the statement, abstractly, the biographer can suffer nothing. Few, however, who read the "Magazine," will, perhaps, have patience, or candour, or discernment to divest the simple narrative of facts of the misleading remarks interwrought with it. For, the truth is, they have had neither the ingenuousness nor courage to come forth openly, and directly accuse doctor Jennings, (the biographer alluded to,) with lack of honesty and imbecility of intellect: they knew that falsehood would be written too plainly on the front of the charge. But, with such subtlety is their statement managed, that a superficial reader is inevitably led to infer the *justness* of such an imputation.

Let it then be distinctly understood that two charges are insinuated against doctor Jennings:

1st. *Mental incompetency to perform the task of composing a biography.*

2ndly. *Retainance of money to which he has no just claim.*

We shall attempt to vindicate him from both these imputations; and shall notice, likewise, the true cause of failure in the projected biography of Mr. Asbury. Preparatory to our argument, we will give a brief history of the circumstances that have led to this vindication. For the sake of comparison, an abstract shall be given of the statements of both parties.

It seems that, in the July Number of 1830, the editors of the "Quarterly" took occasion to express their regret that, though a life of Mr. Asbury had been projected—a biographer employed, and a considerable sum of money expended, the work had never been produced.—"The gentleman, engaged to furnish it, failed in the execution." Doctor Jennings, (the gentleman referred to,) thus publicly mentioned in a way calculated to affect injuriously his reputation, deemed it justifiable to give an exposition of the circumstances of the case.

Without reference to date, of which he had not an exact remembrance, he states the conference to have passed a resolution that Mr. Asbury's life should be written. A committee was, hereupon, appointed, to carry the resolution into effect. Mr. Roszel, whom doctor Jennings supposed to be chairman of the committee, waited upon the doctor with a request that he would undertake the work. After some deliberation, he consented, on condition that, the committee should furnish such documents as would be necessary, and especially, such facts and anecdotes, as would be more particularly requisite to compensate for want of personal knowledge: on condition, also, that, when all the materials should have been selected, the committee should be present to assist in their selection and arrangement. The reasonableness of the terms, was admitted by Mr. Roszel, who promised they should be complied with.*

Mr. McKendree, who alone had access to Mr. Asbury's papers, was absent about that time, on a tour of duty. Nearly, if not quite a whole year elapsed, before an opportunity offered of requesting from him, what materials he could obtain:—and not a single scrawl was furnished. Mr. McKendree, at length, returned, but was able to furnish nothing useful, except the journal, and this, too, after much delay. To add to the biographer's embarrassment, Mr. Hollingsworth, the gentleman from whom Mr. McKendree had procured the journal, soon called and made known to doctor Jennings Mr. Asbury's objection to any attempt to publish his biography, and the pledge which he had given for the publication of Mr. Asbury's journal, stating, that, whatever use the doctor might wish to make of it, he must lose no time; as he was determined to fulfil his engagement with Mr. Asbury, who wished it to be published as soon as practicable.

The journal was found to be deficient in many materials, requisite to the composition of a respectable biography; of which the doctor repeatedly informed Mr. Roszel: adding that, unless further information could be procured, the attempt at a biography would be abortive. Hereupon, at the instance of Mr. Roszel, a general

* Doctor Jennings at that time did not know who were the remaining members of the committee; he saw none of them but Mr. Roszel.

call was made upon the friends of Mr. Asbury throughout the United States, to furnish whatever might be useful.* One annual conference after another passed by, and nothing further was supplied, except a small bundle of papers, of little value to the intended work; one small package sent from the west by Mr. Thomas L. Douglas, and one letter from South Carolina.†

Throughout the time of these delays, Dr. Jennings states, that, "he had written out scraps and paragraphs in prospect of various topics, which he intended to notice in the contemplated work; amounting to several hundred pages: purposing, when the necessary materials should be collected, to submit his scraps, together with the materials, to the judgment of the committee; expecting their assistance in selecting and arranging, according to the understanding with Mr. Roszel."

Having read over the journal and written many extracts from it, he considered it necessary to bring the matter to a close. Waiting upon the conference, at Alexandria, he requested a meeting of the committee; expecting none other than the committee, with one of whose members he had made his engagement. A committee met by order of the conference and sent for the MS.; neither inviting nor summoning him to attend in person. They proceeded to read, examine, and take notes on the MS. as if it had been submitted, ready for publication;—his best effort as the author of Mr. Asbury's life. They finally adjourned, after having rejected the MS. and directed the secretary to serve the Biographer with a copy of the notes. Dr. Jennings deemed these proceedings as unjust as they were offensive, and determined to have nothing more to do with the business.

Subsequently, however, the original committee assembled and invited his attendance. He narrated to them, all the foregoing facts and circumstances, not omitting to state the conditions on which he had engaged to write the Biography. He informed them, likewise, of the feelings with which he viewed their late proceedings. The committee, then, inquired, if he were willing to resume the work. He answered, that, as they had all been committed to the Methodist public, and community at large; he would redeem the common pledge on the same conditions, originally agreed to by him and Mr. Roszel. The committee unanimously assented, and adjourned, sine die. From that day till the General Conference, he heard nothing further from them; nor did he receive any additional materials, except about five or six letters brought by Mr. Emory from England.

Meantime, at the peremptory request of Mr. Hollingsworth, the manuscript journal was sent to the Book-room, at New York, for publication. Hereupon, the Biographer had an interview with

---

*Mr. Roszel was without blame as to that part of the business.

†Doctor Jennings considers Mr. Emory's insinuation as to the possibility of other supplies of materials than those above stated, as being very much out of the way. Let him who furnished any thing more come forward and say what it was.

Mr. Soule; and they, both, were unanimously of the opinion that, the materials furnished, were entirely insufficient.* And finally a messenger from the General Conference of 1824, called for the few remaining papers; and there ended the business.

While the transaction was pending, however, Dr. Jennings states that, Mr. Roszel presented him with $200.

The inferences, correctly deducible from this statement, if true, are that, the Baltimore Annual Conference is not blameable, seeing it made all due exertion to furnish materials; that there is nothing to sustain an impeachment of the Biographer's character, in as much as the want of matter appears to be the only cause, why a sufficient Biography was not composed; and that the judgment or justice of the committee of examination stands implicated, because, they unreasonably passed their opinion upon a MS. submitted for other purposes, as if the author contemplated its immediate publication.

A replication to this statement, appeared in the article in the January number of the Quarterly, to which we have alluded. It professes to be a brief, veracious and complete history of the business.

According to this, the subject of Bishop Asbury's life, being first introduced in the Annual Conference of 1817, held at Baltimore, a Biography was projected, and a committee appointed to superintend the work and employ a compiler. The committee, consisting of Messrs. N. Reed, S. G. Roszel, J. Wells, W. Ryland, and Dr. H. Wilkins, [through Mr. Roszel] subsequently employed Dr. Jennings.

At the Annual Conference in Baltimore, in the spring of 1818, Dr. Jennings came before the conference, and gave, they think, a verbal outline of his plan, which was favorably received.

At the Annual Conference in Alexandria, (D. C.) in March, 1819, Dr. Jennings appeared in person before the conference, and made a verbal communication of his "successful progress" in the Biography. Inferring from the resolution immediately passed, the conference seemed to be under the impression, that the MS. was submitted, ready for the press. The resolution alluded to, was the appointment of a committee of seven, to examine the work with a view to its immediate publication. Messrs. Reed, Roszel, Wells, Burch, Waugh, Griffith, and Emory, constituted this committee.

Meantime, the committee appointed to collect materials, &c. assembled on the 5th of May, 1819, for the purpose of fixing the compensation, to be made to Dr. Jennings, for his services in writing the Life of Bishop Asbury. After an interchange of opinion on the case, it was resolved "to furnish, at present, the sum of $250, to Dr. Jennings, in part for compensation for his services in the above work. According to a subsequent statement made by them, he received only $225.

*And the more especially so, as a Biography written with no other information than the journal afforded, would be so completely forestalled by the publication of the journal.

On the 15th of June, 1819, the committee of examination met in Baltimore: present, Nelson Reed, Joshua Wells, Stephen G. Roszel, Thomas Burch, Alfred Griffith, J. Emory, and B. Waugh. In opposition to the Biographer's direct statement, that the committee sent for his MS. they say it is their ,,*impression*," that he had previously delivered it to a member of the committee. Their "*impression*" would have been correct if they had added, "by request of the member." They read the MS. with great care, devoting more than a week to it, in successive sittings of six hours per day. They say, the examination was conducted with all the "attention, and fidelity, and candor" of which they were capable. They made exact minutes of all their criticisms, with a view of furnishing the Biographer with them, to "afford him an opportunity to avail himself of them, if he chose; and to reconsider, remodel, or rewrite his work, if, on reviewing it with the committee's suggestions, he should think it possible, to make it such a Life of Bishop Asbury, as would be at all acceptable to the Methodist community and the public. They admit, that they neither "invited nor summoned" Dr. Jennings to attend in person, nor asked for note, comment, nor explanation.

After a second reading of the MS. and an examination of their minutes, notes, and criticisms, it was resolved that the following question be propounded, and the sense of the committee be taken upon it:—"can we now recommend the publication of the MS. which has been submitted to this committee?—Their unanimous answer was—No!—"and let it be remembered," say they, "that the work was in truth a folio manuscript *book*, carefully *bound*, regularly *paged*, divided into *chapters*, and *fairly written out for the press*." They marvel greatly, therefore, that the Biographer denies it was presented for publication. We shall have occasion to notice this particularly, hereafter. We have seen the "book," read every "chapter" and every line, and can easily explain with what reason doctor Jennings denies what they wish to be believed.

After the general vote of the committee had been taken, the particular objections of each member were required;—to serve as the basis of a report to be prepared for the conference, by a subcommittee. The report, accordingly was framed, and it was unanimously adopted by the general committee.

At the close of their sittings, they directed the secretary "to inform doctor Jennings of their final judgment, with the reasons thereof; as also, to return the MS. and inform him, that he should be furnished with a copy of the notes of the committee, *if he requested*." They believe a copy of the notes, in fact, was never either asked or "served."

In consequence of information from the committee "for the collection of materials," &c. that doctor Jennings was disposed to resume and finish the Life of Mr. Asbury, the examining committe held another meeting, just previously to the session of the Baltimore Annual Conference, in March, 1820. They then determined, influenced ostensibly by motives of friendship for doctor Jennings, to withhold the report, originally prepared, and frame another and more favourable one, to be presented to the conference. The amount of it was—it was their opinion that the MS. so far as submitted to them, was not prepared for the press. They took the liberty to recommend to the conference, to refer the whole of what had been done in the business, to the disposal and decision of the next General Conference. The subject of Mr. Asbury's Life was accordingly introduced in the General Conference of 1820; when a committee was appointed to consider and report on it. This committee heard part of doctor Jennings' MS. read, and received from him personally, such other information as he thought proper to communicate. They stated in their report, "that they had been led to doubt whether the plan of the work was the most suitable. They recommended, if published, it should be done in two distinct forms; one comprehending Asbury's Life; the other, a concise ecclesiastical history. The conference did not approve the latter project; but appointed a committee of three, to assist doctor Jennings, in furnishing such further facts and information, respecting Bishop Asbury, as could be obtained, and in reviewing the MS.*

"At the General Conference of 1824, little or no progress having been made in the work, a resolution was passed, respectfully to request doctor Jennings, to deliver the materials in his possession, together with the manuscript, so far as he had written it, into the hands of the Rev. William Beauchamp, who was requested by the conference to become the biographer in the place of doctor Jennings." "The true amount of materials," say they, "with which doctor Jennings was furnished, to assist him in preparing a life of bishop Asbury, we do not precisely know. But, if other documents, placed in his hands, exceeded the amount, as stated by him, in the proportion of the five or six letters, brought by Mr. Emory from England, the difference must be pretty considerable." They state that, the exact number of letters is twenty-five; of which twenty were written by Mr. Asbury himself; two, by Mr. Whatcoat; and three by other persons.

The abstract, we have given, will be found to be correct by a reference to the distinct statements of the two parties. The reader has now a fair opportunity for comparison, and a sufficient ground for inference.

After the high-toned preliminary of the Quarterly, on the "barefaced misrepresentations and shameless prevarications" which they seem to have discovered in Dr. Jenning's statement; after so much ostentation of knowledge, of personal information upon the subject, and the seemingly ingenuous profession to give a trust-worthy account of the business—we were prepared to read a statement, at variance in all points, with that of the biographer. What was our astonishment then, to behold the harmony of the two narratives, on the most important points! And, how must the reader be surprised to know, on comparing them, that they differ very little in whatever tends to affect the matter at issue.

*This committee never made any communication to doctor Jennings.

We request the reader candidly and rigidly to compare the two statements. We said, on the most *important* points, they harmonized. These points are,—the character of the contract between Mr. Roszel and the biographer; the quantity of matter, collected for the biography; the circumstances attending the presentation and rejection of his manuscript, and the conclusion of the business. The conditions of the contract between Mr. Roszell and the biographer, as stated by the latter, are not disputed. It is not denied, that subsequently to the rejection of the manuscript, when doctor Jennings, being asked, consented to resume the work, the committee acceded to these conditions. It is not denied, that the materials, furnished, were insufficient, for the compilation of a respectable biography. It is true they take occasion to contradict the biographer in one clause of his statement, and hence very unfairly intimate that he is not over scrupulous in perverting the truth to his own purposes.* Instead of five letters, twenty-five, they assert, were handed to doctor Jennings. The Doctor informs us that he wrote according to his recollection, having reference as he supposes to those alone, which, when he read them, in his opinion appeared to promise him assistance. He cannot account for his recollection having fixed on five or six, in any other way. Let it be remembered, too, that even this additional help was not received until after the composition, examination, and rejection of the first manuscript. If the letters, then, had contained information enough to supply all deficiencies, (which they did not,) they came too late to benefit him in his first essay.

The Quarterly does not say, when doctor Jennings "reported progress" to the conference, he requested his manuscript to be examined for publication; nor does it deny that the Doctor, instead of himself declining the business, was requested by the conference to give up all the papers in his possession and his appointment as biographer. No! All these assertions of doctor Jennings, upon these points, we are bound to accredit;—seeing they are not denied, of course, are tacitly admitted in a narrative, avowedly framed in opposition to him, and naturally disposed to all sustainable contradiction. Ignorance, they cannot plead, as the ground of their admission: for they will not have us suppose that they are unacquainted with any thing pertaining to this subject. "All the members of the committee are yet living;" "the thing, as it was, is fresh in their recollection;" "while such an amount of original and authentic documents is lying before us, that we cannot understand how doctor Jennings" should make such a statement of proceedings. "He must be aware, too, that we are in possession, not only of information on the subject, but of personal knowledge; and, how in view of this, he could persuade himself to put forth such a statement, as he has, is utterly beyond even our power to conjecture, except on the single supposition that his memory had entirely failed him, which, in regard to this matter, we charitably hope

* We shall notice hereafter, particularly this unchristian insinuation against doctor Jennings.

has been the case." The impartial reviewer of both statements will find no difficulty in deciding, that this deed of charity may be readily dispensed with, seeing the correctness of the Doctor's memory is fully evinced, by the consistency of its report with the authentic and veracious account of his opponents. If, after having been taught by us the consequences, derivable from their admission of the most important parts of doctor Jenning's statement, they shall dare to come forth, and deny what, before, they assented to by their silence, then will every one have abundant reason to question the sincerity of their lips.

That there are some discrepancies in the two statements, we acknowledge; but they are unimportant. We shall, however, notice them.

Doctor Jennings, they say, has left the public mind liable to misapprehension, by confounding two distinct committees. The committee for collecting materials, &c. was different from the committee appointed by the conference to examine the manuscript. This, say they, doctor Jennings must have known. This, we say, doctor Jennings did not know, till after the rejection of his work. Nor could he anticipate such a circumstance. One part of the agreement was, that the committee who employed him, should be present, when materials should have been collected, and assist to select and arrange them. We could not but suppose, then, that the committee for collecting, &c. and the committee of examination were identical; especially, when he received no official or private information to the contrary. If doctor Jennings left the reader "liable to misapprehension," he was himself under the same misapprehension, when his manuscript was examined. His not having been informed on this point, is one of the things which he has never yet understood.

"Dr. Jennings," say they, "states erroneously, that Mr. Roszel was chairman of the committee." The Doctor speaks doubtfully: "who was chairman of the committee, perhaps,"—is his phraseology.

They dislike the Doctor should say, "the secretary was directed to serve him with the notes," &c. They acted more politely:—"if the biographer request, the secretary shall furnish him with notes." They "do not believe that a copy was ever either asked or 'served.' " It is true, it was never "asked;" but it was left at his dwelling, or "served," which is a very appropriate term. The notes are now before us; and, on application to doctor Jennings any one will be permitted to see an exact copy of them, which, though ordered to be "furnished, if requested," was "served" without request; perhaps by Mr. Waugh

Doctor Jennings says, that he was presented with $200. The reviewers state, $250 were voted to him, though only $225 were bestowed. The Doctor admits that he may have erred in this,—still he knows not why $250 were voted, and only $225 sent him by the hand of Mr. Roszel.

31

We have thus noticed the principal discrepancies of the two
narratives, and we find them all to be unimportant;—by no means
affecting the matter at issue.   There is one particular in the re-
viewers' account, we have forborne to touch in this comparison;
because, instead of being a legitimate part of the statement, we
believed it, an unproved assumption.   If admitted, it would establish all they wish.   We are therefore, willing, and we think, not
unable to demonstrate its incorrectness.   It is asserted, that the
work, thus presented, was "a folio, manuscript *book*, carefully
bound, regularly *paged*, divided into *chapters*, and *fairly written out
for the press.*"   On this, is based the insinuated charge of mental
incompetency to compose a biography.   Their argument may be
fairly stated thus:—

Doctor Jennings presented to a committee a fairly written out,
manuscript biography, to be examined for publication.   The committee consisted of seven persons, of reputable judgment, knowledge and impartiality.   They were employed more than a week,
in successive sittings of six hours per day, reading the MS twice
over, with all the attention, fidelity and candour of which they were
capable.   They unanimously rejected it, as unfit for publication.
Now, as doctor Jennings had been employed, several years, in the
composition of the biography; and, as the "conference was disposed
to render him prompt encouragement," and the committee to afford
him effectual aid, the conclusion is, that mental incompetency or
culpable indolence on the part of the author, was the veritable
cause of the unfitness of the MS. for publication.

It will, unhesitatingly, be acknowledged, should any one of the
data be false, then is the conclusion false.   If the report of the
candour and intelligence of the committee be unsustained, then
cannot the charge of indolence or incompetence be sustained.   If
adequate and prompt assistance were not rendered him by the conference and committee, then no inference can be drawn against the
character of the biographer.   Although one of these suppositions
could, probably, be supported, and the other certainly established,
we will now notice only the first postulate; believing that we can
show its incorrectness, consequently the fallacy of the whole argument.

We propose, then, to demonstrate, that doctor Jennings did not
submit his manuscript biography, to be examined for publication.
His solemn asseveration in affirmation of this point, will have its
due weight with those acquainted with his character, and with all
impartial men, when it is found not to be contradicted by any testimony.   And it is true that there is no sustained denial of it in
the statement of his opponents.   We glanced at this circumstance
in the comparison of the two narratives: we will now speak more
largely concerning it.   Let us review their account.   "Doctor
Jennings," say they, "reported successful progress in the biography:"—true, but not a termination of his work, or its suitableness
for the press.   "The conference, hereupon, appointed a committee
to examine it, with a view to its publication."   This but shows in
what way the conference construed the report of doctor Jennings:

because *such* was their *construction*, it does not follow certainly, that *such* was the *intention* of the biographer. We appeal again to the statement; we care not for the constructions of conference or committee;—does their own narrative say, either directly or by just implication, that the MS. was presented for *publication?* It does not—"successful progress" only, was reported in the MS.—And what of all this? A mechanic may "report successful progress" in a machine he is framing: is it, therefore, inferred, that his machine is finished, and ready for public examination?

It will be asked, "why did not the biographer, when he understood a committee was appointed to examine his MS., avow it was not his intention to have it published?" Because he fully believed, that the committee, for collecting materials, would be the committee of examination; and they, he knew, were well aware of the condition that sets forth,—"provided also, the committee shall be present, when materials shall have been collected, to assist in selecting and arranging them." He, therefore, confidently believed, that the committee would act in accordance with the implication of that condition;—not examining the MS., as if submitted for the press, but in view of revising and shaping it, as their judgment might dictate. Instead of this a new committee was appointed. This doctor Jennings has never yet understood. That doctor Jennings thought the two committees identical, we have additional evidence from the fact; that he knew Mr. Roszel, who was on the first committee, was also on the second. Mr. Reed, too, a member of the former committee, called upon him for the MS., and did not then state to him, or even give him a hint, that a different committee had been appointed. Nor did he, as before stated, receive official notice or private intimation of this in any way.

Hence we have another argument, that doctor Jennings did not submit his work, ready for the press. The condition that the committee would be present, when the materials should have been collected, to assist him to select and arrange them, precludes even the shadow of a supposition that the MS. was submitted in a fit state for publication.* He, therefore, very properly blames the committee for acting so inconsistently,—so much at variance with the character of the contract. Nor let them say that, being a different committee, they were not obligated by the afore-mentioned conditions; nor, that knowing nothing of them, ignorance would have prevented their fulfilment. The conference acted unjustifiably in

*When Mr. Nelson Reed called for the manuscript and gave no intimation that the writer was expected to accompany it, doctor Jennings was greatly surprised. He expected it until Mr. Reed had received the book and was retiring; when, finding that the committee were about to examine his place-book without his assistance, he was greatly embarrassed, and following Mr. Reed to the door, in a word or two, intimated to him, that the work was not in a fit state to be read by the committee, in that manner. Whether Mr. Reed understood him or not, he cannot know. Mr. Roszel had conducted towards him so properly in every other instance, he thought it unaccountable, that the committee was not informed of the conditions of the existing engagement.

appointing another committee, by which the contract would necessarily be annulled.   Messrs. Reed, Roszel and Wells, constituting three of the five, on the first committee, were appointed members of the second, consisting of seven persons.   They, at least, ought to have known the nature of the agreement.   Mr. Roszel, who was himself the contractor, must have clearly understood the intentions of doctor Jennings in presenting his MS:—and it is curious if he permitted the three remaining members to be ignorant on a point so important.

Beside the evidence, already adduced, we have an irresistable inferential argument, arising from an examination of the MS.   The biography, examined by the committee, embracing 269 pages, which now lie before us, contains no account of the birth, parentage, boyhood, youth, or conversion of Mr. Asbury; nor any information concerning the commencement of his ministerial career. This is not all: it is only extended to the time of his ordination,— we are told nothing of his life posterior to 1784, when he had been only thirteen years in America; in course, the remainder of his life, upwards of thirty years, is wholly untouched; nor have we in it, any account of his death!   Now we ask, is it possible, that any man with common sense could ever have thought of submitting so incomplete a sketch, as a biography, ready *for the press?* Yet this, the Quarterly would have us to believe;—that a *few quires of foolscap paper, roughly bound in boards,* written out by *three different hands* at least, containing a few extracts from the journal of Mr. Asbury, with remarks of the biographer interspersed, and intended as a specimen of what the journal afforded; without a single item, concerning his birth, or death, and omitting thirty of the most important years of his life;—that such a work, on so much paper, thus filled, constituted "a folio manuscript *book,* carefully *bound,* regularly *paged,* divided into *chapters,* and *fairly written out for the press,*" and intended by the writer to be a sufficient biography! Whom here are we to charge with foolishness?   Have we not grounds for implicating both the judgment and candour of the committee, who acted, and the editor of the Quarterly, who attempts to vindicate their doings?   Beside the deficiency of the MS. in facts, there are inaccuracies in its grammar, tautology in some parts, and sometimes inappropriate epithets and language, which, while they argue nothing against the information or good taste of the biographer, indicate the necessity and obvious intention of a revision; and sufficiently prove, that the author could not have deemed it in a suitable state for publication.   We speak this the more confidently, inasmuch as we have seen a second and revised MS. of the work,* in which inaccuracies are corrected, redundancies retrenched, and, in fact, the philological defects of the first

*Immediately after the first committee met and reviewed the engagement with doctor Jennings, he proceeded to correct and rewrite his work.   This revised and rewritten copy of 150 pages, on large sheets, was submitted to the examination of the committee appointed by the general conference of 1820.

MS. satisfactorily amended. Any man who is disposed to doubt any part of this statement, on application to doctor Jennings will be permitted to inspect for himself, when he cannot fail to be satisfied of the truth of this account, in all its details.

"But why so carefully *bound?*"—it is asked. After all, this "carefully *bound*, folio *book*," is no other than a kind of day-book, ROUGHLY bound, and used for convenience. "It is 'regularly *paged*' and 'divided' into *chapters?*" This *is* flat! Who, that is at all acquainted with writing, does not know, that nothing is more common than to page a MS. whether intended or not for the press? And the operation of dividing into chapters and paragraphs becomes a kind of instinct in one who deals much in composition; in truth, is as natural as that he should punctuate regularly: and this too, whether the MS. be intended or not for the press. But there is a peculiar reason for this division into chapters. The work was to be submitted to a committee. The arrangement therefore, of the information and facts collected, in judicious portions, under appropriate captions, was intended to facilitate the labours of the committee in inspecting, selecting, and arranging the materials of the MS. "But why so *fairly written out?*" All that can be said in truth on this point is, that generally, the penmanship is legible, sometimes, however, quite obscure. Besides, as noticed before, three different autographs, at least, are discernible in the MS.

We shall sum up our argument under this head, thus:

1st. Doctor Jennings solemnly affirms, that he did not submit his manuscript biography, as being prepared for the press. In carefully looking over the statement of his opponents, we find nothing to nullify this affirmation. They never once state that he even intimated a wish to have his work examined in view of its publication. Their strongest language is, "he reported successful progress." Now, no matter how conference or committee understood this—their constructions, or rather misconstructions, avail nothing: we are bound to accredit the unqualified and *uncontradicted* affirmation of the biographer.

2d. The nature of the agreement, between Mr. Roszel and the biographer, affords another argument. By this agreement the committee were obligated to be present when materials should have been collected, to assist in preparing the MS. for the press, by *selection, arrangement, &c.* Doctor Jennings could not, therefore, have contemplated the immediate publication of his work.

3d. Our last argument arises from a view of the character of the MS. It gives us no account of more than thirty years, which in course included by far the most important and interesting events in the life of Mr. Asbury. It has various extempore inaccuracies of style and grammar, and is not unfrequently incorrect in its reference to dates and authorities. Now, supposing doctor Jennings to possess common sense, he could not have thought of submitting so incomplete and defective a composition as a biography, to be examined with a view to its publication;—"his best effort as the author of Mr. Asbury's life."

We therefore, conclude that so far, the charge of incompetence against the biographer is invalid, since the MS. was not a fair sample of the author's ability.

"Why then," they ask, "was not his work *prepared for publication!*" "Surely he had time sufficient, and great encouragement: why did he not *make* his MS. *ready for the press?*" We trust we can answer this in a manner, which shall convince every one that the defectiveness of the MS. *biography* was attributable to other causes than to the *inability* or *indolence* of its author. We say, then, the reason was, *want of necessary materials;* which we will prove.

1st. Inferentially from the fact, that though the committee, who employed doctor Jennings, must have known the amount and kind of materials furnished, they have not, in the slightest particular, contradicted his statement concerning the sparsity of requisite information; except in one, and this we have noticed. We allude to the letters brought from England by Mr. Emory. That it may be borne in mind, however, by the reader, we repeat, these letters were never furnished, till after doctor Jennings had consented to resume the biography, of course, cannot be included in the amount of materials, out of which the biographer framed his first MS. We cannot but notice, here, the ungracious insinuation of the "Quarterly," conveyed in the following: "The true amount of 'materials,' with which doctor Jennings was furnished, to assist him in preparing a life of Bishop Asbury, we do not precisely know. But if other documents placed in his hands exceeded the amount as stated by him, in the proportion of the 'five or six letters brought by Mr. Emory from England,' the difference must be pretty considerable." If the Quarterly be here the organ of speech for the committee, we are compelled to believe that the "difference" between their *words* and *truth*, "is pretty considerable." What! engaged to furnish the necesssary anecdotes, facts and documents, and not "know" the "quantity" of information furnished! Impossible! "Their memories must have entirely failed them," "which, in regard to this matter, we charitably hope has been the case," or they have stooped to a degrading untruth, to blast the reputation of an innocent man. If the Editor of the "Magazine" be the speaker, we appeal to an enlightened community to determine, whether he does not act beneath the character of a christian, and a gentleman, when possessing sufficient "information," and "personal knowledge," to detect falsehood, if there were any, he ventures an unsupported and malignant insinuation against the veracity of a christian minister?

2d. So far as the testimony of a respectable minister of the Methodist Episcopal Church will go, we have another evidence of the *want of materials.* The biographer, after the reception of the letters from England, affording him the last information he obtained, had an interview with Mr. Soule, who entirely accorded with the Doctor in opinion, that the materials, already furnished, were *insufficient.*

3d. The proceedings of the General Conference of 1820, in reference to the biography, affords another very conclusive proof. The Quarterly says, a committee of three was appointed "to assist doctor Jennings in furnishing such other facts and information, as could be obtained, respecting Bishop Asbury." Would the conference have done this, unless with the belief, that the facts and information, already gathered, were insufficient for the compilation of a respectable biography? Is it not a plain confession, there was *a lack of materials?*

4th. The character of the MS. bears strong presumptive evidence of this same dearth of materials. Would any man, in his right mind, giving a biography of another, neglect to insert, in the account, the most important particulars of his history, if they were obtainable. Had doctor Jennings have known any thing satisfactory of Mr. Asbury's birth, his conversion, call to the ministry; of his correspondences with other ministers—his address to the conferences, &c. &c. would he not have communicated it in his MS. It is true, that a sermon was preached by Mr. Snethen and printed, affording some information on some of these subjects; inasmuch, however, as it was incomplete, and in a degree unauthentic, Dr. Jennings determined to defer any account of these matters, till he should lay his MS. before the committee, who might from authentic and sufficient documents supply the deficiency.

We are compelled then to conclude,—from the character of the MS. from the avowed opinion of one of their principal ministers, (Mr. Soule,) from the uncontradicted statement of doctor Jennings, and from their own account, that there was a *want of materials;*— and *this* was why a sufficient biography was never compiled.

"Why, then, did the doctor request a meeting of the committee, and submit his work in so incomplete a state, to their inspection?" The answer is plain:—he wished to bring the business to a close. From the MS., which ought to have been considered as a common-place-book, prepared for that particular purpose, when laid open before them, the committee might learn how much information had been collected, and how much was still needed. If no more materials could be furnished, he wished to know what course they would advise him to pursue. And if the design of framing a Biography was not to be abandoned, the committee would then perceive more fully the necessity of bestirring itself in the obtainment of the necessary information.

It is strange that blame should be bestowed on the Biographer, for persevering in his purpose of writing a Biography. "If," says the Quarterly, "Doctor Jennings, even after engaging to become the Biographer of Bishop Asbury, on becoming convinced that, with his want of sufficient personal acquaintance with the subject, the documents and materials were altogether inadequate, had thought proper to decline the task, with any reasonable notice to the committee, and without subjecting them to useless expense, we apprehend no censure would or could have been attached to him from any quarter. This would have been the only course of propriety." We take the liberty to differ from the Quarterly. Had doctor Jennings have been convinced, not only that the "documents and materials," *already* furnished, were "*inadequate*," but that an *adequate* supply *never* could be furnished, then was his course plain—by all means he should have declined the task. But he waited in hope: he depended on the committee who employed him, for such documents and facts as should be necessary; and the discouragements which afterwards were multiplied, had scarcely commenced when he received the money;—and, therefore, does he deserve much praise for maintaining to the last his agreement with the committee, under so many disadvantages. Contending with a multiplicity of impediments, he continued patiently and perseveringly to perform his part of the task, as well as circumstances would permit. Had the committee done likewise, a Biography, most probably, would not now be wanting. It was *their* business to determine the possibility or impossibilty of procuring the necessary materials, and if convinced of the impossibility, it became *them*, and not the Biographer, "to decline the task." They should have communicated "reasonable notice," to the conference who appointed them, and have satisfied the author whom they had employed, and we apprehend no censure could or would have attached to them from any quarter, if they had abandoned the work. They were at no additional expense after the two hundred or two hundred and twenty-five dollars were sent by Mr. Roszel, the receipt of which served to impose perseverance upon the doctor.

We think we have fully confuted the insinuated charge of incompetency or indolence on the part of the Biographer; established the fact of a dearth of materials being the cause why a sufficient Biography was never written; satisfactorily shown the object of the author in requesting a meeting of the committee; and proved the propriety of doctor Jennings' conduct in not declining the task under so many inauspicious circumstances.

The second insinuated charge is retainance in his hands of money, to which he has no just claims. Was doctor Jennings entitled or was he not, to a compensation for his services? The answer to this question depends on a single circumstance;—whether or not the Biographer failed to perform his part of the task. From what we have said, any unprejudiced person will feel warranted in answering—he did not fail. He did all, that any man could have been justly required to perform, with the means afforded him. The committee failed in supplying necessary materials; they dismissed him from their employment, as Biographer; not *he himself:* consequently, they, alone, violated the contract—and be became justly entitled to a proper compensation. Even could it be proved, (which is very far from the truth,) that doctor Jennings was incapable of writing a Biography, he could still, with justice, retain any remuneration made to him; on the same principle that an artist could hold legal claim to money, voluntarily and unconditionally paid him in advance for services, which subsequent trial, should prove him unable to perform to entire satisfaction of both parties;—except some specific condition in the contract hindered. But doctor Jennings stoops not to such a refuge. The MS. he offers to the inspection of any one who may wish to examine it; convinced that its character will fully sustain the credit of his competency and the justness of his claim to remuneration.

A compensation was, then, due to the Biographer: The next question concerns the amount. We here appeal to the judgment of the impartial; for, as no specific compensation was determined on by the committee, equity alone must decide the question.

Let it be known, then, that the MS. submitted to the inspection of the committee of examination, &c, contained two hundred and sixty-nine folio pages. This the committee admits. A portion of the Biography, consisting of seventy-nine pages, was written out, but not presented, with the other, to the committee. Subsequently to the rejection of the 269 pages, by the examining committee, and the second meeting of the first committee, when he consented to recommence the Biography, he revised the original MS. and rewrote one hundred and fifty pages. "But whence so much work with so few materials?" "How could so voluminous a MS. be wrought out of so sparse and imperfect information?" It is easily answered. Doctor Jennings, considering on the imperfection of the facts, documents and anecdotes furnished, and the tedious monotony of Mr. Asbury's journal, perceived the necessity of introducing appropriate extraneous matter, in order to give any thing like interest or utility to his Biography. Contemplating Mr. Asbury as the great apostle of Methodism in America, he deemed it would neither be irrelative nor uninteresting to discourse somewhat on the peculiar system, with which he was identified. In doing this, he was led to bestow some attention on the circumstances, attending its origin; by which he was still further conducted to an investigation of the general causes of reformation, and the method in which it is most frequently effected. Hence, for the sake of illustration, he glances cursorily at the different religious changes of ancient and modern times, in view principally of the fact, that unofficial, individual exertion, is the general agent in operating reformations.

This is the reason why the MS. was so voluminous. And when we consider the toil and time which must have been expended in so extensive an investigation, together with the labour of penning, correcting and transcribing *four hundred and ninety-four folio pages*, (the sum total of pages written out,) will any one be so iniquitous as to pronounce two hundred and twenty-five dollars a more than equivalent compensation? Certainly not. *Justly* then does doctor Jennings retain the two hundred and twenty-five dollars; which as before stated, is the only remuneration he ever received.

Here would end the "chapter," if permitted by the Quarterly. But, "we would like to know," says its editor, "how it happens that doctor Jennings comes to be still in possession, as he intimates, of 'two volumes of manuscript which he wrote in view of Mr. Asbury's Life?'" Why, thus it happens. Having been dismissed from his employment by an act of the General Conference,

32

and no arrangement having been made respecting the completion of the work, which had the least respect to the feelings or reputation of doctor Jennings, was it reasonable to suppose that he would let go his manuscripts, which could not have been used in a manner consistent with his design, unless he had been in some way concerned in completing them; especially as he had every good reason to fear they would be disposed of, in a manner unsatisfactory to himself, since so much of his work as had been read by the committee, had been formally condemned; and no attention had been paid to him, by either of the committees, appointed to aid him in procuring materials? He determined, very properly, therefore, that they ought to remain in his possession. It is said, however, the MS. was paid for by the committee and was their property. It was condemned by the committee, whilst the materials were in a crude and an unfinished state, and the money paid to him was an inadequate compensation for the toil and time which he had then devoted to the work. Besides, the dismissal in the manner in which it was done, was arbitrary and insolent;—such as justified resistance; a violation of the agreement made with him; by which he considers all right to the MS. forfeited on their part, even on the supposition that the remuneration for his services had been much more satisfactory.* It is presumed that the subject was so considered by them, since they have made no subsequent call. And it is believed we should have heard no more about it, had not doctor Jennings become active and conspicuous in the work of reform.

In conclusion we beg leave to submit an hypothesis, concerning the reason why the work of the biographer was unacceptable to his employers, and one which is another good reason, why he ought not to have delivered it, upon such an application. It is this, that the principles frequently advocated in the MS. biography, and the general spirit of it, were greatly at variance with the now known opinions of the committee. The principles and spirit evinced throughout the work are all liberal: they look frowningly upon priestly aspirations for power and the enforced servility of laymen. Is it not easy to understand, then, why the members of the committee, who, at this day are staunch advocates of the powers, that be, looked not with pleasure on the work? This is not altogether hypothesis. Among several other reasons, (not very reasonable,) for the rejection of the MS., they declare this to be one; "it contains a variety of sentiments, on doctrines and *ecclesiastical polity*, which we deem at least questionable." We do indeed, believe this was their strongest reason. And what wonder? Even at that period "reform" began to be so much talked about, they became very sensitive to whatever bore an ill aspect toward a clerical monopoly of power.

*Dr. Jennings informs the writer of this appendix, that the call for the manuscript and papers, was altogether out of the way. No interview was asked or demanded for the purpose of fixing upon any preliminaries, respecting their delivery. After the rising of the conference, a most unceremonious call was made, and all but the manuscripts were delivered to the messenger of Mr Beauchamp.

7

In looking over their notes, too, we find them generally taking exceptions to those passages, which we would naturally suppose unsavoury to an Episcopal Methodist. For instance, in remarking on one passage they ask, "does not this indicate too great a desire to have a stroke at the priests?" In another place they query, "whether the private members of the church were made guardians of true orthodoxy, &c. &c. But the MS. and the committee's notes may be seen any time, on application to doctor Jennings, so that any one who is inquisitive may learn for himself, what probably was the true cause of the rejection of his work.

Thus have we seen the unfair treatment of doctor Jennings by the committee; who first did him injustice by passing their opinion on his work, as if submitted, ready for publication; and then, endeavouring to vindicate themselves through the medium of the Quarterly, cruelly aspersed both his moral and intellectual character; subjecting his honesty, as well as competency to foul suspicion. We think the impartial reader will acknowledge, that we have fixed the charge of unfair and cruel dealing upon the committee, and have wiped away the aspersions made by them, on the character of a christian minister.

THE END.

CPSIA information can be obtained
at www.ICGtesting.com
Printed in the USA
BVHW071416280819
556943BV00022B/3030/P